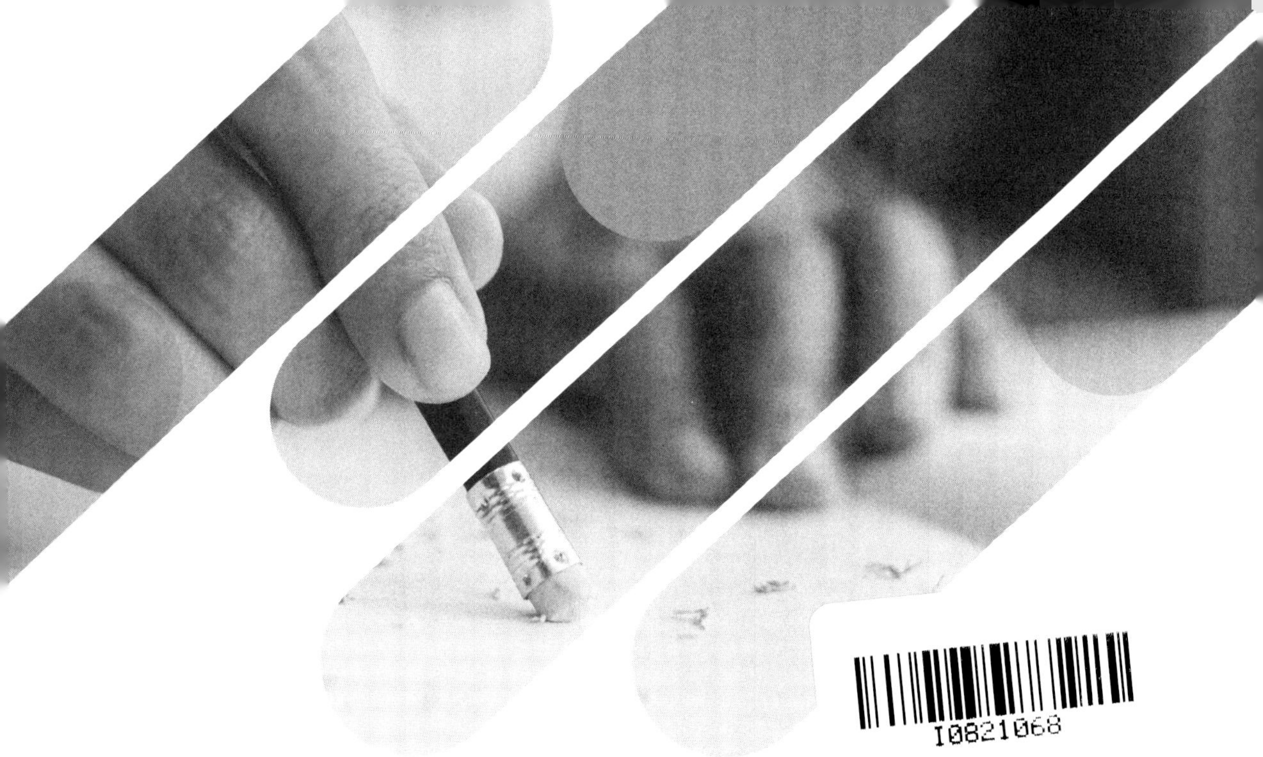

ASSESSMENT LITERACY

for Educators

Rethinking the What, Why, and How of Assessment and Grading

Robert J. MARZANO Michael D. EVANS Julia A. SIMMS

Copyright © 2026 by Marzano Resources

Materials appearing here are copyrighted. With one exception, all rights are reserved. Readers may reproduce only those pages marked "Reproducible." Otherwise, no part of this book may be reproduced or transmitted in any form or by any means (electronic, photocopying, recording, or otherwise) without prior written permission of the publisher and the authors. This book, in whole or in part, may not be included in a large language model, used to train AI, or uploaded into any AI system.

555 North Morton Street
Bloomington, IN 47404
888.849.0851
FAX: 866.801.1447

email: info@MarzanoResources.com
MarzanoResources.com

Visit **MarzanoResources.com/reproducibles** to download the free reproducibles in this book.

Printed in the United States of America

Library of Congress Control Number: 2025027757

ISBN: 978-1-943360-67-3

Production Team

Publisher: Kendra Slayton
Associate Publisher: Todd Brakke
Acquisitions Director: Hilary Goff
Editorial Director: Laurel Hecker
Art Director: Rian Anderson
Managing Editor: Sarah Ludwig
Copy Chief: Jessi Finn
Developmental Editor: Laurel Hecker
Copy Editor: Mark Hain
Proofreader: Anne Marie Watkins
Text and Cover Designer: Kelsey Hoover
Content Development Specialist: Amy Rubenstein
Associate Editor: Elijah Oates
Editorial Assistant: Madison Chartier

Table of Contents

Visit **MarzanoResources.com/reproducibles** to download the free reproducibles in this book.

About the Authors

Robert J. Marzano, PhD, is cofounder and chief academic officer of Marzano Resources in Denver, Colorado. During his fifty years in the field of education, he has worked with educators as a speaker and trainer and has authored more than fifty books and two hundred articles on topics such as instruction, assessment, writing and implementing standards, cognition, effective leadership, and school intervention. His books include *The New Art and Science of Teaching*, *Five Big Ideas for Leading a High Reliability School*, *The Marzano Academies* series, *Improving Teacher Development and Evaluation*, *Leading a High Reliability School*, *The Classroom Strategies* series, *A Handbook for High Reliability Schools*, and *Marzano Mastery Approaches*. His practical translations of the most recent research and theory into classroom strategies are known internationally and are widely practiced by both teachers and administrators.

Dr. Marzano received a bachelor's degree from Iona College in New York, a master's degree from Seattle University, and a doctorate from the University of Washington.

To learn more about Robert J. Marzano, visit www.marzanoresources.com.

Michael D. Evans, EdD, has spent over thirty years working in education, serving in the roles of teacher, counselor, principal, and district administrator. Throughout his career, he has focused on helping schools move toward personalized competency-based education models.

Dr. Evans has hands-on experience implementing standards-based learning and High Reliability Schools frameworks in multiple districts. He has seen firsthand what works—and what doesn't—when schools attempt to transform their practices. As an associate with Marzano Resources, Dr. Evans brings a practical perspective to schools and districts across the United States, helping them navigate the challenges of educational change. Dr. Evans is a contributing author of *Leading the Evolution: How to Make Personalized Competency-Based Education a Reality* and continues to advocate for educational approaches that put student learning at the center.

Dr. Evans holds a bachelor of education degree from Missouri Southern State University, a master of science in counseling from Missouri State University, a doctorate in educational administration from Lindenwood University, and a specialist degree in educational administration from William Woods University.

To book Michael D. Evans for professional development, contact pd@MarzanoResources.com.

Julia A. Simms is vice president of Marzano Resources. A former classroom teacher, she now serves on a team that develops research-based books and resources. Her expertise includes effective instruction, learning progressions and proficiency scales, assessment and grading, argumentation and reasoning skills, and literacy development. She has authored or coauthored sixteen books, including *The Marzano Synthesis*, *A Handbook for High Reliability Schools*, *Marzano Mastery Approaches*, *The New Art and Science of Teaching Reading*, *Where Learning Happens*, and *Guide on the Side*.

Simms received a bachelor's degree from Wheaton College and master's degrees in educational administration and K–12 literacy from Colorado State University and the University of Northern Colorado.

Introduction

REVISITING ASSESSMENT PRACTICES

In 1991, Rick Stiggins introduced the term *assessment literacy* to K–12 educators. He described it as the knowledge and understanding necessary to produce high-quality achievement data and to critically evaluate and use those data. He emphasized that assessment-literate individuals can distinguish between sound and unsound assessment practices. Over the next three decades, the concept of assessment literacy became an important part of the landscape of K–12 education.

In 2016, the U.S. Department of Education issued *Assessment Literacy Defined*, a report by the National Task Force on Assessment Education for Teachers. This task force was designed to "address the need for assessment-literate educators in a positive way" (p. 1) and consisted of three advisers and twenty-four educators from seventeen states. The task force's goal was "to be a collective voice that elevates the national dialogue on assessment education, develops innovative approaches to assessment literacy, and advances existing best practices in assessment" (p. 1). The task force and its report formalized the need for educators at all levels to increase their knowledge of the nature of assessments and how best to use them.

To that end, several organizations and authors have developed assessment literacy frameworks; assessment experts Yelisey A. Shapovalov and Carla M. Evans synthesized many of these frameworks in 2022. Although each

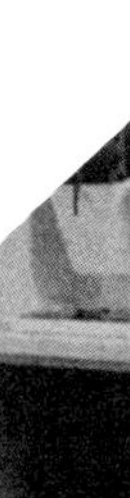

of these frameworks takes somewhat differing perspectives, they all focus on what might be thought of as the technical aspects of assessment literacy, such as types of validity, types of reliability, and the like. These are important issues, and the frameworks have addressed them well. This book does not duplicate those efforts, although we do address technical aspects of assessments. Instead, this book adds to previous discussions by focusing on three categories of assessment.

1. Large-scale assessment
2. Classroom assessment
3. Grading practice

To a certain extent, previous books on assessment literacy for educators focused on understanding and interpreting large-scale assessments and then made applications to classroom assessments. Here, we address some of these same issues about large-scale assessments, but our focus is on classroom assessments. Further, we make the case that the generalizations and principles that are appropriate to large-scale assessments are not automatically transferable to classroom assessments. Indeed, in many cases, entirely different generalizations and principles must be applied to classroom assessments. The last category—grading practice—is often ignored in discussions of assessment literacy, despite the fact that grades are the "most common educational measure" (Brookhart et al., 2016, p. 803). We submit that this is perhaps the first assessment literacy book to acknowledge the proper place of grading in the grand scheme of assessment. Additionally, this book addresses the underlying—but often tacit—beliefs that have guided assessment development in the United States for decades. Finally, this book articulates basic tenets designed to inform the design, use, and interpretation of assessments.

We should note that the assessment literacy perspective we articulate in this book has been developed through research and development over the course of thirty years. Specifically, the concepts we present here were introduced and developed in the following books.

- *A Comprehensive Guide to Designing Standards-Based Districts, Schools, and Classrooms* (Marzano & Kendall, 1996)
- *Transforming Classroom Grading* (Marzano, 2000)
- *Classroom Assessment and Grading That Work* (Marzano, 2006)
- *The New Taxonomy of Educational Objectives* (Marzano & Kendall, 2007)

- *Making Standards Useful in the Classroom* (Marzano & Haystead, 2008)
- *Designing and Assessing Educational Objectives* (Marzano & Kendall, 2008)
- *Formative Assessment and Standards-Based Grading* (Marzano, 2010)
- *Making Classroom Assessments Reliable and Valid* (Marzano, 2018)
- *The New Art and Science of Classroom Assessment* (Marzano, Norford, & Ruyle, 2019)
- *Leading a Competency-Based Elementary School* (Marzano & Kosena, 2022)
- *Teaching in a Competency-Based Elementary School* (Marzano & Abbott, 2022)
- *Test-Specific Thinking* (Marzano et al., 2025)

Educators across the United States have implemented and tested the concepts from these texts, and when appropriate, we use examples from these books. Each of these texts provides greater depth regarding many of the topics addressed in this book, in addition to addressing assessment-adjacent topics (such as instruction and curriculum), which are outside the scope of this work. This book brings together the cumulative knowledge articulated in previous works into a comprehensive and cohesive theory base for assessment that modern educators can use to address modern issues of large-scale assessments, classroom assessments, and grading.

The Troubling Genesis of Testing in the United States

Testing has always been a part of the educational process. Many trace the advent of formal testing to around 600 AD in China. During oral examinations, aspiring bureaucrats were required to demonstrate their knowledge of governmental rules (U.S. Congress, Office of Technology Assessment, 1992). In the United States, the genesis of formalized testing had a different focus. In the late 19th and early 20th centuries, U.S. educators sought to measure students' intelligence using tests and examinations. We argue that this idea—that a test can measure human intelligence—is coded into the United States' assessment DNA and that true assessment literacy requires a thorough understanding of the thinking and beliefs that underpinned the development of intelligence tests.

Intelligence Tests

In 1904, under the direction of the French Ministry of Public Instruction, Alfred Binet created the first intelligence test. Contrary to the ministry's intention, which was to divert students with lower intelligence out of regular classrooms, Binet wanted to use his test and scoring scales to identify and track children's developmental progress. Notably, Binet's scales were culturally biased, resulting in strong correlations between a child's social class and their performance on Binet's intelligence test (Sacks, 1999). For example, figure I.1 shows one scale from Binet's test.

When one breaks something belonging to another, what must one do?	A. One must pay for it and ask to be excused.	B. One must pay for it or replace it.	C. Mend it and give it back.

Source: Adapted from Binet & Simon, 1916.

FIGURE I.1: Culturally biased scale example from Binet's intelligence test.

According to Binet, the most correct answer is A, "One must pay for it and asked to be excused," and the least correct answer is C, "Mend it and give it back." But quite naturally and problematically, a child's socioeconomic status (SES) will likely influence their response. For high-SES children, it might make the most sense to pay for a broken item. But for low-SES children, who likely do not have excess money, it might make the most sense to fix the broken item and return it. Nonetheless, this response is considered incorrect on Binet's test. The notion of seeking forgiveness adds an additional cultural nuance; while it might be intuitive to some children, it is unreasonable to expect a child to include that element in their response in order to be correct.

Another example of the inherent bias in early 20th century intelligence tests involves the influence of language. Alfred Binet and Théodore Simon (1916) acknowledged that "language played a part in a good many of the tests" (p. 320) and that "the children of the rich are in a superior environment from the point of view of language" (p. 320). They also observed that children "of the poorer class are shorter, weigh less, have smaller heads . . . less often reach the high school [, and] are more often behind in their studies" (p. 318). While some aspects of these statements may be true, Binet and Simon interpreted them incorrectly, revealing their own biases and stereotypes regarding intelligence. Instead of considering how students' economic differences impacted their test scores, they positioned their data as evidence of the intellectual superiority of high-SES students.

In the United States, psychologist Lewis M. Terman (1916) adapted Binet's scales to create a single test that would identify the "feeble-minded" (p. 5), believing the following:

> In the near future intelligence tests will bring tens of thousands of these high-grade defectives under the surveillance and protection of society. This will ultimately result in curtailing the reproduction of feeble-mindedness and in the elimination of an enormous amount of crime, pauperism, and industrial inefficiency. It is hardly necessary to emphasize that the high-grade cases, of the type now so frequently overlooked, are precisely the ones whose guardianship it is most important for the State to assume. (pp. 6–7)

Intelligence tests in the early 20th century also influenced the development of the United States Army's Alpha test during World War I; it was used to identify the jobs for which army recruits were allegedly best suited (Kaestle, 2013). Arthur Otis, a student of Terman, is credited with developing the Alpha test. According to psychologist Leon J. Kamin (1977), scores for 125,000 draftees were analyzed to determine the typical performance by different subgroups. The National Academy of Sciences published the results in *Memoirs of the National Academy of Sciences: Psychological Examining in the United States Army* (Yerkes, 1921). One chapter of *Memoirs*, "Relation of Intelligence Ratings to Nativity," focuses on a test of about 12,000 draftees who reported that they were born outside of the United States. *Memoirs* noted the following:

> The range of differences between the countries is a very wide one. . . . In general, the Scandinavian and English speaking countries stand high in the list, while the Slavic and Latin countries stand low. . . . The countries tend to fall into two groups: Canada, Great Britain, the Scandinavian and Teutonic countries . . . [as opposed to] the Latin and Slavic countries. (Yerkes, 1921, p. 699)

Like Binet's intelligence test, the Army Alpha tests were culturally biased (Sacks, 1999). English-speaking draftees took one version of the test (the Alpha version), while non-English-speaking draftees took a different version (the Beta version). The Beta version attempted to measure intelligence through items that were, theoretically, not dependent on language skills. For example, the Beta version presented pictures that were missing important components (such as a hand missing a finger) and asked draftees to fix them. While some of the pictures were straightforward, others were not. Specifically, many pictures involved elements that might only be recognized by higher-SES individuals: a tennis court with no net or a bowler with no bowling ball. Other pictures, such as a letter with no stamp or return address, required the draftee to be familiar with U.S. postal rules (Sacks, 1999). Additionally, Beta test instructions were given using a blackboard example with pantomime and a very limited set of English words, such as *yes, no, fix it, do it,* and so on. Unsurprisingly, scores on the Beta test were lower than scores on the Alpha test.

Eugenics

Conclusions drawn from the Army Alpha and Beta tests and from Terman's use of Binet's scales added to the influence of eugenics in the late 19th and early 20th centuries. Termed as such in 1883 by Sir Francis Galton (cousin of Charles Darwin), *eugenics* asserted that the best way to improve the genetic quality of the human population was through selective breeding. The concept of selective breeding to improve human traits dates back to Plato and Aristotle in ancient Greece, but in the late 19th and early 20th centuries, eugenics gained significant support and attention in the United States and Europe. Indeed, eugenics was so well accepted in the United States that in 1910, geneticist and biologist Charles Davenport established the Eugenics Record Office (ERO) in Cold Spring Harbor, New York. The ERO only lasted until 1939, but it was instrumental in promoting the principles of eugenics during its almost thirty-year tenure (Lawrence, 2011).

Though he later revised his views, Princeton professor and creator of the Scholastic Aptitude Test (SAT), Carl C. Brigham (1923), used eugenics as an interpretational framework to compare U.S.-born White draftees to foreign-born White draftees and Black Americans. He concluded that drafted officers scored highest, followed by White draftees born in England, foreign and U.S.-born White draftees, and finally, Black Americans. Brigham argued that his comparison "proved . . . a progressive decrease in the intellectual level of immigrants coming to [the United States] in each succeeding five-year period since 1902" (p. 199).

The final sections of Brigham's (1923) book focused on using the results of the Army Alpha and Beta tests in an attempt to argue the superiority of what he described as the "Nordic" race as opposed to the "Alpine" and "Mediterranean" races (p. 157). For Brigham, the Nordic race consisted primarily of immigrants from Sweden, the Netherlands, England, and Scotland and represented the first stage of American immigration, which was later supplanted by immigrants from Alpine and Mediterranean regions. He concluded that "data from the army tests indicate clearly the intellectual superiority of the Nordic race group" (p. 207). In Brigham's view at the time, the results of the Army Alpha and Beta tests supported the idea that race played a dominant role in intellectual ability, to the exclusion of familiarity with English, literacy, time spent in the United States, or bias within the test itself.

Later in his career, Brigham changed his mind. In an unpublished document in 1934, as quoted by Nicholas Lemann (2000), Brigham wrote the following:

> The test movement came to this country some twenty-five or thirty years ago accompanied by one of the most glorious fallacies in the history of science, namely, that the tests measured *native intelligence* purely and simply without regard to training or schooling. I hope nobody believes that now. The test scores very definitely are a composite including schooling, family background, familiarity with English, and everything else, relevant and irrelevant. The "*native intelligence*" hypothesis is dead. (p. 34; emphasis in original)

Unfortunately, significant damage had already been done to the American testing psyche. Beliefs that tests measure innate intelligence in a pure and accurate way and consequent conclusions that various races and ethnicities differed significantly in their levels of intelligence were firmly entrenched in the minds of U.S. educators and measurement specialists.

Single-Trait Theory

The single-trait theory added to the growing beliefs and assumptions about intelligence and testing. Sir Francis Galton (1883) proposed and developed the idea that human intelligence can be reduced to a single factor called *general intelligence* (represented by the letter *g*). It was a short step from this idea to eugenics: If intelligence is a single trait, then those who possess more of it will outperform those who have less. Galton reasoned that if specific races or ethnic groups systematically outperformed other races or ethnic groups, then those higher-performing groups most probably inherit their intelligence genetically.

Obsessed with the idea of intelligence as a singular characteristic, Galton (1889) developed statistical methods for analyzing the linear relationship between the characteristics of parents and their offspring. Using scatterplots, he was able to determine the extent that one could predict the level of a specific trait in children from the extent that the parents possessed the trait. These analyses formed the basis for mathematical models to compute correlations and conduct regression analyses, techniques that were then applied to measurement theory by Karl Pearson (1896) and Charles Spearman (1904). These two psychometricians, with others, made it common practice to determine the effectiveness of tests by examining their correlations with criterion variables. For example, the predictive validity of a test is typically determined by the extent that scores on the test correlate with scores on some accepted criterion measure of the trait. Certain types of reliability (for example, test-retest reliability) are defined by correlations. In sum, the early work of Galton seeking a single factor for intelligence laid the groundwork for judging the effectiveness of tests through their correlations with single traits. Over time, one of the primary tenets of test development was that all tests should be *unidimensional*, which means that tests should be designed to measure a single trait only.

In the 1920s and 1930s, Louis Leon Thurstone (1928, 1931, 1934) further promoted single traits by developing a statistical technique called *factor analysis*. Factor analysis allowed researchers to determine the extent to which items on a test all measured one common trait. Thurstone postulated that in education and psychology, traits being measured are *latent*; that is, they cannot be directly observed. Only through intentional testing could educators infer students' expertise with such latent traits.

The work of the psychologist Georg Rasch further advanced the concept of latent traits in educational measurement during the middle of the 20th century. Rasch (1960) developed the Rasch model, also known as the *one-parameter logistic model* or *Rasch measurement theory*. Rasch's model provided a mathematical framework for understanding latent traits in educational and psychological assessments and allowed for the measurement of latent traits, such as ability or proficiency, based on observed item responses.

Throughout this book, we will occasionally revisit the assumption that tests can measure unobservable traits, as it still plays a role in modern testing. For example, many tests still assume that the trait they measure cannot be directly observed; rather, the percentage of items answered correctly on the test can accurately place the test taker on a latent-trait continuum.

One can find strong arguments for the validity and utility of single-trait theory (also called *g-factor theory*) nearly all the way through the 20th century. Arthur R. Jensen's 1980 book, *Bias in Mental Testing*, was widely read in the United States. Perhaps revealing his bias, Jensen dedicated the book to Galton, Binet, and Spearman. The book is a detailed psychometric argument grounded in g-factor theory; it positions standardized tests as highly accurate indicators of differences in intelligence and competence between both individuals and groups. While Jensen speaks out strongly and eloquently against discrimination, a thorough examination of his book leaves the reader with the message that there are differences in general intelligence that are highly correlated with factors such as ethnicity, socioeconomic status, and so on. Jensen (1980) ultimately reached the following conclusion about standardized tests:

> Most current standardized tests of mental ability yield unbiased measures for all native-born English-speaking segments of American society today, regardless of their sex or their racial and social-class background. The observed mean differences in test scores between various groups are generally not an artifact of the tests themselves, but are attributable to factors that are causally independent of the tests. (p. 740)

While the legacy of single-trait theory continues to influence contemporary assessment practices, it remains crucial to critically examine its assumptions and implications, particularly regarding the potential for reinforcing societal biases in educational measurement.

Multiple Dynamic Traits

Despite his promotion of the single-trait theory through factor analysis, Thurstone also offered an alternative to single-trait theory. After analyzing data from fifty-six intelligence tests, Thurstone identified an array of mental abilities that could be said to constitute intelligence (Myers, 2009). Said differently, he used more sophisticated versions of the mathematical techniques that established single-trait theory to demonstrate its limitations and offer a multidimensional alternative. Later theories of intelligence, such as Howard Gardner's (1993) notion of multiple intelligences, expanded the number and types of traits associated with intelligence.

By the year 2000, the concept of intelligence had broken the bonds of single-trait theory and the psychometric and mathematical models used to create it. Instead, researchers and theorists explained intelligence and human thought in ways that single-trait theory and its descendants could not. For example, neuroscientists Eduardo Camina and Francisco Güell (2017) and Sruthi Sridhar, Abdulrahman Khamaj, and Manish Kumar Asthana (2023) offered explanations of human thought and intelligence based on models of long-term memory and its subcomponents, like explicit memory and implicit memory. *Explicit memory* is information that we can volitionally (and explicitly) remember. *Implicit memory* is unconscious; it includes all the memories we have but can't explicitly remember and all the skills we have learned so well that we can perform them without explicitly thinking about them. Likewise, the field of artificial intelligence (AI) has developed neural networks that cast new light on human competence. Computer scientists Chellammal Surianarayanan, John Jeyasekaran Lawrence, Pethuru Raj Chelliah, Edmond Prakash, and Chaminda Hewage (2023) observed the following:

> It is clear that neuroscience lays the foundation for the design of artificial neural networks (ANNs), which consist of nodes structured in input, hidden, and output layers. Hence, it is realized that there is a complementary relationship between neuroscience and AI, irrespective of their different end purposes or goals. (p. 2)

In summary, 21st century conceptions of intelligence from diverse fields describe intelligence and human behavior in terms of multiple dynamic traits that interact in complex ways. As science examines intelligence in greater detail, it is clear that a single or even a small set of traits can never explain human competence and behavior.

The Residual Effects of Early Beliefs About Intelligence

So what does this dark history have to do with assessment literacy and assessment practices? Fortunately, historical levels of bias and racism in testing have abated. Unfortunately, vestiges of the beliefs that led to that bias and racism persist. We assert that basic assumptions that led to egregious abuses of testing and test data in previous centuries are still hardwired into American educational measurement practices. The genesis of testing in the United States spawned beliefs that continue to shape assessment practice well into the 21st century. Specifically, there are three beliefs that still exert a strong influence.

1. **Standardized tests can effectively quantify intelligence:** The early use of intelligence tests laid the foundation for a belief in fixed, measurable intelligence that could be used to categorize individuals, often reinforcing stereotypes and perpetuating social inequalities.
2. **There is a genetic component to intelligence:** Although eugenics has been discredited, its legacy continues to haunt contemporary

education, with vestiges of its ideas still influencing how tests are interpreted and how students are categorized based on performance.

3. **Intelligence is reducible to a single quantifiable trait:** The influence of single-trait theory persists in educational testing practices, reinforcing the notion that intelligence is a singular trait measurable in a standardized manner.

Even though views of intelligence have changed dramatically in the 21st century, we assert that early views still influence test administration and interpretation. Most obviously, the education system continues to categorize and label students. For example, consider the following categories and labels that are commonly used in K–12 education.

- Attention-deficit/hyperactivity disorder (ADHD)
- Specific learning disabilities (for example, dyslexia)
- Emotional/behavioral disorders
- English learners or multilingual learners
- Gifted and talented
- Economically disadvantaged
- Behavioral or disciplinary categories
- Ethnic or racial categories

While sorting students into categories may provide some useful information for educators, many (perhaps all) of these classification systems have potential negative effects on students because of inferences about them such labels may prompt.

There are other more subtle, residual effects of early beliefs about intelligence. One is the commonly tacit presence of *deficit thinking* (Valencia, 2010, 2019). According to educational researchers Sacha Cartagena and Lindsey Pike (2022):

> Deficit thinking is a theory that describes the phenomena of unconscious or implicit biases (Valencia, 2010). Labeling or categorizing others as disadvantaged or disabled is an example of deficit thinking. . . . Educators may unconsciously relieve themselves of any responsibility for providing adequate academic or behavioral support to students with disabilities or students from other marginalized populations (Reed, 2020).
>
> Naming is a prerequisite for defining and eventually categorizing people, often leading to relegation to particular classes and the inherent consequences of membership in specific groups (Wehmeyer, 2013). . . . Just as an

> individual's name is a powerful identifier (Moore, 2020), society's process of naming conveys a variety of messages about perceived human value and relationships. (pp. 104–105)

Deficit thinking might manifest as educators assuming that certain students are incapable of learning certain types of knowledge. While that might occasionally be true on an individual level, it is also true that the human mind is capable of making up for deficits that might logically appear as insurmountable obstacles at first blush. An assessment and instruction system that seeks to develop the potential of every student should perhaps err on the side of assuming students can accomplish difficult tasks until overwhelming evidence proves otherwise. A deep understanding of the uses and limitations of various types of assessments can be instrumental to this end.

What You Will Find in This Book

This book is divided into three parts: (1) large-scale assessments, (2) classroom assessments, and (3) grading practice. Each section discusses pertinent history relative to a particular type of assessment and best practices for further use. Part I, on large-scale assessments, consists of chapter 1, "The Influence of Large-Scale Assessments," and chapter 2, "Technical Characteristics of Large-Scale Assessments." The first chapter explains the role of large-scale assessments in education, while the second addresses the potential sources of error in using large-scale assessments as a source of information about students. Part II covers classroom assessments and contains three chapters. Chapter 3, "Rethinking Classroom Assessments," shows how explicit knowledge continuums form the basis for effective classroom assessments. Chapter 4, "Scoring Classroom Assessments," reviews how teachers score individual assessments, while chapter 5, "Aggregating Classroom Assessment Scores," recommends best practices for using multiple assessments to calculate overall scores within a measurement topic. Part III's two chapters discuss grading practice. Chapter 6, "Grading Systems," explores methods of calculating and reporting course grades. Finally, chapter 7, "Competency-Based Systems," delves into the possibilities for grading and promoting students based on mastery rather than seat time.

Throughout each chapter, we present tenets that underlie our paradigm of assessment literacy for educators. A *tenet* is a generalization or awareness that educators should understand to be literate about assessment in K–12 education. We close the introduction with our first tenet.

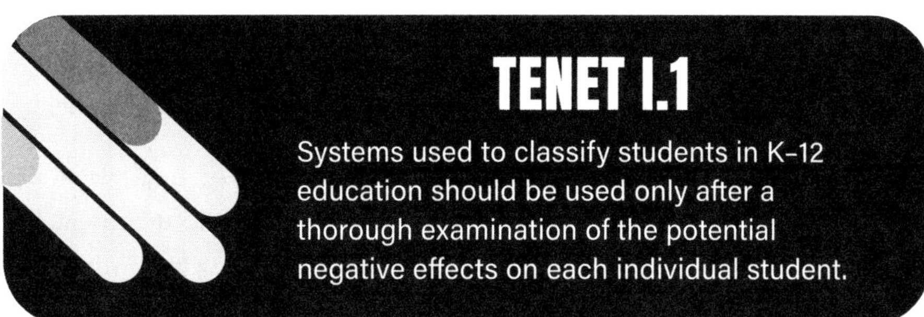

Each tenet has implications for assessment definition and use. For example, implications of tenet I.1 might include the following.

- **Risk of reinforcing bias and stereotyping:** Classification systems, such as those for students with learning disabilities, students with behavioral issues, or English learners, can unintentionally reinforce societal biases and stereotypes. For example, students from lower socioeconomic backgrounds may be disproportionately labeled with learning disabilities or behavioral problems, leading to lower expectations and a lack of appropriate support. These labels can affect how teachers and peers perceive a student's potential, possibly leading to a self-fulfilling prophecy where the student is treated as less capable or less deserving of advanced educational opportunities.
- **Impact on student self-perception and motivation:** The labels assigned to students can affect their self-esteem and academic motivation. A student categorized as "gifted" may feel immense pressure to perform at high levels, while a student categorized as "at risk" or "below grade level" might internalize the label and struggle with feelings of inadequacy. These labels can shape how students view their own abilities, potentially affecting their effort, engagement, and overall academic achievement.
- **Overreliance on labels for educational decisions:** Relying on classification systems without careful consideration of their long-term impact can result in missed opportunities for individualized learning. For instance, students identified as "gifted" might not

> receive the full support they need in areas outside of their intellectual strengths, while students categorized as having learning disabilities might be placed in remedial tracks that do not challenge them appropriately. A more nuanced, flexible approach is needed to ensure that each student receives the support and opportunities that align with their unique needs, rather than being defined solely by a label.

This introduction has laid out an accounting of the history of intelligence testing and the beliefs that guided its development. In many cases, the foundational beliefs were not conducive to helping students develop to their fullest potential. Rather, the trajectory of those beliefs was to sort students into well-defined categories that had well-defined limitations. While those limiting foundational beliefs are no longer always salient or explicit, they still have a lingering influence on how tests are used and interpreted. The remaining chapters disclose many of these influences and provide concrete ways to mitigate their impact.

PART I

Large-Scale Assessments

Chapter 1

THE INFLUENCE OF LARGE-SCALE ASSESSMENTS

Large-scale assessments have been a part of public education for quite some time. By *large-scale assessments*, we mean standardized tests that are typically administered to students across a district, state, or nation. Examples include state tests (for example, Colorado Measures of Academic Success), national tests (for example, the SAT, ACT, or NAEP), and international tests (such as PISA or TIMSS). They are designed to measure student performance against established academic standards.

As early as 1877, the impact of large-scale assessments was evident to Henry Latham, a priest and tutor at Trinity Hall in Cambridge, England. In his book *On the Action of Examinations Considered as a Means of Selection*, Latham (1877) documented how testing influences "the prevalent views of life and work among young [people], and how it affects parents, teachers, the writers of educational books, and the notions of the public about education" (p. 2). A few decades later, in the 1890s, Joseph M. Rice (1897) administered the first large-scale assessments in the United States, measuring the spelling ability of about thirty-three thousand students in grades 4 through 8.

While Rice's intent was to establish a baseline of student learning based on the work of the best teachers, he also compared the results from each school participating in the study. He wanted to find out if schools with more progressive instruction performed better than schools with more traditional instruction. While these purposes have merit, Rice's tests presaged a system of large-scale testing in the United States wherein testing data are not always used for such productive purposes. In this chapter, we examine the limitations of large-scale assessments and the role that interim assessments play in the current educational landscape.

The Development and Proliferation of Large-Scale Assessments

The first high-profile and widespread manifestation of a large-scale assessment in the United States was in 1926, when the Scholastic Aptitude Test (SAT) was introduced. It soon became a de facto entrance exam for college admissions, as did the American College Test (ACT), which was created in 1959 as a response to the SAT. The next highly influential large-scale national assessment emerged in 1969, when the National Assessment of Educational Progress (NAEP) was administered across the United States, with results compiled and reported in what is known as the Nation's Report Card (Volante et al., 2020). Finally, more focused types of tests, like the Iowa Test of Basic Skills (ITBS) and the Cognitive Abilities Test (CogAT), and international assessments (such as those listed in table 1.1, arranged by frequency of administration) have also been used on a large-scale basis to measure students' academic learning and cognitive abilities.

In 2001, the National Research Council published *Knowing What Students Know: The Science and Design of Educational Assessment*, which began to change perceptions of large-scale assessments by advocating a balance between classroom and large-scale assessments. This increased the credibility of classroom assessments and weakened the dominance of large-scale assessments. James W. Pellegrino and Naomi Chudowsky (2003) applauded this recommendation, explaining that large-scale assessments "do not focus on many aspects of cognition that research indicates are important, such as students' organization of knowledge, problem representations, use of strategies, self-monitoring skills, and individual contributions to group problem solving" (p. 107). Subsequently, many states added interim assessments throughout the school year to supplement the large-scale tests administered every

TABLE 1.1: International Large-Scale Assessments Used in the United States

Acronym	Title of Test	Content Tested	Frequency
PISA	Program for International Student Assessment	Reading, mathematics, and science	Every three years
TIMSS	Trends in International Mathematics and Science Study	Mathematics and science	Every four years
ICILS	International Computer and Information Literacy Study	Computer and informational literacy, computational thinking	Every five years
PIRLS	Progress in International Reading Literacy Study	Reading	Every five years
PIAAC	Program for the International Assessment of Adult Competencies	Literacy, numeracy, problem-solving, and workplace skills	Every ten years

spring. Despite these efforts, many schools have still narrowed their curriculum and instruction in ways that led education scholar Louis Volante and colleagues (2020) to observe that "what gets tested gets taught" (p. 25) in American schools.

Beginning in 2010, groups within the United States sought to establish common learning standards in English language arts (ELA), mathematics, and science (National Governors Association Center for Best Practices [NGA] & Council of Chief State School Officers [CCSSO], 2010a, 2010b; NGSS Lead States, 2013). To provide large-scale assessments aligned to these standards, the federal government funded two consortia: the Partnership for Assessment of Readiness for College and Careers (PARCC) and Smarter Balanced. While the tests produced by these consortia were an improvement on previous end-of-year assessments, they were—like all large-scale assessments—still limited in their ability to provide useful feedback to educators to inform everyday classroom teaching and learning (Volante et al., 2020). The Every Student Succeeds Act (ESSA; 2015) allowed a limited number of states to innovate on their assessment systems, but whether those innovations are able to strike an improved balance between providing data for large-scale purposes (such as accountability) and data that are useful to inform classroom practice remains to be seen.

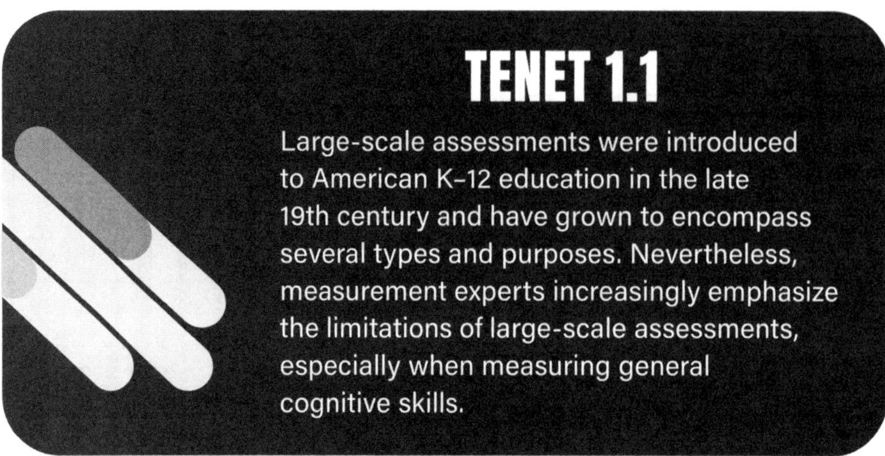

Implications of tenet 1.1 might include the following.

- **Increased focus on accountability at the expense of instructional quality:** The proliferation of large-scale assessments over time has led to a stronger emphasis on standardized testing as a measure of student and school performance. This can result in a narrowing of the curriculum, as teachers focus primarily on the content and skills that are tested. As the adage "What gets tested gets taught" suggests, teachers may feel pressured to prioritize test preparation over fostering broader critical thinking, creativity, and problem-solving skills, ultimately undermining the richness of the educational experience for students.
- **Limited usefulness for classroom instruction:** Despite the expansion of large-scale assessments, measurement experts continue to point out that these tests are not always effective tools to inform day-to-day teaching. They often fail to assess important aspects of student cognition, such as problem-solving strategies, metacognitive skills, and the application of knowledge in novel contexts. This limits their ability to provide meaningful feedback to educators, making it difficult for teachers to address students' individual learning needs, especially when assessments are only administered annually or at discrete intervals.

The Role of Interim Assessments

Interim assessments, also known as *benchmark assessments*, are designed to augment year-end large-scale assessments. Like year-end assessments, interim assessments are standardized, formal, and purportedly aligned to state standards. In contrast with year-end assessments, interim assessments are usually administered multiple times over the course of a school year and are intended to address the cumulative nature of the curriculum in a given subject area (Crane, 2010; Perie, Marion, & Gong, 2009). The frequency of administration and the scope of the standards addressed by interim assessments vary by manufacturer.

An important distinction within interim assessments is between adaptive assessments and fixed assessments. An *adaptive assessment*, also known as *computerized adaptive testing*, is a type of assessment that adjusts to the test taker's ability level: The difficulty of the questions presented to the test taker changes in real time based on their performance. As the test taker answers questions correctly, the questions become more difficult. Conversely, if the test taker struggles with a question, the next question will be easier. Theoretically, this adaptive approach ensures that each test taker is challenged at an appropriate level, providing a more personalized and accurate assessment of their knowledge and skills.

A *fixed assessment*, also known as a *fixed form assessment* or *static assessment*, is a type of test in which all participants are asked the same questions, in the same order, regardless of their skills, abilities, or responses to previous questions. Year-end assessments—wherein all students at a particular grade are assessed on the standards for that grade level—are a common example of fixed assessment. The decision to use adaptive or fixed interim assessments should align with how schools and districts will use the data from the assessment. For example, a school district might choose a fixed assessment to measure all students' understanding of specific mathematics concepts at the end of a semester to ensure consistency in evaluating their progress. On the other hand, an adaptive assessment might be more appropriate to identify each student's individual proficiency level in reading at the beginning of the school year because it adjusts the difficulty of questions based on their previous responses to provide a more personalized evaluation of their skills. Marianne Perie, Scott Marion, and Brian Gong (2009) identified three purposes for interim assessments: (1) instructional, (2) evaluative, and (3) predictive.

Instructional Purposes

Many educators see interim assessments filling the gap between high-stakes, end-of-year assessments and ongoing classroom assessment (Herman, 2017). Like classroom assessments, interim assessments measure student understanding of the learning expectations at multiple points throughout the academic year and provide data that are intended to help teachers make instructional decisions at the classroom level. However, like year-end assessments, results from interim assessments are commonly aggregated beyond the classroom level to the building or even district level (Perie, Marion, Gong, & Wurtzel, 2007).

By providing data at various points throughout the year, interim assessments enable educators to identify trends in student performance across different classrooms or grade levels. This shared information allows teachers to collaborate more effectively, discussing strategies, interventions, and best practices that may be needed to support students who are struggling or excelling. Furthermore, when used thoughtfully, interim assessments can assist in tailoring professional development efforts, helping educators refine their instructional practices to better meet student needs. Through this continuous cycle of data collection, analysis, and reflection, interim assessments help create a more responsive and adaptable learning environment.

Evaluative Purposes

Because they occur several times during a school year, interim assessments are more useful than year-end assessments for evaluating the quality of curriculum and general classroom instruction. Interim assessments can provide schools and districts with data to make long-term decisions, "not with the intention of intervening but for evaluating the effectiveness of a program, strategy, or teacher" (Perie et al., 2007, p. 5). This evaluative use of interim assessments focuses on programs, not individual students (Shepard, 2009).

Interim assessments can never take the place of classroom assessments. Although interim assessments are easier to implement than classroom assessments, they do not provide teachers with the same level of information. As Marianne Perie, Scott Marion, Brian Gong, and Judy Wurtzel (2007) explained, "Districts putting in place interim assessment systems may be getting important and actionable data, but they are rarely getting the power of true formative assessment practices" (p. 2). Nevertheless, because the data from interim assessments can be aggregated beyond the classroom, school and district leadership teams can use the data in many of the same ways collaborative teacher teams use data, but at a larger scale, to answer questions such as the following.

- Are there standards or concepts that some schools are more successful teaching than others?
- Are there common standards or concepts that all students across the district tend to struggle with on an ongoing basis?
- How well do classroom assessments align with the expectations expressed by the standards?

Predictive Purposes

The predictive use of interim assessments is aimed at determining how students will score on large-scale assessments, such as state assessments, graduation exams, and the ACT or SAT (Perie et al., 2009). While it is doubtful that many interim assessments are created with the sole purpose of predicting future outcomes, schools and districts continue to use this function of interim assessments to identify students who may not be successful on the high-stakes assessments required by state and federal legislation. Unfortunately, as Lorrie A. Shepard (2009) pointed out, there are practical problems with the predictive quality of interim assessments. Depending on the format of the assessment, it is not unusual for students to be tested on standards that have not been taught, which "leads to the problem of diagnosing as weaknesses topics that have not yet been taught" (Shepard, 2009, p. 36). Thus, while interim assessments are often used to predict student performance on high-stakes tests, their predictive value is compromised by issues such as misalignment with the curriculum, which can lead to inaccurate diagnoses of student weaknesses.

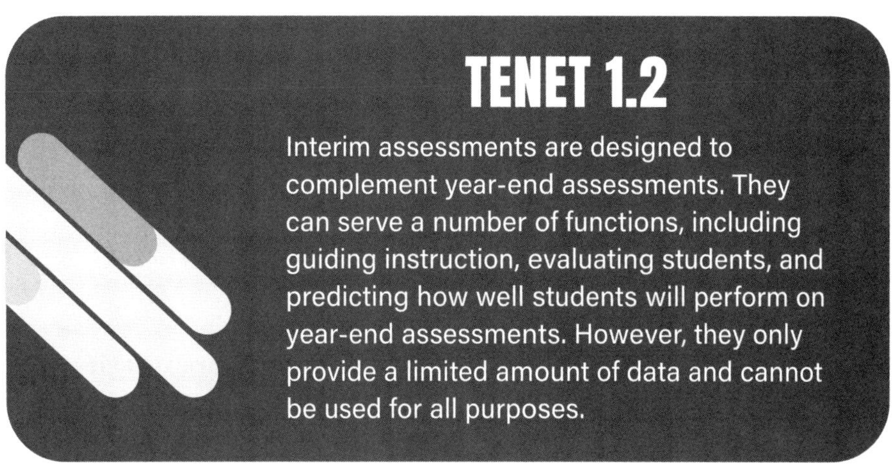

Implications of tenet 1.2 might include the following.

- **Complements to, not substitutes for, classroom assessments:** Interim assessments serve as an important bridge between large-scale assessments and classroom assessments, filling the gap by offering data on student progress at various points throughout the year. However, they should never replace high-quality classroom assessments. Classroom assessments provide a more detailed, context-rich understanding of individual student progress, which is critical for making daily instructional decisions. Therefore, while interim assessments offer valuable insights, they cannot fully replace a robust system of ongoing, targeted classroom assessments.
- **Careful analysis of adaptive versus fixed assessments:** Teachers and school leaders must be mindful of the differences between adaptive and fixed interim assessments when analyzing the data. Adaptive assessments, which adjust the difficulty based on student responses, provide a more detailed profile of where each student is on the learning continuum. In contrast, fixed assessments offer a uniform approach to assessing all students, which may not reveal as nuanced a picture of individual performance. Understanding these differences ensures that educators make informed decisions based on the type of data each assessment provides.
- **Cross-references with interim assessment data:** To ensure the validity and reliability of the data, interim assessment scores should be compared not only to results from the year-end large-scale assessments but also to classroom assessment scores. By triangulating data from all three sources, schools can help validate the predictive power of the interim assessments and ensure that instructional practices align with the intended standards and expectations.
- **The danger of overuse for predictive purposes:** While interim assessments can be useful for predicting student performance on high-stakes assessments, their ability to do so accurately is limited. These assessments may test standards not yet taught, leading to incorrect conclusions about student readiness for end-of-year tests. As such, schools and districts should use interim assessments for prediction with caution and ensure that their predictive value is corroborated by other data sources, such as classroom assessments

and large-scale assessments. Overreliance on interim assessments for predictions could result in misguided interventions or misplaced focus on areas that do not reflect actual student needs.

Summary

In this chapter, we highlighted the long history and pervasive influence of large-scale assessments in education, from their early use in the 19th century to their central role in modern testing systems like the SAT and ACT. Despite their widespread use, large-scale assessments face significant criticisms, particularly their narrow focus on measurable skills, which can limit broader learning objectives like critical thinking and problem solving. While interim assessments have emerged as a potential solution to provide more frequent feedback and guide instruction, the challenge remains in balancing these tests with meaningful, holistic feedback that supports student growth.

Chapter 2

TECHNICAL CHARACTERISTICS OF LARGE-SCALE ASSESSMENTS

In this chapter, we explore the technical characteristics of large-scale assessments. While such characteristics might not seem immediately useful to a classroom teacher, understanding them allows teachers to see how they do and don't transfer to classroom assessments. In effect, understanding large-scale assessment characteristics will enrich teachers' understanding of how classroom assessments can mitigate some of the possible negative influences of large-scale assessments.

Uses and Misuses of Large-Scale Assessment Data

The first thing to remember about any assessment—large-scale or classroom—is that one assessment (or one type of assessment) can never answer all one's questions. Educators should be sharply aware of the types of questions a specific assessment can and cannot answer. For example, measurement experts Amy I. Berman, Edward H. Haertel, and James W. Pellegrino (2020) emphasized that many stakeholders want large-scale assessments to answer a wide variety of questions. Families frequently want to know the following:

> How is my child doing?
>
> What are my child's strongest and weakest subjects?
>
> Have my child's test scores improved from last year?
>
> How [do] my child's test scores compare to others looking to go to college?
>
> Should I move to this school zone? (Berman et al., 2020, p. 9)

District administrators seek answers to questions such as the following:

> How do the assessment scores of schools within our district compare?
>
> How are our English learner students doing compared with our native English speakers?
>
> Are we closing the achievement gap?
>
> How do our assessment scores compare to others within the state? (Berman et al., 2020, p. 9)

And state administrators and policymakers are curious to find out the following:

> How do our kids measure up to kids in other states?
>
> [How do our kids measure up to other kids] within districts?
>
> How are the scores of various student subgroups changing over time? (Berman et al., 2020, p. 9)

Despite how frequently various stakeholders ask these questions of large-scale assessments, Berman and colleagues (2020) were adamant that large-scale assessments are not designed to answer all of them. Volante and colleagues (2020) explained the following about the large-scale assessments spawned by the No Child Left Behind Act (NCLB; 2002) and the Every Student Succeeds Act (2015):

> [These assessments are] primarily informed by research focused on psychometric models and represent content domains as the end points of learning (Shepard, 2019). *Such assessments are not designed for instructional purposes, and so have little utility for informing ongoing teaching and learning in the classroom* (Perie, Marion, & Gong, 2009). (p. 25; emphasis added)

This statement—and others like it—shakes the foundations of common understandings of assessment literacy. Educators and other stakeholders frequently try to use large-scale assessment data to answer questions that large-scale assessment data cannot legitimately answer. There are many reasons why large-scale assessment data do not adequately reflect the strengths and needs of individual students relative to specific subject areas at specific grade levels; we address those reasons in this chapter. However, the fact that large-scale assessments are limited in the types of questions they can answer warrants a tenet of assessment literacy.

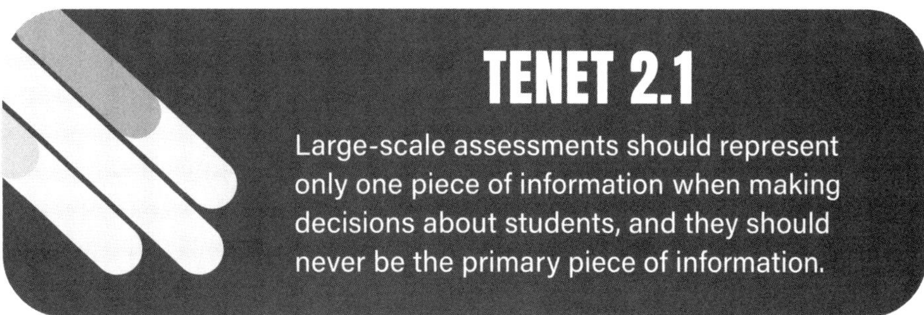

Implications of tenet 2.1 might include the following.

- **Educating stakeholders on the role of large-scale assessments:** Schools and districts should prioritize educating stakeholders, including families, teachers, and administrators, about the purpose and limitations of large-scale assessments. This understanding helps ensure that everyone involved recognizes these assessments as one tool among many to assess student progress. Stakeholders should be informed about how large-scale assessment results contribute to decisions and how they fit into the larger picture of a student's overall educational experience.
- **Preparing for stakeholder questions with broader data:** Leaders and educators need to be prepared to answer the types of questions posed by stakeholders using a variety of data sources beyond large-scale assessments. Establishing clear goals for student improvement, along with multiple methods for measuring progress, reinforces that large-scale assessments are just one piece of the puzzle and that a more nuanced approach to student assessment is necessary.

- **Highlighting the limitations of large-scale assessments in measuring progress:** It's important to help stakeholders understand that large-scale assessments are not designed to provide detailed insights into specific aspects of student learning. Leaders should be transparent about the limitations of these assessments, particularly when it comes to informing day-to-day instruction. By focusing on ongoing assessment practices that align more closely with classroom needs, educators can demonstrate how large-scale assessments fit into a broader strategy for supporting student growth.

Sampling

Sampling, also called *content sampling*, refers to the process of selecting a representative subset of topics and skills from a broader curriculum or content domain. When designing large-scale assessments, sampling is supposed to ensure that an assessment adequately measures the range of knowledge and abilities intended to be assessed. But, because of length restrictions, this mission is almost always doomed to failure. Consider the Common Core State Standards (NGA & CCSSO, 2010a, 2010b), which contain (on average) about twenty-five standards per grade level per subject area. According to Julia A. Simms (2016), each of those standards may contain from three to seven discrete elements of knowledge and skill. If each element of knowledge and skill is allotted one item (which is likely insufficient), then a test covering one subject at one grade level would need to contain a minimum of about 125 items to even begin to claim to adequately "cover" the content.

Sampling is widely acknowledged as a primary source of measurement error (Berman et al., 2020; Volante et al., 2020) and often prevents educators from making truly valid judgments about the performance of individual students on specific learning targets or standards. According to Volante and colleagues (2020), large-scale assessments involve "sparse sampling of content and [have] rare validity studies relative to the policy uses intended (Baker, [Chung, & Cai,] 2016)" (p. 26). That is, they aren't nearly detailed enough to provide the level of precision and specificity often attributed to them. Put another way, large-scale assessments create a data mirage; stakeholders think the information they yield is far more accurate than it actually is. When large-scale assessment data are used for high-stakes decisions—such as students' placement in college or career programs, or whether a teacher should be retained or released—the negative consequences can be severe.

Even if enough items were present on a test to cover all the important topics at a given grade level, it is also necessary to use a variety of task types on an assessment for each topic assessed. This is because one particular item may not (for a number of reasons) allow a student to demonstrate their actual knowledge and skill regarding a particular standard or learning target. Mark Wilson and Richard Wolfe (2020) stated the following:

> A student's knowledge and skill match up idiosyncratically with the demands of the test items. Items that are generally easy may be especially hard for some students. . . . Items that are generally difficult may be especially easy for some students. (p. 110)

In theory, an ideal assessment would include multiple items for each element of knowledge and skill being assessed to protect against this form of measurement error. But such protection comes at a cost: Such an assessment would almost certainly need to contain upward of 250 items, even if it were only addressing one content area at one grade level. This is not manageable from a test development or administration perspective, nor is it defensible to regularly use instructional time for the administration of such an extensive instrument.

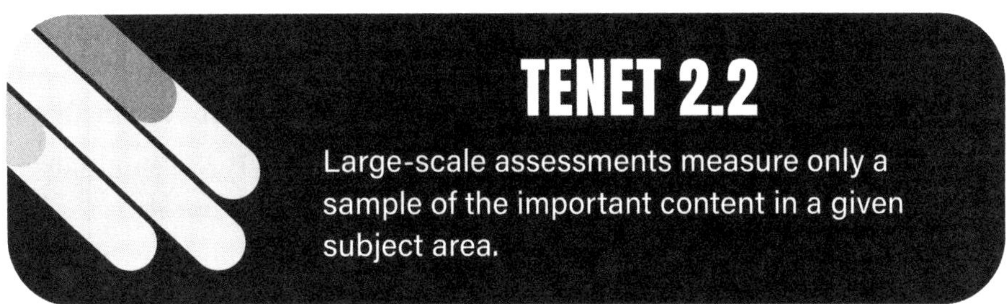

Implications of tenet 2.2 might include the following.

- **Inaccurate reflection of content importance:** The sampling of standards on large-scale assessments gives teachers a sense of which topics they should prioritize in their teaching, but this prioritization is often influenced by the number of items assigned to each standard on the assessment. Unfortunately, the decisions about which standards to assess are not always aligned with the actual importance or complexity of the standard. Some standards may be difficult to assess using the selected-response format commonly found on large-scale assessments, leading test manufacturers to exclude them or assess only portions of the standard that are easier to measure. This can narrow teachers' understanding of the full scope of the standard, potentially resulting in an incomplete or skewed representation of the curriculum in the classroom.

- **Risk of teaching to the test:** When educators align their instruction too closely with the topics sampled on large-scale assessments, they may narrow their focus inappropriately (a situation often called "teaching to the test"). This can undermine the broader educational goals of the curriculum, as teachers may focus more on the assessed standards while neglecting other important content areas not represented on the test blueprint. It is crucial to remember that just because the assessment blueprint does not explicitly include certain standards, it does not mean those standards are not important.
- **Increased measurement error and misleading results:** Given that large-scale assessments measure only a limited subset of content, they are prone to measurement error, which can distort the accuracy and reliability of the results. Educators and policymakers might mistakenly assume that the data produced by these assessments are more precise than they actually are, leading to misinformed decisions. These assessments often fail to fully capture a student's performance across all important areas of the curriculum, especially when only certain aspects of standards are assessed. As a result, high-stakes decisions based solely on these assessments may not reflect an accurate or comprehensive picture of a student's abilities or the effectiveness of instruction.

Alignment

Many people assume that large-scale assessments align with the standards they purport to measure. That is, they think that large-scale assessments measure what students have been taught in a particular content area at a particular grade level. But this is not always so. As an example, take the SAT and ACT tests, which are often used in the United States to determine admissions for colleges and universities and are required for graduation in some states (Erwin, Brown, & Mann, 2023). These large-scale assessments are not based on any particular state's content standards (Camara, Mattern, Croft, Vispoel, & Nichols, 2019). Rather, "both tests are designed to measure the important skills that research has determined to be most essential for college and career readiness" (Way & Croft, 2020, p. 28). Using these tests, or data from these tests, to determine whether a state, district, school, or teacher is meeting their goals may or may not be justified, depending on the degree of alignment between state standards and the content and skills the test is assessing.

The remedy for alignment issues is to conduct an alignment study. In an alignment study, educators and content experts typically gather evidence to show how test items match content in standards documents. There are at least three formal methods for doing this: the Norman L. Webb (1997, 2007) alignment model, the Surveys of Enacted Curriculum approach (Porter, 2002), and the Achieve, Inc. (2006) approach. Table 2.1 provides a brief description of each, in chronological order of development. (Interestingly, although Webb is best known in education for his Depth of Knowledge [DOK] framework, test alignment and validation are his actual areas of expertise, and the DOK framework is only a single element of Webb's more comprehensive test alignment model.)

TABLE 2.1: Methods for Conducting Alignment Studies

Method	Description
Webb alignment model	Determines the strength of alignment based on four criteria: 1. **Categorical concurrence**—Are there enough items measuring each standard? 2. **DOK consistency**—Is the cognitive demand of each item equivalent to the difficulty and complexity indicated by the standards? 3. **Range-of-knowledge correspondence**—Do the items on an assessment adequately reflect the range of information encompassed by a standard? 4. **Balance of representation**—Does an assessment give equal attention to each objective in a given standard?
Surveys of Enacted Curriculum approach	Compares an assessment to the curriculum teachers report they are teaching, taking into account both standards and curriculum materials
Achieve, Inc. approach	Reviews six criteria to determine the level of alignment: 1. Accuracy of the test blueprint 2. Content centrality 3. Performance centrality 4. Challenge 5. Balance 6. Range Additionally, this approach requires that each assessment item corresponds to at least one standard, examines cognitive complexity of items and standards, and evaluates construct-irrelevant variance and range of difficulty as appropriate to the grade level.

However, alignment studies only offer a partial remedy to the alignment problem, for at least two reasons. First, alignment studies are based on human judgments, and humans are not always reliable, consistent, and rigorous. Catherine J. Welch and Stephen B. Dunbar (2020) pointed out the following:

> Given that most approaches for measuring the alignment between a test and standards rely on judgmental evaluations by groups of educators familiar with the curricular standards, these approaches frequently result in *unreliable and inconsistent results and not at the same level of rigor* that is expected of assessments with respect to reliability or classification consistency. (p. 8; emphasis added)

Morgan S. Polikoff (2020) stated, "Alignment analyses are hard and require actual humans to carry out. . . . [They] feel more 'art' than 'science,' perhaps because there is no obvious right answer or criterion" (p. 18). Researchers in the field of educational measurement and assessment developers typically rely on statistical calculations and computer-generated models to provide precise quantitative data relative to a large-scale assessment's psychometric properties. But with alignment performed by groups of humans, this is often difficult or impossible.

Second, there are strong incentives to ignore unpleasant findings of alignment studies. If the study shows gaps between the content in the standards and on the test, or misalignment between the two, what should test developers and state-level decision makers do? Adding items to a test presents problems in terms of the time required to administer it; longer tests take longer to administer, cutting into instructional time more and more. Also, Walter D. Way and Michelle Croft (2020) noted that "some standards do not lend themselves to being assessed as part of a summative assessment" (p. 29), and therefore, there is no way to add items to address content that might be missing. And cost is always a consideration. Changing a test's blueprint (number of items, types of items, and so on) affects all the psychometric calculations and validations previously conducted. Plus, there are costs associated with item development; writing and validating new items are expensive.

In light of the challenges with alignment studies and the potential misalignment between large-scale assessments and state or local standards, it becomes clear that large-scale assessments are not necessarily aligned with the specific content taught in schools. This misalignment can undermine their accuracy in evaluating educational progress and student readiness.

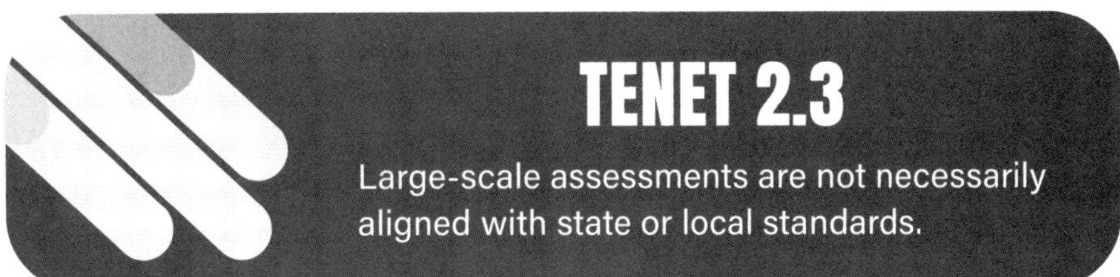

Implications of tenet 2.3 might include the following.

- **Questionable use of assessment data for accountability:** If large-scale assessments are not aligned with state or local standards, using the results of these assessments to evaluate the performance of schools, districts, or teachers may be problematic. The data from these tests may not accurately reflect whether students are meeting specific learning goals defined by local or state standards. This misalignment could lead to misinformed decisions regarding educational accountability and resource allocation.
- **Challenges in curriculum design and instructional planning:** Educators rely on assessments to gauge student progress and adjust their teaching strategies. If large-scale assessments do not match the content in state or local standards, there may be a disconnect between what teachers are expected to teach and what is being tested. This could create confusion in curriculum development and may lead to a focus on topics or skills that are not directly relevant to the learning objectives of the standards.
- **Limited utility for policy and educational improvement:** Policymakers often use data from large-scale assessments to drive educational reform and improvement efforts. However, if large-scale assessments are not aligned with the standards, this misalignment hinders efforts to assess whether educational reforms are truly having the desired impact on student learning.

Comparability

Different large-scale assessments are usually not comparable with one another, even though educators commonly assume that they are. As a case in point, consider two international large-scale literacy assessments: the Program for International

Student Assessment (PISA) and the Program for the International Assessment of Adult Competencies (PIAAC). Francesca Borgonovi (2022) examined the scores of teenagers who took both assessments and found that "estimates of literacy gender gaps in the two assessments are different" (p. 239). On PISA, boys scored significantly lower than girls. But on PIAAC, there is no gender gap. Yet both assessments purport to assess literacy. Clearly, "literacy" as assessed on PISA is different from "literacy" as assessed on PIAAC.

Stakeholders (and educators) sometimes assume two things: (1) that aggregate scores from different large-scale assessments can be compared and (2) that individual student scores from the same large-scale assessment can be compared. But these are unfounded (if not dangerous) assumptions. As Berman and colleagues (2020) asserted, "Countless factors influence assessment scores . . . including different item pools, timing of the administration (a few weeks' difference can make a big difference in students' opportunity to learn), test administration conditions, and accommodations" (pp. 2, 4). The number of variables that must match for comparisons to be viable is excessive. Berman and colleagues (2020) further noted the following:

> In general, comparisons are most defensible when the same assessment is given under substantively the same conditions to similar student samples at the same point in time. The legitimacy of comparisons thus becomes less certain as the assessment, the assessment conditions, student samples, and the time of administration diverge. Thus, there is a continuum where comparisons for certain purposes are appropriate and reasonable and some comparisons should not be made. (p. 4)

Educators and stakeholders often assume that aggregate and individual scores from different assessments can be meaningfully compared, but such comparisons are fraught with challenges. Multiple factors, such as test conditions, sample differences, and timing, can impact the validity of comparisons. Thus, comparisons should be avoided to prevent misleading conclusions.

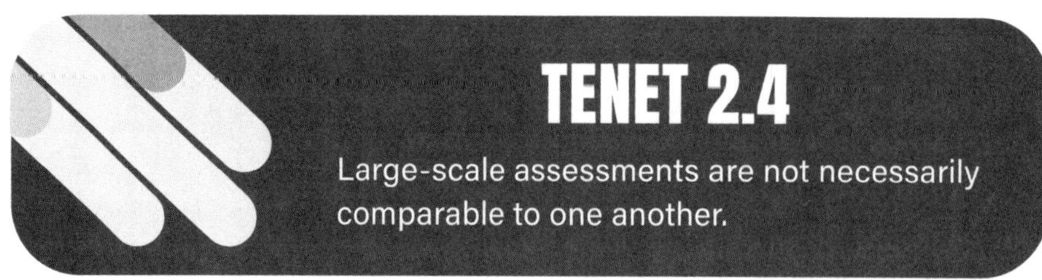

Implications of tenet 2.4 might include the following.

- **Risk of misleading comparisons:** Given the significant variability in the content, administration, and timing of large-scale assessments, comparing results across different assessments, whether aggregate or individual scores, can lead to inaccurate conclusions. Educators and policymakers must be mindful of these differences and avoid making cross-assessment comparisons that may not accurately reflect student performance or educational outcomes.
- **Need for context-specific interpretation of data:** When using large-scale assessments to evaluate educational outcomes, it is crucial to consider the context in which the data were collected. Comparisons between assessments with different conditions (for example, different student populations, testing environments, or time frames) may not be valid. As such, educators and researchers must carefully interpret data within the specific context of the assessment's design and implementation to avoid drawing inappropriate conclusions about student performance or educational effectiveness.

Construct-Irrelevant Variance

One of the most underreported and problematic aspects of large-scale assessments is construct-irrelevant variance. *Construct-irrelevant variance* is variation in test scores due to factors other than a student's knowledge and skill of the achievement construct being tested. An *achievement construct* is "the concept or characteristic that a test is designed to measure" (American Educational Research Association [AERA], American Psychological Association [APA], & National Council on Measurement in Education [NCME], 2014, p. 11). To illustrate, knowledge of seventh-grade mathematics would be the achievement construct for a test designed to measure a state's seventh-grade mathematics standards. If the test had to be completed in a specific amount of time, students' ability to answer items quickly could cause construct-irrelevant variance. Students who could not answer the items quickly but understand seventh-grade mathematics would receive low scores—not because of their lack of knowledge but because they couldn't answer the items in the allotted time.

Construct-irrelevant variance is such a problem for large-scale assessments that the *Standards for Educational and Psychological Testing*, edited jointly by AERA, APA, and NCME (1999, 2014), addressed it three times.

> **Standard 4.16.** The instructions presented to test takers should contain sufficient detail so that test takers can respond to a task in the manner that the test developer intended. When appropriate, sample materials, practice or sample questions, criteria for scoring, and a representative item identified with each item format or major area in the test's classification or domain should be provided to the test takers prior to the administration of the test, or should be included in the testing material as part of the standard administration instructions. (p. 90)
>
> **Standard 6.5.** Test takers should be provided appropriate instructions, practice, and other support necessary to reduce construct-irrelevant variance. (p. 116)
>
> **Standard 8.2.** Test takers should be provided in advance with as much information about the test, the testing process, the intended test use, test scoring criteria, testing policy, availability of accommodations, and confidentiality protection as is consistent with obtaining valid responses and making appropriate interpretations of test scores. (p. 134)

As seen in *Standards*, testing conditions and item formats are significant sources of construct-irrelevant variance, so familiarizing students with testing conditions and item formats can mitigate those problems. Charles DePascale and Brian Gong (2020) explained the following:

> If two students have equal levels of content knowledge and skills but differ in their familiarity with the item formats and tools used in the assessment, it is likely that the student who is more familiar and comfortable with the assessment will earn a higher test score. The observed difference in student performance would be attributed to construct-irrelevant variance (i.e., familiarity with the assessment). (p. 41)

In sum, construct-irrelevant variance poses a significant challenge to the validity of large-scale assessments, as it can lead to test score differences that reflect factors unrelated to a student's actual knowledge or skills. To minimize this issue, it is critical to ensure that students are adequately prepared for the assessment's specific conditions and formats.

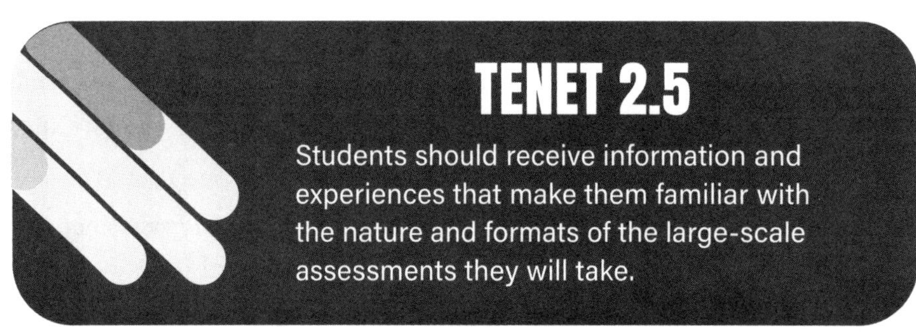

Implications of tenet 2.5 might include the following.

- **Reduction in construct-irrelevant variance:** Providing students with information and experiences that familiarize them with test formats and conditions mitigates the variance caused by unfamiliarity. This allows test scores to better reflect students' true knowledge and skills related to the achievement construct being tested rather than differences in how well they can navigate the specific test format.
- **Improved test fairness and equity:** Students from diverse backgrounds, with varying levels of prior exposure to standardized testing, may perform differently, not because of differences in knowledge but due to their comfort with the test format. Ensuring that all students have access to practice materials and clear instructions contributes to more equitable outcomes.

Engaged and Operating Achievement Levels

Another underreported characteristic of large-scale assessments is the fact that a test taker's level of engagement when answering the items on the test has a huge impact on how well the test taker will perform on the test. According to Steven L. Wise and G. Gage Kingsbury (2022), "the goal of achievement testing is to measure engaged achievement level, which represents the knowledge, skills, and abilities of a fully engaged (i.e., maximally performing) student" (p. 273). Stated differently, engaged achievement level represents a student performing to the best of their abilities, without interference from any construct-irrelevant variance.

As with most ideals, engaged achievement level occurs sporadically or even rarely. In many cases, the daily life challenges of an individual student get in the way, leading to an achievement level that is less than engaged. As Wise and Kingsbury (2022) explained, "factors often have a negative effect on test performance, and to the degree they are present a student's operating achievement level will be different (usually lower) than their engaged achievement level" (p. 273). Therefore, recognizing and minimizing these factors are crucial to ensuring that assessments more accurately reflect a student's true potential.

When interpreting test scores, educators (and psychometricians) typically assume that, for each item, the student's operating achievement level and engaged achievement level are equal. But this is almost never the case. Again, Wise and Kingbury (2022) explained, "To the extent that construct-irrelevant factors are present, operating achievement level will differ from engaged achievement level, and the resulting test score is likely to be a biased indicator of maximum performance" (p. 273). In this way, engaged versus operating achievement level is a specific form of construct-irrelevant variance that threatens the validity and fairness of large-scale assessments.

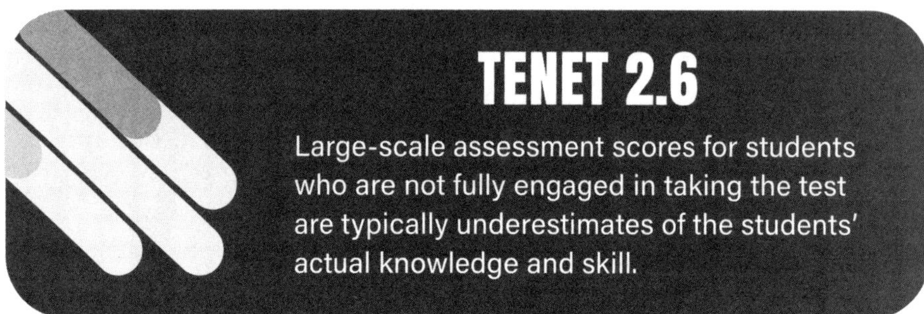

Implications of tenet 2.6 might include the following.

- **Need for engagement strategies:** Educational systems can implement strategies to increase student engagement during large-scale assessments. This could involve designing tests that are more interactive or offering breaks to reduce fatigue, ensuring that students can perform closer to their engaged achievement level and leading to more accurate reflections of their abilities.
- **Limitations of test scores as indicators:** Test scores should not be viewed as definitive measures of a student's potential, especially for those who are disengaged during testing. Educators may need to consider additional assessments or alternative methods, such as portfolios or observational evaluations, to obtain a more complete picture of a student's true academic capabilities.
- **Improvements to test design:** Test developers should consider how to minimize factors that cause disengagement, such as excessive test length, unclear instructions, or irrelevant content. Addressing these issues could help reduce the gap between a student's operating and engaged achievement levels, leading to more valid and fair assessment outcomes.

The Influence of Measurement Error

Educators frequently talk about the precision of tests, but they rarely talk about the underlying dynamic of precision. More precisely, the precision of a test refers to how much or how little error can be expected in the scores the test produces. The more familiar educators are with the concept of error, the more capable they are of determining how precise a given assessment might be.

There are many types of measurement error. One important type is *systematic error*. The defining feature of systematic error is its predictability; once you identify the source of systematic error, you can predict how it will manifest. This is not true of other types of error, such as *random error*, which is unpredictable. Because systematic error is predictable, one can take steps to mitigate or eliminate it. Thomas M. Haladyna and Steven M. Downing (2004) described systematic error as coming in two types.

1. **Constant error for all members of a particular group:** For example, if two raters score student responses, and one rater is harsher than the other, all students whose papers were scored by the harsher rater will be subject to systematic error. As another example, if there are two forms of a test, and one form is more difficult, all students who take the more difficult form will be subject to systematic error.
2. **Over- or underestimation of individual examinee scores:** For example, if a test requires reading comprehension to demonstrate a target construct related to science knowledge, two students with equal science achievement might receive different scores because one is better at reading comprehension than the other. In this case, reading comprehension skills are a source of systematic error when measuring science achievement.

Heather M. Buzick, Jodi M. Casabianca, and Melissa L. Gholson (2023) suggested a list of error sources that includes what they call a student's *personal characteristics*:

> By personal characteristics, we mean sociocultural factors that are relevant to learning and personal development. Examples include abilities to access and interact with the tested content and respond to test items (Mislevy et al., 2013); cultural and racial-identities (Paschall et al., 2018; Randall, 2021); motivation and engagement (CAST, 2018); and contextual factors that vary

> across individuals in the tested population such as opportunities to learn (Moss et al., 2008), rural education (Graves et al., 2021; Johnson, 2019), economics (Henry et al., 2020) and more generally, prior experiences (Mislevy, 2018). (p. 5)

Berman and colleagues (2020) highlighted two groups of students who are particularly vulnerable to systematic error: English learners and students with disabilities. Regarding English learners, they explained the following:

> EL students, by definition, are still developing their proficiency in English. Thus, it is important to provide accommodations designed to help them demonstrate their construct-relevant knowledge and skills without being hampered by construct-irrelevant limitations in language skills. (p. 7)

Regarding students with disabilities (SWD), they stated the following:

> For SWD, a disability may interact with the assessment situation to give rise to construct-irrelevant variance in their test scores. Minimizing such irrelevancies is the reason testing agencies provide accommodations to the standardized testing situation for SWD. (p. 182)

Both English learners and students with disabilities require thoughtful accommodations to ensure that assessments more accurately reflect their true abilities, free from the influence of factors unrelated to the constructs being measured.

As illustrated by these examples, systematic error arises from a wide range of sources. When these sources of systematic error are not addressed, students' scores on tests can be highly misleading about students' knowledge of the content being tested.

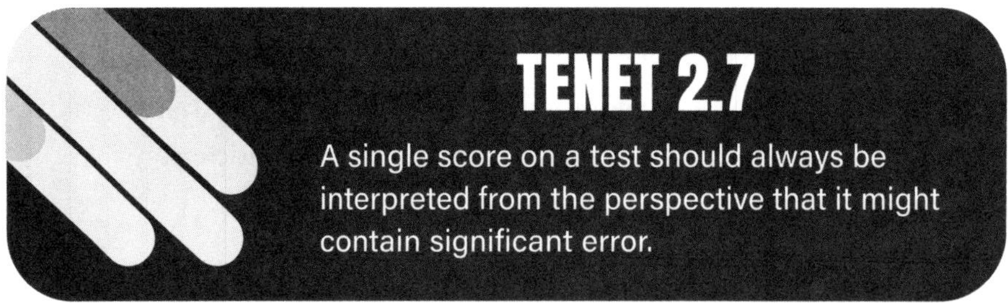

Implications of tenet 2.7 might include the following.

- **Increased need for multiple measures:** Relying on a single score to evaluate a student's abilities can be misleading due to systematic error. This highlights the importance of using multiple assessments or multiple forms of assessment to provide a more accurate and reliable understanding of a student's knowledge and skills.

- **Targeted accommodations:** The identification and mitigation of systematic errors—such as those related to language proficiency in English learners or disability-related factors—demand that educators provide tailored accommodations. This ensures that assessments measure the intended constructs, not irrelevant factors, for vulnerable student populations.
- **Critical interpretation of test results:** Test results should always be interpreted with caution, understanding that error is inherent. This perspective encourages educators and policymakers to consider the broader context of students' backgrounds and test-taking conditions, reducing the likelihood of misjudging a student's true abilities based on a single, potentially flawed measure.

Cut Scores

Cut scores can present significant problems for educators when making decisions about individual students. A *cut score* is the point below which scores indicate failure and above which scores indicate success. Clearly, this binary classification can oversimplify a student's abilities, overlooking the nuances of their performance and potentially leading to decisions that do not fully reflect their true potential or areas of need.

There are two ways that psychometricians set cut scores. The first is the William H. Angoff (1971) method, where a group of judges try to "think of a number of *minimally acceptable persons* . . . who would answer each item correctly" (p. 515; emphasis added). The second is the bookmark method (Mitzel, Lewis, Patz, & Green, 2001), wherein a panel of judges each receives a booklet with all the items on a test arranged from easiest to most difficult. Each judge then attempts to find the page (and put a bookmark there) that they believe represents "the divide between items that a student at the threshold of a performance level (the minimally qualified student) should master from those items that are not necessary to master" (Mitzel et al., 2001, p. 254). Both methods aim to establish a cut score that accurately reflects the threshold of minimal competency, though they differ in their approach to determining that standard.

While these judgments are made with as much precision and expertise as possible, it is easy to see that they involve a healthy dose of subjectivity and potential for human error. Howard T. Everson and Ellen Forte (2020) noted the following:

> Connecting the language of learning and achievement to the reporting metrics of any kind—raw scores, scale scores, or percent proficient—is always an exercise in needle threading, requiring groups of educators and other stakeholders to agree not only on abstract concepts such as degrees of proficiency but also on what constitutes "enough" when describing test-based performances of examinees.
>
> Even in those contexts where a single cut score is used to benchmark "passing" or "proficiency," nuances in the language used to describe performances above and below the cut-score pose challenges to agreement among panelists on where to draw that line. And, this has serious consequences for those whose educational and professional opportunities are altered because of where their scores fall in relation to that focal point on the scale. (p. 7)

Ultimately, the subjective nature of setting cut scores highlights the inherent challenges in translating abstract concepts of proficiency into measurable outcomes. These challenges can lead to disagreements among stakeholders, with significant implications for individuals whose futures depend on these decisions. Therefore, it is crucial to recognize the limitations and potential consequences of cut score judgments in assessment systems.

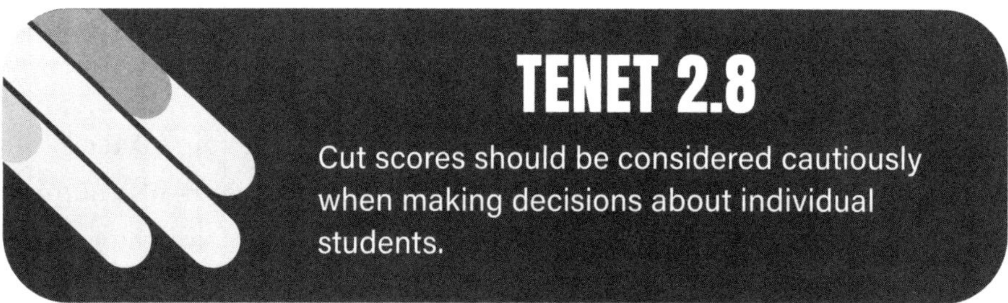

Implications of tenet 2.8 might include the following.

- **Risk of oversimplification:** Relying heavily on cut scores may lead to an oversimplified view of a student's abilities, reducing a complex set of skills and knowledge to a binary decision of success or failure. This could ignore the nuances of a student's overall performance, potentially overlooking strengths in areas that are not captured by the cut score.

- **Unintended consequences for students:** The application of cut scores in decision making may result in negative consequences for students who are marginally below the cut score. These students may be labeled as failures or underachievers, which could hinder their future educational opportunities, self-esteem, and motivation, despite their potential for growth in other areas.
- **Subjectivity in decision making:** The subjective nature of how cut scores are set introduces variability in decision making. Different panels of educators or psychometricians may set different cut scores based on their interpretations of "minimal competency" or proficiency, leading to inconsistencies and a lack of fairness in determining student outcomes across contexts or testing conditions.

Subscores

Educators often pay a great deal of attention to subscores from large-scale assessments. *Subscores* are scores that are nested within broad content areas. For example, a large-scale assessment might report students' overall scores for mathematics and then subscores for areas within mathematics, such as number sense, algebraic thinking and reasoning, and so on. These subscores are derived from *subtests*—distinct sections of an assessment designed to measure specific skill domains or content areas within the broader subject. While subscores purport to provide more detailed insights into specific areas of student performance, they should be interpreted with extreme caution, as they rarely live up to this promise.

Psychometricians and measurement experts have made the point repeatedly that, given the current architecture of large-scale assessments, subscores are so unreliable as to be almost useless. Joseph A. Rios and Alejandra A. Miranda (2021) reported that "some researchers have concluded that without massive changes in test development, reporting subscores may not be a worthwhile endeavor (Wainer & Feinberg, 2015)" (p. 69). Rios and Miranda (2021) continued:

> This assertion is based on numerous analyses of operational subscore utility, which have shown that, in practice, *subscores are often lacking technical adequacy* due to high intersubdomain correlations and/or low reliability (e.g., Haberman, 2008; Sinharay, 2010; Sinharay, Haberman, & Puhan, 2007).
>
> One major reason for a lack of subdomain distinctiveness is that testing programs are often retrofitting subscores from essentially unidimensional assessments that were not designed specifically to provide information at the subtest level (Luecht, Gierl, Tan, & Huff, 2006).

> Furthermore, due to operational constraints (e.g., testing time), subtest lengths are often short. As an example, Goodman and Hambleton (2004) found some testing programs to report subscores based on as few as five items, whereas simulation studies have suggested that a minimum of 20 items are necessary for adequately reliable subscores (Feinberg, 2012; Sinharay, 2010). (p. 69; emphasis added)

In effect, Rios and Miranda (2021) are saying the subscores are accurate pieces of information about students only if test makers have intentionally designed the subsections of a test to focus on specific knowledge and skills and have ensured that the subsection contains enough items to represent a valid sampling of the content. Unfortunately, this is commonly not the case.

In 2007, Gregory J. Cizek provided a dramatic illustration of the dangers of using subscores to make decisions about individual students. He explained that the total score reliability for the mathematics portion of a state test at the fourth-grade level was 0.87—certainly an acceptable level of reliability. That test also reported students' scores in subareas: algebra, data analysis and probability, estimation and mental computation, geometry, and problem-solving strategies. The reliability of these subscale scores ranged from 0.33 to 0.57—a completely unacceptable level of reliability when making decisions about individual students. Cizek (2007) memorably stated the following:

> In many cases, a teacher who flipped a coin to decide whether to provide the pupil with focused interventions in algebra (heads) or measurement (tails) would be making that decision about as accurately as the teacher who relied on the examination of subscore differences in the two areas. (p. 104)

In conclusion, while subscores may seem to offer a more detailed understanding of student performance, their reliability is often too low to be used meaningfully. As a result, educators should be extremely cautious when presented with subscores, as they likely do not provide accurate insights.

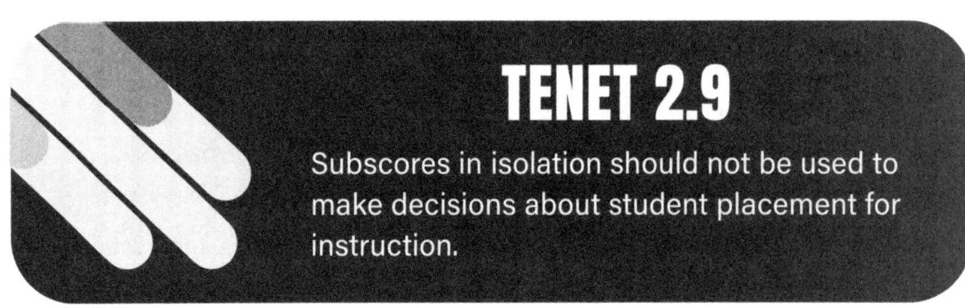

Implications of tenet 2.9 might include the following.

- **Educational decisions based on broader data:** Given the low reliability of subscores, educators should avoid using them as the basis for making decisions about student placement in specific instructional programs or interventions. Instead, they should incorporate a broader range of assessment data, including classroom performance, classroom assessments, and teacher observations, to make more informed decisions.
- **Advocacy for improved test design:** Schools and districts should advocate for changes in assessment design, such as longer subtests and better-defined subdomains, to ensure that subscores, if reported, offer more accurate and actionable information. Without such changes, the current system may continue to mislead educators about student strengths and weaknesses.

Accommodations

As we briefly mentioned in our discussion of construct-irrelevant variance, it behooves educators to make assessment accommodations for the specific needs of individual students. Stephen Sireci and Maura O'Riordan (2020) noted the following:

> The purpose of test accommodations is to allow students to demonstrate their performance in a manner such that confounding factors . . . are minimized. The logic is that accommodations will remove, or at least reduce, any obstacles inherent in a standardized testing situation that will prevent an examinee from demonstrating their proficiency with respect to the construct measured. (p. 182)

Berman and colleagues (2020) explained:

> Ideally, an accommodation would function in such a way that, if it were provided to all students, it would improve the scores of students with disabilities who needed it without affecting the scores of other students (interaction hypothesis).
>
> If this ideal cannot be attained, then the accommodation should at least improve the scores of those needing it more than it improves the scores of other students (differential boost hypothesis).

> When properly designed and used, accommodations promote fairness by helping to ensure that the test measures the same intended construct for all students. (p. 7)

Accommodations are designed to level the playing field and reduce the effects of construct-irrelevant variance on the scores of individual students.

However, as Sireci and O'Riordan (2020) noted, accommodations entail some problems. For example, a student with a language barrier receives a translation dictionary during a reading comprehension test. While this accommodation helps the student understand the text, it may inadvertently shift the focus of the test from assessing reading comprehension to evaluating the student's ability to navigate the dictionary and translate terms. This could result in a performance outcome that reflects the student's translation skills rather than their actual reading comprehension ability, introducing construct-irrelevant variance.

To help mitigate the problems caused by accommodations, plans for accommodations often include universal test design. *Universal test design* is an approach to test construction that seeks to create a flexible testing situation that does not require accommodations (Thompson, Blount, & Thurlow, 2002; Thurlow, Lazarus, Christensen, & Shyyan, 2016). It achieves this by focusing on principles such as removing time limits, reducing unnecessary language load, and ensuring all the options in multiple-choice items are plausible distractors.

Buzick and colleagues (2023) also recommended that test designers identify personal characteristics that cause construct-irrelevant variance and analyze them to determine how to address them. In one situation, a personal characteristic might be deemed inseparable from, but irrelevant to, the achievement construct. In this case, test designers might expand the achievement construct to eliminate construct-irrelevant variance:

> If a personal characteristic is not separable but is also both irrelevant to and interactive with the intended construct, then steps should be taken to clearly define or even redefine the construct to incorporate how these characteristics may be considered, especially during the scoring process.
>
> For example, suppose a test measuring science content knowledge requires a test taker to respond to an open-ended prompt with a written explanation. While the rubric clearly describes what aspects of the response should be used to determine the score on the essay, an expanded set of scoring instructions might emphasize that writing skills are not part of the measured

> construct and use of different writing styles, such as African American vernacular English, should not result in a lower rating or a penalty.
>
> For these situations, expanding both the construct definition and the scoring rules promotes the explicit acknowledgment of the possibility for personal characteristics that are not separable from the construct (as in this case where a written response is required) but also should not be used to evaluate the test taker (only their knowledge of science should be used). (Buzick et al., 2023, p. 8)

In a different situation, a personal characteristic might be deemed inseparable from, but relevant to, the achievement construct. In this case, test designers might consider revising the definition of the construct to be more inclusive of specific personal characteristics:

> If a personal characteristic is not separable but relevant according to the existing construct definition, consider revising the construct to precisely reflect the interaction or redefining the construct anew. Doing so may also require revising the purpose and intended use of the test. The former can be thought of as personalizing the construct itself.
>
> Returning to the use of African American vernacular English as an example, suppose the test is an assessment of writing skills and aspects of writing are part of the scoring rubric. Standard English would be expected in written responses, but there should be a discussion on whether the features of writing that would differ for those using African American vernacular English or other types of vernacular are relevant aspects to be evaluated and should be included as acceptable responses. (Buzick et al., 2023, p. 8)

As with the other characteristics of large-scale assessments, accommodation-related complications demonstrate that large-scale assessments pose many obstacles to estimating students' true levels of knowledge and skill in a given subject.

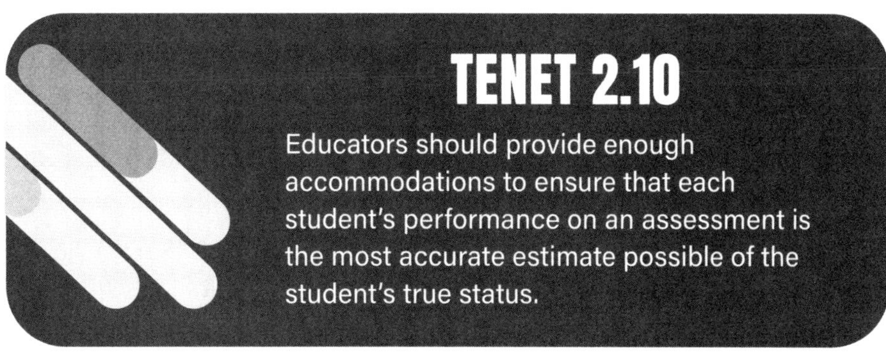

Implications of tenet 2.10 might include the following.

- **Fairness and equity in assessment:** Accommodations should be provided to ensure all students, especially those with disabilities or other unique needs, can demonstrate their abilities on a level playing field. This means recognizing and reducing barriers that might otherwise skew test results, such as language difficulties or the need for extra time. Without such accommodations, students' scores might not accurately reflect their true capabilities but rather their ability to navigate the specific challenges of the test format itself.
- **Personalized support for diverse learners:** Accommodations must be tailored to individual student needs, reflecting the variety of challenges students face. This could involve changes in test format (for example, text read aloud, extra time) or adjustments in how test content is measured (for example, expanding a construct definition to include different forms of language expression).
- **Construct clarity and consistency:** Educators must have a clear understanding of the construct being measured (for example, fluency versus comprehension) and how accommodations might affect that measurement. Educators need to carefully design accommodations to ensure they do not inadvertently change the nature of the construct being assessed. This highlights the importance of intentionality in test design and the application of accommodations that respect the integrity of what is being tested.

Summary

In this chapter, we examined the technical characteristics of large-scale assessments, which, while integral to educational policy, often fail to provide a full and accurate picture of student learning. These assessments can be biased, narrowly focused, and inconsistent, raising concerns about their fairness and reliability. We also explored the shortcomings of subscores and the importance of considering a broader range of data, including classroom assessments, to make more informed decisions about student progress. Additionally, we emphasized the necessity of carefully planned accommodations to ensure equity in assessment practices. This chapter set the stage for the next type of assessment that comprises assessment literacy, and the next part of the book: classroom assessments. Classroom assessments are a powerful strategy to move away from traditional, large-scale, one-size-fits-all assessments and adopt more inclusive, holistic, and reflective assessment approaches that truly support all students in their academic and personal growth.

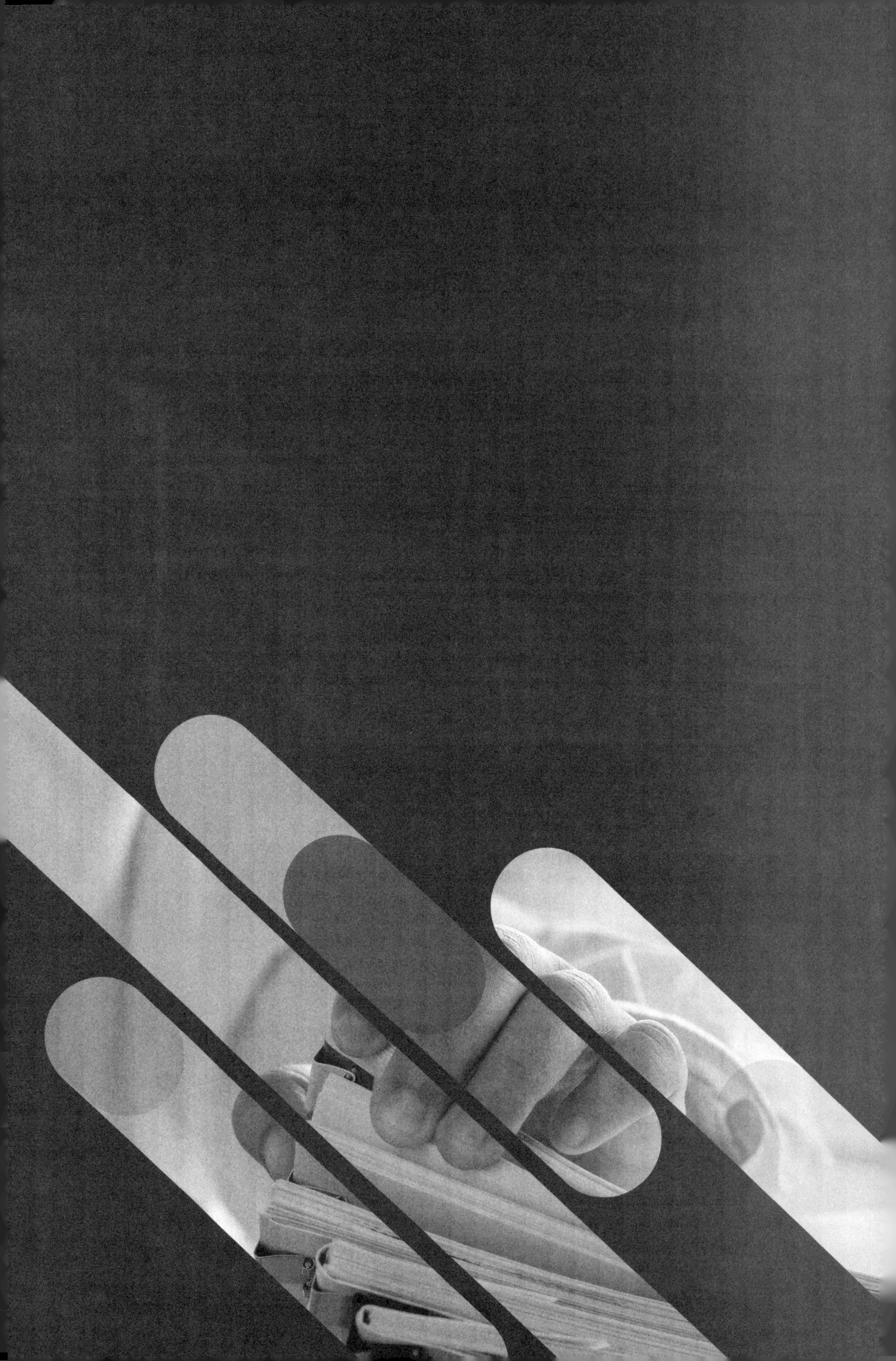

PART II
Classroom Assessments

Chapter 3

RETHINKING CLASSROOM ASSESSMENTS

For as long as teachers have been teaching, they've been designing and administering tests to their students. Thus, classroom assessments have always been one of the most common forms of assessments in K–12 education. Nevertheless, classroom assessment was rarely mentioned in the technical literature on assessment during the 20th century. James H. McMillan (2013) noted the following:

> Throughout most of the 20th century, the research on assessment in education focused on the role of standardized testing. . . . It was clear that the professional educational measurement community was concerned with the role of standardized testing, both from a large-scale assessment perspective as well as with how teachers used test data for instruction in their own classrooms. (p. 4)

McMillan further noted that an entire 1983 issue of the *Journal of Educational Measurement*, which claimed to focus on the state of the art in testing and instruction, did not bother to address teacher-made tests (Burstein, 1983). Additionally, the first three editions of the book *Educational Measurement* (Lindquist, 1951; Linn, 1989; Thorndike, 1971), each of which purported to be an up-to-date collection of all of the extant knowledge on assessment, paid little, if any, attention to classroom assessment. It wasn't until the fourth edition

(Brennan, 2006) that a chapter addressed classroom assessment. That chapter was simply and appropriately titled "Classroom Assessment" (Shepard, 2006). Finally, both editions of the *Standards for Educational and Psychological Testing* (AERA et al., 1999, 2014), which were designed to set standards for testing in psychology and education, made little explicit reference to classroom assessment.

We assert that assessment literacy requires that classroom assessment play a vastly more prominent role in making decisions about individual students. As such, classroom assessments will be increasingly judged from the perspective of measurement and psychometric theory, and assessment-literate educators will understand and use technical language to discuss classroom assessments. Table 3.1 summarizes some technical definitions from measurement theory that will facilitate these conversations about classroom assessment. Table 3.1 contains five terms that are best understood as a set. Specifically, the terms *assessment*, *test*, *score*, and *scale* are all components of the overarching term *measurement*. In effect, measurement is the context in which the other terms make sense.

TABLE 3.1: Technical Definitions for Measurement Terms

Term	Technical Definition
Assessment	"Any systematic method of obtaining information, used to draw inferences about characteristics of people, objects, or programs; a systematic process to measure or evaluate the characteristics or performance of individuals, programs, or other entities, for purposes of drawing inferences; sometimes used synonymously with *test*" (AERA et al., 2014, p. 216).
Test	"A collection of tasks; the examinee's performance on these tasks is taken as an index of [the examinee's] standing along some psychological dimension" (Lord, 1959, p. 473).
Score	"Any specific number resulting from the assessment of an individual, such as a raw score, a scale score, an estimate of a latent variable, a production count, an absence record, a course grade, or a rating" (AERA et al., 2014, p. 223).
Scale	"1. The system of numbers, and their units, by which a value is reported on some dimension of measurement. 2. In testing, the set of items or subsets used to measure a specific characteristic (e.g., a test of verbal ability or a scale of extroversion-introversion)" (AERA et al., 2014, p. 223).
Measurement	"The assignment of numerals to objects or events according to rules" (Stevens, 1946, p. 677). In education, numerals typically represent a position on some continuum of knowledge and skill.

Source: Adapted from Marzano, 2018.

If we translate the technical definitions in table 3.1 into less formal language, *assessment* is the act of collecting evidence. Thus, assessment is a very broad term and can be executed in a wide variety of ways. As we shall see, teachers do many things that qualify as assessments. The evidence gleaned from an assessment is used to make inferences about students. A *test* is a collection of tasks and is one form of assessment. Of course, in the classroom, such tasks commonly ask students to respond to various item types and probes. In subsequent chapters, we introduce many different forms of tasks that can be used in tests. A *score* is a numeral that represents a student's performance or status. A score is typically translated into some point on a scale, and the *scale* represents different levels of status on the dimension being measured. As we will see, this relationship has historically been problematic for classroom assessments because scores on different types of classroom assessments can mean very different things in terms of a student's status on a given dimension. Finally, *measurement* represents the rules that are used to assign scores on a specific scale.

Measurement is the ultimate purpose for creating and scoring assessments of various types; you are seeking to place a student on some continuum of knowledge and skill relative to a topic being measured. Historically, classroom assessments have not adhered to a tight system of measurement rules. In the paradigm of assessment literacy this book describes, they must. In addition to understanding technical language, assessment-literate educators must be familiar with classroom assessment concepts. One of the most important is unidimensionality.

Unidimensionality

One of the most critical but undervalued aspects of classroom assessment is that a student's score on a particular assessment should represent a student's status on one particular construct. A number of measurement experts have affirmed this. As noted in table 3.1, Frederic M. Lord (1959) explained that a test is "a collection of tasks; the examinee's performance on these tasks is taken as an index of [the examinee's] standing along some psychological dimension" (p. 473). Over forty years later, David Thissen and Howard Wainer (2001) explained:

> Before the responses to any set of items are combined into a single score that is taken to be, in some sense, representative of the responses to all of the items, we must ascertain the extent to which the items "measure the same thing." (p. 10)

A decade after that, Jay Parkes (2013) stated, "Any single score from a measurement is to represent a single quality" (p. 107). This is the essence of *unidimensionality*: An assessment that yields a single score should measure "only one dimension or only one latent variable" (AERA et al., 2014, p. 225).

Without unidimensionality, a score on a test is difficult to interpret. To illustrate, consider figure 3.1. Assume that two students receive a score of 70 on the same test, but that test measures two dimensions. One dimension is the topic of patterns. It is represented by the black shading in the figure. The other dimension is data analysis. It is represented by the gray shading in the figure.

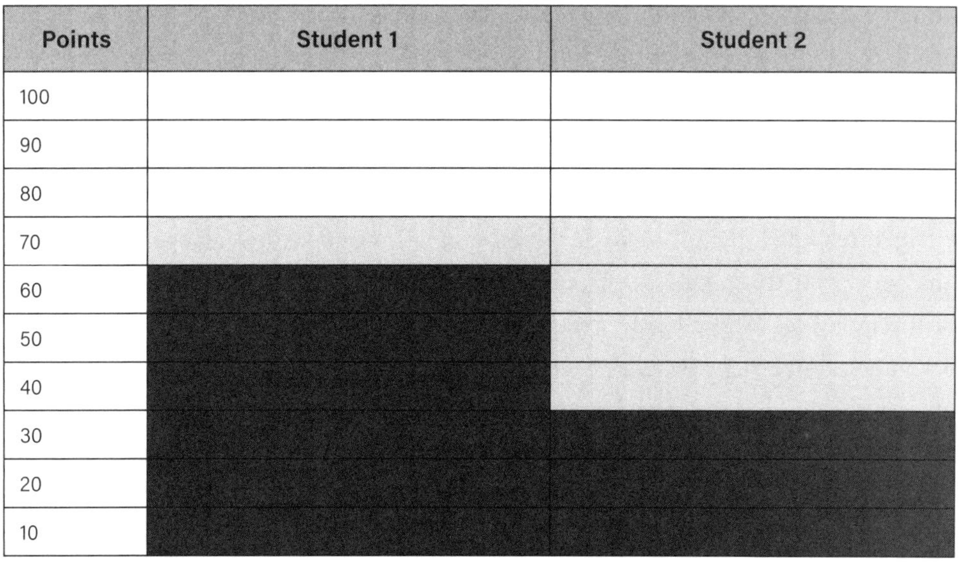

Points	Student 1	Student 2
100		
90		
80		
70		
60		
50		
40		
30		
20		
10		

Note: Black = patterns; gray = data analysis. Total possible points for black (patterns) = sixty; total possible points for gray (data analysis) = forty.

Source: Marzano, 2018, p. 23.

FIGURE 3.1: Two students' scores on a two-dimensional test.

In figure 3.1, each student received a total score of 70 on the test. At face value, a teacher might conclude that both students know the content on the test equally well. However, this conclusion would be inaccurate, since the test was designed in such a way that sixty points were allocated to the topic (or dimension) of patterns and forty points to the topic (or dimension) of data analysis. Student 1 received sixty out of sixty points for the topic of patterns but only ten out of forty points for the topic of data analysis. In contrast, student 2 received thirty out of sixty points for the topic of patterns and forty out of forty points for the topic of data analysis. *Although both students received the same overall score, they had very different levels of knowledge regarding the two dimensions on the test.* As this example illustrates, the overall score on a test that measures more than one dimension is uninterpretable in terms of students' knowledge and skill regarding specific content.

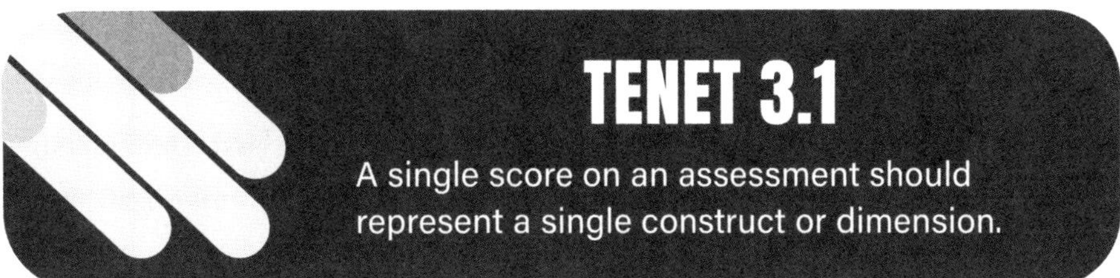

Implications of tenet 3.1 might include the following.

- **Clarity in assessment design:** Educators must ensure that assessments are designed to measure only one specific topic or dimension at a time. If an assessment is meant to evaluate a student's understanding of a single topic, it should be carefully crafted to focus exclusively on that content. This avoids the confusion that arises when multiple unrelated dimensions are measured by the same score. By focusing on a single dimension, teachers can more easily interpret the results and determine whether students have mastered the intended material.
- **Detailed feedback for targeted learning:** When assessments do measure multiple dimensions or standards, it is important to report separate scores for each dimension rather than combine them into one overall score. Providing distinct scores for each dimension helps students and teachers identify specific strengths and weaknesses. This type of feedback allows for more personalized learning and can guide both teaching practices and student effort more effectively than a single aggregated score.
- **Alignment and review of existing assessments:** Teachers and teams should regularly review their assessments to ensure they align with the topics or dimensions they are intended to measure. If an assessment inadvertently combines multiple topics or dimensions, the overall results may be misleading or difficult to interpret. By regularly evaluating assessments and aligning them to clear, specific learning goals (which might even be explicitly articulated at the beginning of the assessment), educators can improve the

unidimensionality of their assessments, ensuring that each score accurately reflects student status in a particular area.

Points and Percentages

Historically, one of the biggest problems associated with classroom assessments involves assigning a score to students based on how many items they answered correctly. The inherent problems with this approach were first acknowledged in the early 20th century by Edward L. Thorndike, a pioneer of measurement theory. Thorndike (1904) emphasized that the measurement of learning and knowledge is neither a concrete nor an objective process, for three reasons: "[1] the absence or imperfection of units in which to measure, [2] the lack of constancy in the facts measured and [3] the extreme complexity of the measurements to be made" (p. 5). Thorndike demonstrated these three issues using Rice's (1897) spelling test (which we discussed at the beginning of chapter 1) as an example:

> If, for instance, one attempts to measure even so simple and mechanical a thing as the spelling ability of ten-year-old boys, one is hampered at the start by the fact that there exist no units in which to measure. One may, of course, arbitrarily make up a list of 10 or 50 or 100 words and measure ability by the number spelled correctly. But if one examines such a list, for instance the one used by Dr. J. M. Rice . . . one is or should be at once struck by the inequality of the units. Is 'to spell *certainly* correctly' equal to 'to spell *because* correctly'? In point of fact, I find that of a group of about 120 children, 30 missed the former and only one the latter. All of Dr. Rice's results which are based on the equality of any one of his 50 words with any other of the 50 are necessarily inaccurate. (Thorndike, 1904, p. 5)

Thorndike's comments shed light on the futility of using "number of items answered correctly" as the metric for measuring students' performance on a test. Further, assigning the same point value to the correct spelling of the word *certainly* and the word *because* makes little sense in terms of accurately representing an individual student's spelling ability. Counting all responses on a test as the same in terms of the information they provide about spelling ability introduces significant amounts of error to the score. This constitutes the first problem Thorndike (1904) articulated: the absence or imperfection of units in which to measure.

In an attempt to correct this problem, many teachers try to weight items on a test. That is, they assign different numbers of points to different items based on the importance of each item. For example, a teacher designs a test that has ten items.

The first four items are worth five points each. The next four items are worth ten points each, and the final two items are worth twenty points each. The test has a total of one hundred possible points. Figure 3.2 depicts the pattern of scores for a student named Laurel.

Item Number	Possible Points	Points Earned by Laurel
1	5	5
2	5	5
3	5	5
4	5	5
5	10	5
6	10	10
7	10	5
8	10	10
9	20	10
10	20	10
Total	**100**	**70**

FIGURE 3.2: Points earned by Laurel.

As figure 3.2 shows, Laurel answered the first four items completely correctly and earned five points for each. On items 6 and 8, the teacher awarded Laurel the full ten points for each item, since Laurel's responses indicated a thorough understanding of the content. However, for items 5 and 7, Laurel's responses were only half correct, so the teacher awarded only half the possible points for each. Similarly, Laurel's responses to items 9 and 10 were also only half correct, so again the teacher awarded half the possible points for each. Thus, Laurel earned seventy of the possible one hundred points, or 70 percent.

One major problem associated with this type of point scoring is the criteria used to assign points to those items for which a student provides a partially correct answer. The more points an item is worth, the more difficult it is to accurately assign partial points. With Laurel, this was not too much of an issue because she provided either a totally correct answer or an answer that was half correct. Unfortunately, students' answers on classroom test items don't always follow such a clear pattern, and when that is the case, it is very difficult to assign partial points in a systematic way. For example, consider the two twenty-point items. It might be easy to discern student responses that should receive all twenty points (everything is correct) or responses that should receive zero points (nothing is correct). It might even be relatively easy to discern student responses that should receive ten points (half correct). But how does a teacher make distinctions between responses that should receive eleven, twelve, or thirteen points?

A second issue associated with this type of scoring is the assignment of total possible points for each item. Changing the total possible point value for various items on a test can dramatically change the percentage score for a student. Let's consider Laurel's overall score if the first four items on the test were worth four points, the second four items were worth six points, and the last two items were worth eight points, for a total point value of fifty-six points. Using the same answer pattern as shown in figure 3.2 (page 63), the student would have received forty-two of fifty-six possible points, for a percentage score of 75. Most students, teachers, and families would say there is a significant difference between receiving a score of 70 percent versus a score of 75 percent. This difference would be even larger with other changes in point values for specific items.

The type of point scoring this example illustrates is not an anomaly; in fact, it might be considered the norm in K–12 schools in the United States. Many educators believe that effective execution of the measurement process involves the following steps.

1. Assign points to items.
2. Award points for correct and partially correct answers.
3. Add up the points awarded.
4. Translate the number of points awarded to a percentage score.

But when one considers the technical meaning of measurement table 3.1 (page 58) describes, it becomes clear that the points-and-percentages method falls significantly short of placing students along some continuum of knowledge and skills. If simply changing the point value of items on a test creates significantly different scores for students, then the results of an assessment are completely equivocal and meaningless in terms of useful information about a student.

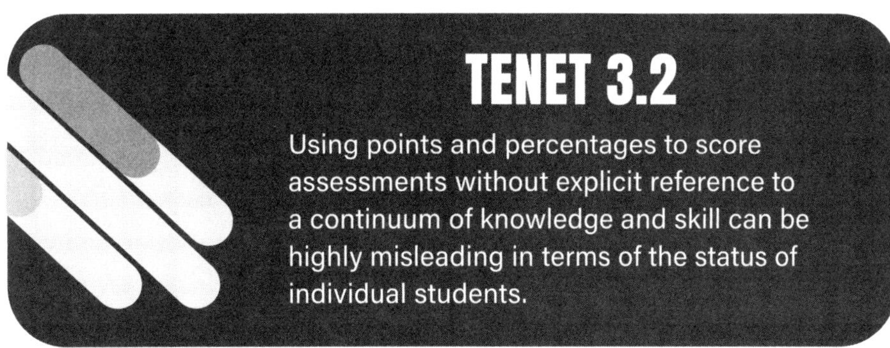

Implications of tenet 3.2 might include the following.

- **Inaccurate representation of student learning:** The traditional use of points and percentages oversimplifies the assessment process, failing to capture the complexity of a student's understanding. Without recognizing a continuum of knowledge, assessments are likely to inaccurately represent a student's mastery of content. For example, a student who scores 70 percent might appear to be struggling, but that score may mask the fact that the student has mastered foundational concepts while only partially understanding more complex material. This distortion can undermine the accuracy of performance evaluations and the usefulness of the assessment as a tool for understanding student learning.
- **Inability to differentiate between levels of understanding:** The points-and-percentages method does not account for the varying levels of difficulty among test items. A correct answer on a simple, foundational question may carry the same weight as a correct answer on a more complex question. As a result, students who perform well on basic tasks but struggle with more complex ones may receive the same percentage score as a student who performs moderately well in all areas. This lack of differentiation fails to convey a clear picture of where each student stands in their progression along a continuum of knowledge and skills.
- **Missed opportunities for instructional improvement:** Using points and percentages without context or a deeper understanding of the student's knowledge limits the potential of assessments to

guide instruction. When teachers view assessments through the lens of percentages alone, they miss the opportunity to focus on specific skills or concepts that need further attention. Instead of identifying specific gaps or misconceptions, teachers may simply see a score and make assumptions about a student's overall ability. This prevents targeted interventions or differentiated instruction that could address the nuances of individual student needs based on their mastery of different types of content.

Explicit Knowledge Continuums

As discussed in the introduction, assessment in the U.S. educational system is founded on beliefs and assumptions that can be traced to attempts to measure intelligence at the start of the 20th century. One of these assumptions was that intelligence was latent; it could not be observed. This assumption spilled over onto the knowledge and skills taught in schools; educators assumed that knowledge and skills were also latent and could not be observed directly. This made it seem reasonable to use test items and percentages as a proxy for positioning students along a continuum of knowledge or skill (Galton, 1883; Pearson, 1896; Spearman, 1904; Thurstone, 1928, 1931, 1934). But the assumption that knowledge and skills are latent traits is wrong. Furthermore, it breeds uncertainty and destroys precision when trying to determine a student's status relative to a particular topic or aspect of knowledge or skill. As long as the "knowledge as latent trait" perspective is used as a measurement model in education, there can be little precision in classroom assessments. Fortunately, there is an alternative perspective. Unlike the latent-trait perspective—which is rooted in the dark history of intelligence testing and eugenics—the *item-specification* perspective springs from 21st century test development theory (Downing & Haladyna, 2006; Haladyna, 1994; Haladyna & Rodriguez, 2013; Mehrens & Lehmann, 1991; Nitko & Brookhart, 2011; Popham, 2017). At its core, item specification seeks to identify the relative complexity of various test items by articulating the underlying continuum of knowledge or skill being measured.

A direct approach to articulating underlying continuums of knowledge is to create *proficiency scales*. Since 1996, Robert J. Marzano and colleagues have developed and refined the format and use of proficiency scales (Marzano, 2000, 2006, 2010; Marzano & Kendall, 1996; Marzano, Norford, Finn, & Finn, 2017; Simms,

2016). To create proficiency scales, you must first generate measurement topics for each subject area at each grade level. Focus statements can expedite this process significantly.

Focus Statements and Measurement Topics

Robert J. Marzano, Jennifer S. Norford, and Mike Ruyle (2019) recommended that educators rewrite standards statements in such a way that they provide a clear and unequivocal focus for classroom instruction and assessment. These rewritten standards statements are referred to as *focus statements*. To illustrate, consider table 3.2. The focus statements in table 3.2 extract the content from each standard that will be the focus of instruction and assessment. Focus statements should be detailed enough to provide guidance for assessment without adding unnecessary complexity. One or more focus statements are associated with each measurement topic. A *measurement topic* consists of a few words or a phrase; it is a shorthand name for a category of content that is "considered important enough to assess multiple times at the school level or district level in an effort to determine the most accurate scores for individual students" (Marzano et al., 2019, p. 19). The right column in table 3.2 lists the measurement topic for each focus statement.

TABLE 3.2: Standards With Focus Statements and Measurement Topics

Subject	Standard	Focus Statement	Measurement Topic
Science (K–2)	Students understand that the sun supplies heat and light to earth.	Knows the relationship between the sun and the earth	The Sun and the Earth
Physical Education (K–2)	Students use control in travel activities on a variety of body parts (for example, travel in backward directions and change directions quickly and safely, without falling; change speed and direction in response to various rhythms; combine traveling patterns to music).	Executes control of various body parts while engaging in different bodily activities	Body Control
Mathematics (3–5)	Students understand the basic concept of a sample (for example, a large sample leads to more reliable information; a small part of something may have unique characteristics but not be an accurate representation of the whole).	Knows characteristics of a sample	Samples

continued →

Subject	Standard	Focus Statement	Measurement Topic
Geography (3–5)	Students know patterns on the landscape produced by physical processes (for example, the drainage basin of a river system, the ridge-and-valley pattern of the Appalachians, vegetation on the windward and leeward sides of a mountain range).	Knows specific types of landscape patterns	Landscape Patterns
Health (3–5)	Students set personal health goals and make progress toward those goals.	Executes the process of setting goals regarding personal health	Personal Health Goals
Technology (3–5)	Students use proper fingering for all keys, beginning from the home row, maintaining proper posture while using the keyboard.	Executes the process of keyboarding	Keyboarding
Dance (5–8)	Students demonstrate a range of movement qualities.	Executes two or more movement qualities in the context of a single dance (for example, collapse, percussive, suspended)	Dance Movements
U.S. History (7–8)	Students understand the circumstances that shaped the Civil War and its outcomes (for example, differences between the economic, technological, and human resources of both sides; impact of the Emancipation Proclamation on the outcome of the war)	Knows events that caused the Civil War and the outcomes of that war	Causes and Outcomes of the Civil War
Language Arts (9–12)	Students use reading strategies and skills to understand a variety of informational texts (for example, textbooks, biographical sketches, letters, diaries, directions, procedures, magazines, essays, and primary sources).	Executes specific reading strategies and skills	Reading Strategies

Subject	Standard	Focus Statement	Measurement Topic
Civics (9–12)	Students know the major ideas of republicanism (for example, government of a republic seeks the public or common good rather than the good of a particular group or class of society; civic virtue of citizens is essential, with citizens putting the public or common good above their private interests).	Knows characteristics of republicanism	Republicanism
Economics (9–12)	Students understand that most federal tax revenue comes from personal income and payroll taxes, and these taxes are used to fund education, public welfare, road construction and repair, and public safety.	Knows the source and use of federal taxes	Federal Taxes
Foreign Languages (9–12)	Students use the target language and its idioms to demonstrate appropriate cultural responses (for example, expressing gratitude, extending and receiving invitations, closing a conversation, negotiating solutions to problems).	Executes the process of using idioms and language to demonstrate appropriate cultural responses	Using Idioms

Source for standards: McREL, 2024.
Source: Adapted from Marzano et al., 2019.

Notice that focus statements are worded in such a way as to highlight the type of knowledge they represent. Those that begin with the word *knows* are examples of declarative knowledge. Those that begin with the word *executes* are examples of procedural knowledge. We address the distinction between declarative knowledge and procedural knowledge in depth in the next section (page 74). For now, we simply note that different subject areas have differing proportions of declarative and procedural knowledge. This was demonstrated in a study conducted at Mid-continent Research for Education and Learning (McREL, 2024), with researchers analyzing standards in fourteen subject areas to determine the distribution of declarative and procedural knowledge in each. Seventy-seven percent of the standards in this study involved declarative content and 23 percent involved procedural content (for additional details about the McREL study, please see Marzano et al., 2019, p. 21). That noted, there is some significant variation from subject area to subject area. For example, physical education, life skills, arts, and foreign language are about equal in terms of their distribution of declarative and procedural content, whereas civics and economics have no procedural content.

Proficiency Scales

Once focus statements and measurement topics have been identified, each measurement topic may be more fully defined by a proficiency scale. As mentioned previously, the format and use of proficiency scales have progressed over three decades of development and use (Marzano, 2000, 2006, 2010; Marzano & Kendall, 1996; Marzano et al., 2017; Simms, 2016). Proficiency scales fully define each measurement topic by articulating the continuum of knowledge or skill for that topic. Figure 3.3 shows one example of a proficiency scale.

4.0	The student will: • Use mental computation and estimation strategies to assess the reasonableness of an answer at different stages of solving a problem (for example, when given that a boy has 374 more baseball cards than a friend who has 221 baseball cards, and when given that he then buys another 186 cards, use rounding to estimate that the number of baseball cards the boy started with should be close to 600 and the number of cards he ended up with should be close to 800).
3.5	In addition to score 3.0 performance, partial success at score 4.0 content
3.0	The student will: **Round a given number to the nearest 10 or 100** (for example, round the numbers 23, 50, 95, 447, 283, 509, and 962 to the nearest 10 and the nearest 100).
2.5	No major errors or omissions regarding score 2.0 content, and partial success at score 3.0 content
2.0	The student will recognize or recall specific vocabulary (for example, ***digit, estimate, hundreds, number line, ones, place, place value, round, round down, round up, tens, thousands***) and perform basic processes such as: • Identify multiples of 10 and 100. • Identify relationships between place values. For example, explain that ten 1s are equal to one 10 and that ten 10s are equal to one 100. • Explain that rounding a number to a given place estimates or approximates the value of the number to the nearest multiple of that place. For example, rounding a number to the nearest 10 approximates the value of that number to the nearest multiple of 10. • Explain that rounding a number to a given place will leave a value of zero in each place that is smaller than (to the right of) the targeted place. For example, rounding a number to the nearest 100 will leave a value of 0 in the tens and ones places. • Use a number line to find the nearest multiple of a specified place for a given number. For example, when given the number 146 represented on a number line, identify 100 as the closest multiple of 100. • Explain that a number will be rounded up to a given place if the digit in the place immediately to the right is greater than or equal to 5, and will be rounded down if the digit is less than or equal to 4. • Identify situations in which rounding might be useful. For example, explain that rounding two addends and quickly calculating their sum can be useful for assessing whether or not the calculated sum of the unrounded addends is accurate.

1.5	Partial success at score 2.0 content, and major errors or omissions regarding score 3.0 content
1.0	With help, partial success at score 2.0 content and score 3.0 content
0.5	With help, partial success at score 2.0 content but not at score 3.0 content
0.0	Even with help, no success

Source: © 2021 by Marzano Resources. Used with permission.

FIGURE 3.3: Proficiency scale for estimation (grade 3).

The proficiency scale in figure 3.3 is for the mathematics measurement topic of *estimation* at the third-grade level. A proficiency scale has nine score values that range from 0.0 to 4.0. Each of the nine score values in this proficiency scale represents a level of competence relative to the content of the measurement topic of estimation. However, only three values of a proficiency scale involve specific content.

The fulcrum of a proficiency scale is the explicit content at the score 3.0 level. It is the desired state of knowledge or skill relative to the measurement topic. Many teachers think of this level as the learning objective or learning target for students. In figure 3.3, that content involves rounding to the nearest 10 or 100. The score 3.0 level also typically provides specific examples of the content that would demonstrate proficiency. In figure 3.3, those examples include tasks like rounding the numbers 23, 50, 95, 447, 283, 509, and 962 to the nearest 10 and the nearest 100.

The score 2.0 level of a proficiency scale contains important vocabulary that will be taught directly. It also identifies basic processes and information that will be addressed. The vocabulary at the score 2.0 level includes those terms and phrases for which students need a general (but not in-depth) understanding to achieve score 3.0 status (see Marzano & Kendall, 2007). The basic processes at the score 2.0 level include information and skills such as identifying multiples of 10 and 100 and using a number line to find the nearest multiple.

The score 4.0 content involves an example of a specific task that could be used to demonstrate competency beyond the target content. These tasks typically require students to apply the content at the score 3.0 level in some manner.

In addition to the three levels of explicit content for a given measurement topic, proficiency scales also contain score values of 1.0 and 0.0, but these do not involve new content. These levels represent partial understanding or understanding with help. Specifically, a score value of 1.0 indicates that a student has partial success with score 2.0 and 3.0 content with help. The score value of 0.0 indicates that even with help, a student does not demonstrate even partial success with any of the content.

Proficiency scales can also include half-point scores. Student performances at the half-point scores indicate partial movement to the next level of the scale. For example, a score of 2.5 indicates that a student has partial competence with the score 3.0 content. In the next chapter, we introduce a version of the proficiency scale that involves quarter-point intervals. However, this version of the scale is more typically used to report summative scores across a series of assessments than to score individual assessments, where half- and whole-point scores suffice.

In effect, a proficiency scale allows the three levels of explicit content (that is, score values 2.0, 3.0, and 4.0) to be translated into nine different score values. The score values of a scale that do not involve explicit content allow teachers to determine what the student knows and can do independently or with assistance. Stated differently, they allow the teachers to identify students' independent levels of knowledge and skill and their instructional levels for specific topics (for a detailed discussion, please see Marzano, 2006).

One of the more powerful aspects of proficiency scales is that they eliminate guessing about the continuum of knowledge underlying a specific trait. When a proficiency scale is in place for a measurement topic, the continuum of knowledge is explicit. To operationalize this idea, consider table 3.3. We have added proficiency scale definitions to the technical definitions presented at the beginning of this chapter. When a proficiency scale is used, each of the five measurement concepts can be defined concretely and unequivocally relative to a specific measurement topic.

TABLE 3.3: Proficiency Scale Definitions for Measurement Terms

Term	Technical Definition	Proficiency Scale Definition
Assessment	"Any systematic method of obtaining information, used to draw inferences about characteristics of people, objects, or programs; a systematic process to measure or evaluate the characteristics or performance of individuals, programs, or other entities, for purposes of drawing inferences; sometimes used synonymously with *test*" (AERA et al., 2014, p. 216).	Any system a teacher uses to collect information about a student's status on the various levels of a proficiency scale
Test	"A collection of tasks; the examinee's performance on these tasks is taken as an index of [the examinee's] standing along some psychological dimension" (Lord, 1959, p. 473).	A specific type of assessment—usually written—involving items that pertain to various levels of a proficiency scale

Term	Technical Definition	Proficiency Scale Definition
Score	"Any specific number resulting from the assessment of an individual, such as a raw score, a scale score, an estimate of a latent variable, a production count, an absence record, a course grade, or a rating" (AERA et al., 2014, p. 223).	A number assigned to an assessment that indicates a student's status on a proficiency scale as indicated by the student's performance on the assessment
Scale	"1. The system of numbers, and their units, by which a value is reported on some dimension of measurement. 2. In testing, the set of items or subsets used to measure a specific characteristic (e.g., a test of verbal ability or a scale of extroversion-introversion)" (AERA et al., 2014, p. 223).	The explicit description of levels of knowledge and skill for a specific dimension within a specific content area at a specific grade level
Measurement	"The assignment of numerals to objects or events according to rules" (Stevens, 1946, p. 677). In education, numerals typically represent a position on some continuum of knowledge and skill.	The process of using evidence from a student's performance on a specific assessment to assign a score on a proficiency scale

Source: Adapted from Marzano, 2018.

Proficiency scales offer a clear and explicit continuum for understanding student performance at various levels. By articulating a progression of knowledge and skill for each measurement topic, proficiency scales guide the measurement process, helping educators more accurately assess and support student learning.

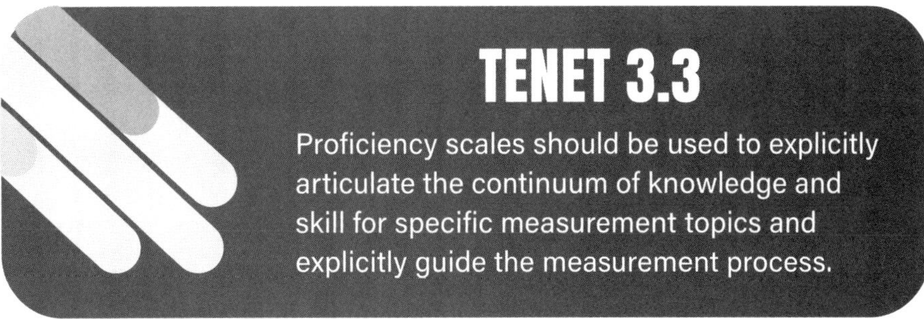

Implications of tenet 3.3 might include the following.

- **Enhanced precision in assessment:** By explicitly defining the continuum of knowledge and skill within proficiency scales, assessments can move beyond vague or generalized indicators of student performance. Teachers and students can more clearly understand where students fall on the continuum, whether they are mastering basic concepts or working at more advanced levels. This explicit articulation reduces ambiguity in grading and assessment, allowing for more targeted feedback and improving the accuracy of measuring student understanding.

- **Clearer instructional goals:** The use of proficiency scales directly ties assessment to specific learning goals. Since the scale shows the learning targets at each level, it serves as a road map for instruction, enabling teachers to design lessons and activities that closely align with the goals for each measurement topic. This clarity helps students focus on their progress and understand exactly what they need to do to improve.
- **Differentiation of learning levels:** Proficiency scales allow educators to identify students' independent capabilities and the areas where they may require additional support. By categorizing students' understanding within the scale, teachers can more effectively differentiate instruction to meet students' varying needs. This approach also highlights where students are making progress (even at partial levels), thus providing a more nuanced view of their learning journey compared to traditional judgments based solely on test scores.

While proficiency scales by their very nature provide educators with a great deal of focus, they can be made even more granular if they are tailored to one of three specific types of knowledge: declarative, mental procedural, or psychomotor procedural. The following sections detail proficiency scale design for each type of knowledge.

Proficiency Scales for Declarative Knowledge

In our discussion of focus statements and measurement topics, we noted that a standard usually focuses primarily on either declarative knowledge or procedural knowledge; focus statements for declarative knowledge typically begin with *knows*, whereas those for procedural knowledge begin with *executes*. In the coming pages, we explore more fully the distinction between declarative and procedural knowledge through the lens of proficiency scale design. We begin in this section with declarative knowledge.

Declarative knowledge commonly involves understanding the defining characteristics of something. To illustrate this, consider the proficiency scale in figure 3.4

4.0	In addition to score 3.0 performance, the student will demonstrate in-depth inferences and applications that go beyond what was taught. For example, the student will: • Describe a real-world problem in the school that the student might address by surveying a sample of students (for example, identify a problem such as the cafeteria wants to reduce the amount of food that students throw away, describe the sample that the school might use to help address this issue, and explain why the sample is appropriate).
3.5	In addition to score 3.0 performance, partial success at score 4.0 content
3.0	The student will: • Understand the defining characteristics of a sample.
2.5	No major errors or omissions regarding score 2.0 content, and partial success at score 3.0 content
2.0	The student will recognize or recall specific vocabulary (for example, *sample, data set, random sample, population*) and perform basic processes, such as: • Explain that samples can be used to make logical guesses about a larger set of people or things. • Explain that sometimes you need a sample because it is impossible to use the entire set of a population or things. • Demonstrate that you can get a simple random sample by pulling names out of a hat. • Explain why usually a larger sample is better than a smaller sample. • Describe why a small part of a group (a small sample) may not represent the whole group accurately.
1.5	Partial success at score 2.0 content, and major errors or omissions regarding score 3.0 content
1.0	With help, partial success at score 2.0 content and score 3.0 content
0.5	With help, partial success at score 2.0 content but not at score 3.0 content
0.0	Even with help, no success

Source: Marzano et al., 2019, p. 30.

FIGURE 3.4: Proficiency scale for samples (grades 6–7).

for the measurement topic of samples. Notice that the content at the score 3.0 level is a general statement—"The student will understand the defining characteristics of a sample"—derived from the focus statement for the grades 3 through 5 mathematics standard in table 3.2 (page 67). Some of these defining characteristics are listed at the score 2.0 level of the scale. However, being proficient at the score 3.0 level goes well beyond simply listing characteristics of a sample; it also involves knowing how the various characteristics fit together and interact. For example, it does not suffice to know that a sample can be generated by pulling names out of a hat. Students must also understand that even randomly generated samples can be subject to biases that prevent them from representing a larger population accurately.

According to Marzano and colleagues (2019), there are eleven different types of declarative knowledge that standards statements frequently include. The following list presents examples of each.

1. Abstract concepts and principles (samples)
2. Specific person (Abraham Lincoln) or type of person (U.S. presidents)
3. Specific organization (NAACP) or type of organization (civil rights groups)
4. Specific intellectual or artistic product (*Guernica*) or type of intellectual or artistic product (paintings)
5. Specific naturally occurring object (American Linden) or type of naturally occurring object (trees)
6. Specific naturally occurring place (Arctic Ocean) or type of naturally occurring place (oceans)
7. Specific animal (Secretariat) or type of animal (racehorses)
8. Manmade object (wampum beads)
9. Manmade place (Machu Picchu)
10. Naturally occurring phenomenon or event (solar eclipse)
11. Manmade phenomenon or event (light pollution)

Of these eleven types, abstract concepts and principles are the most common (Marzano et al., 2019). The proficiency scale in figure 3.4 (page 75) exemplifies the abstract concept of a sample, and table 3.4 lists other examples of abstract concepts and principles found in standards (for examples of the other ten types of declarative knowledge in standards statements, please see Marzano et al., 2019, pp. 109–120 [appendix A]).

TABLE 3.4: Examples of Standards Focused on Abstract Concepts and Principles

Content Area	Grade Levels	Standard
Physical education	K–2	Understands the benefits of physical activity (for example, good health, physical endurance)
ELA	3–5	Understands the defining features and structures of fantasies and fables

Content Area	Grade Levels	Standard
Mathematics	3–5	Understands the basic characteristics of mixed numbers
Foreign language	3–5	Understands the basic concept of an oral message
Civics	5–8	Understands the basic characteristics of the adversary system
Science	6–8	Understands the principle that energy cannot be created or destroyed but only changed from one form to another
Health	6–8	Knows situations that require professional health services (for example, management of health conditions such as asthma, diabetes)
Economics	6–8	Understands that the national debt is the total amount of money that the government has borrowed over all the years it ran deficits that have not been repaid
Technology	6–8	Knows that the design process relies on different strategies, such as creative brainstorming, evaluating the feasibility of various solutions, and troubleshooting the selected design
History	9–12	Understands the defining characteristics of slavery
Geography	9–12	Understands ways to use the concept of a region to simplify the complexity of earth's space

Source for standards: McREL, 2024.
Source: Adapted from Marzano et al., 2019.

Each of the eleven types of declarative knowledge has specific characteristics that are important to understanding it. For example, to understand an abstract concept or principle, a student would likely need to know the following.

- Examples or types of the concept or principle (for example, types of *debt*)
- Necessary conditions for the concept or principle (for example, the conditions necessary for something to be considered *valid*)
- Situations in which the concept or principle is necessary or important (for example, situations where *precision* is important)
- The features of the concept or principle that distinguish it from other concepts and principles (for example, *mixed numbers* versus other types of numbers)
- The superordinate category to which the concept or principle belongs (for example, *anger* is a type of emotion)

Table 3.5 lists these characteristics for each of the eleven types of declarative knowledge. As described next, teachers can use these characteristics when crafting content for the various levels of a proficiency scale.

TABLE 3.5: Important Characteristics for Types of Declarative Knowledge

Type	Characteristics
Abstract concepts and principles	• Examples or types of the concept or principle • Necessary conditions for the concept or principle • Situations in which the concept or principle is necessary or important • The features of the concept or principle that distinguish it from other concepts and principles • The superordinate category to which the concept or principle belongs
Specific person or type of person	• Accomplishments associated with the person or type of person • Events associated with the person or type of person • Physical or psychological traits common to the person or type of person • Places associated with the person or type of person • Requirements for becoming the person or type of person • The time period associated with the person or type of person • Typical actions or behaviors associated with the person or type of person
Specific organization or type of organization	• Beliefs associated with the organization or type of organization • Events associated with the organization or type of organization • People associated with the organization or type of organization • Places associated with the organization or type of organization • The purpose associated with the organization or type of organization • The time period associated with the organization or type of organization
Specific intellectual or artistic product or type of intellectual or artistic product	• Beliefs and values associated with the product or type of product • Events associated with the product or type of product • People associated with the product or type of product • Places associated with the product or type of product • The process associated with the product or type of product • The purpose or use associated with the product or type of product • The time period associated with the product or type of product

Type	Characteristics
Specific naturally occurring object or type of naturally occurring object	• Events associated with the object or type of object • People associated with the object or type of object • Physical traits associated with the object or type of object • Places associated with the object or type of object • The color, number, quantity, or dimension associated with the object or type of object • The system associated with the object or type of object • The time period associated with the object or type of object • Uses associated with the object or type of object
Specific naturally occurring place or type of naturally occurring place	• Events associated with the place or type of place • People associated with the place or type of place • Physical traits associated with the place or type of place • The color, number, quantity, or dimension associated with the place or type of place • The location associated with the place or type of place • The process by which the place or type of place is formed • The time period associated with the place or type of place • Uses of the place or type of place
Specific animal or type of animal	• Events associated with the animal or type of animal • People associated with the animal or type of animal • Physical traits associated with the animal or type of animal • Places associated with the animal or type of animal • The color, number, quantity, or dimension associated with the animal or type of animal • The system associated with the animal or type of animal • The time period associated with the animal or type of animal • Uses associated with the animal or type of animal
Manmade object	• Events associated with the object • People associated with the object • Physical traits associated with the object • Places associated with the object • The color, number, quantity, or dimension associated with the object • The process by which the object was designed and made • The system associated with the object • The time period associated with the object • Uses associated with the object

continued →

Type	Characteristics
Manmade place	• Events associated with the place • Locations associated with the place • People associated with the place • Physical traits associated with the place • The color, number, quantity, or dimension associated with the place • The process by which the place was designed and made • The time period associated with the place • Uses associated with the place
Naturally occurring phenomenon or event	• Places associated with the naturally occurring phenomenon or event • The causes or consequences of the naturally occurring phenomenon or event • The process associated with the naturally occurring phenomenon or event • The sequence of actions involved in the naturally occurring phenomenon or event • The time period or time frame associated with the naturally occurring phenomenon or event
Manmade phenomenon or event	• Places associated with the manmade phenomenon or event • The causes or consequences of the manmade phenomenon or event • The process associated with the manmade phenomenon or event • The sequence of actions involved in the manmade phenomenon or event • The time period or time frame associated with the manmade phenomenon or event

Source: Adapted from Marzano et al., 2019.

With proficiency scales for declarative knowledge, the score 2.0 content will most probably consist of details. To illustrate, assume the score 3.0 content in a proficiency scale involves declarative knowledge for the concept of the water cycle at the middle school level. That score 3.0 content in the proficiency scale might be stated, "The student will understand the water cycle and the sources of energy that power it (for example, create a diagram of the water cycle and explain how the movement of water between various sources is powered by either solar energy or gravitational force)."

Details for this topic at the score 2.0 level would likely involve factual information. A teacher might note that the concept of the water cycle is a type of naturally occurring phenomenon or event. Using the list of important characteristics for that type of declarative knowledge in table 3.5, the teacher might identify the following score 2.0 content.

- **Places:** Identify sources of water on earth (for example, clouds, oceans, glaciers, snowpack, lakes, rivers, streams, watersheds, soil, water tables, aquifers).
- **Causes or consequences:** Know the different states of water (ice, liquid, vapor).
- **Causes or consequences:** Know the role of the sun in the water cycle.
- **Causes or consequences:** Know the role of gravity in the water cycle.
- **Causes or consequences:** Know the role of organisms in the water cycle (plants and animals).
- **Process:** Know the water cycle as the flow of water between various sources.
- **Process:** Know how water on the surface of the earth enters the atmosphere (evaporation and transpiration).
- **Sequence of actions:** Know how water moves from the atmosphere to the surface of the earth (condensation and precipitation).

Score 2.0 content in the proficiency scale might also include terms like *clouds*, *glaciers*, *lakes*, *oceans*, *rivers*, *snowpack*, *soil*, *streams*, *watersheds*, and *water tables*. It is important to know, when identifying the vocabulary terms for the score 2.0 level, that these terms will be taught directly, and the expectation after such instruction is that students will be able to associate the word with its general meaning—they will not necessarily have an in-depth understanding of the word. As mentioned previously, for the purposes of a proficiency scale, vocabulary terms are intended to establish general background knowledge for students as opposed to creating in-depth knowledge for each term.

The general expectation at the score 4.0 level is that a student is able to make inferences and applications that go above and beyond the score 3.0 content. The complete proficiency scale for the water cycle in figure 3.5 (page 82) depicts our preferred method of articulating score 4.0 content. The description begins with the general statement that the student demonstrates in-depth inferences and applications that go beyond what was taught. This statement is then followed by a sample task. Sample tasks at the score 4.0 level typically involve content that was directly taught at the score 3.0 level or even the score 2.0 level. However, at the 4.0 level, students are expected to provide examples or applications that were not directly taught. For a more detailed discussion, consult *Making Classroom Assessments Reliable and Valid* (Marzano, 2018).

Score	Description
4.0	In addition to score 3.0 performance, the student will demonstrate in-depth inferences and applications that go beyond what was taught. For example, the student will: • Provide an example of a water cycle in a natural context and explain how this particular water cycle is affected by various elements such as the sun, gravity, and plants or animals.
3.5	In addition to score 3.0 performance, partial success at score 4.0 content
3.0	The student will: • Understand the water cycle and the sources of energy that power it (for example, create a diagram of the water cycle and explain how the movement of water between various stores is powered by the sun or the force of gravity).
2.5	No major errors or omissions regarding score 2.0 content, and partial success at score 3.0 content
2.0	The student will recognize or recall specific vocabulary (for example, ***atmosphere*, *cloud*, *condensation*, *evaporation*, *gas*, *gravity*, *lake*, *liquid*, *ocean*, *precipitation*, *rain*, *respiration*, *river*, *sources*, *water cycle*, *watershed*, *water table*, *water vapor***) and perform basic processes, such as: • Identify the different states of water (ice, liquid, vapor). • Identify sources of water on earth (for example, clouds, oceans, glaciers, snowpack, lakes, rivers, streams, watersheds, soil, water tables, aquifers). • Describe the water cycle as the flow of water between various sources. • Explain how water moves from the atmosphere to the surface of the earth (condensation and precipitation). • Explain how water on the surface of the earth enters the atmosphere (evaporation and transpiration). • Describe the role of the sun in the water cycle. • Describe the role of gravity in the water cycle. • Explain the role of organisms in the water cycle (plants and animals).
1.5	Partial success at score 2.0 content, and major errors or omissions regarding score 3.0 content
1.0	With help, partial success at score 2.0 content and score 3.0 content
0.5	With help, partial success at score 2.0 content but not at score 3.0 content
0.0	Even with help, no success

Source: Marzano et al., 2019, p. 33.

FIGURE 3.5: Proficiency scale for the water cycle (grades 3–4).

In sum, proficiency scales for declarative knowledge delineate various levels of proficiency with content that students must know or understand, from recognizing basic vocabulary and facts to demonstrating a deeper understanding and application of the concepts in real-world contexts. In contrast, proficiency scales for procedural knowledge are constructed slightly differently, a process we discuss next.

Proficiency Scales for Mental Procedural Knowledge

Mental procedures involve skills and processes that are executed mentally (as opposed to carried out physically). For example, converting fractions to decimals is a mental procedure. Table 3.6 lists examples of mental procedures found in standards.

TABLE 3.6: Examples of Standards Focused on Mental Procedures

Content Area	Grade Levels	Standard
Reading	K–2	Creates mental images from pictures and print
Physical education	K–2	Follows rules and procedures (for example, playground, classroom, and gymnasium rules) with little enforcement
Mathematics	3	Adds and subtracts within 1,000 using strategies and algorithms based on place value, properties of operations, or the relationship between addition and subtraction
Foreign language	3–5	Understands the basic ideas of oral messages and short conversations based on simple or familiar topics appropriate at this developmental level (for example, favorite activities, personal anecdotes, simple instructions)
Health	3–5	Sets a personal health goal and makes progress toward its achievement
Technology	3–5	Troubleshoots simple problems in software (for example, reboots, uses help systems)
Writing	6–8	Evaluates own and others' writing (for example, applies criteria generated by self and others, uses self-assessment to set and achieve goals as a writer, participates in peer response groups)
Geography	6–8	Uses thematic maps (for example, patterns of population, disease, economic features, rainfall, vegetation)
Life skills	6–8	Identifies and questions false analogies
Music	9–12	Reads an instrumental or vocal score of up to four staves

Source for standards: Adapted from McREL, 2024; NGA & CCSSO, 2010b.
Source: Adapted from Marzano et al., 2019.

Proficiency scales for mental procedures have some unique characteristics. To illustrate, look at the proficiency scale for the mental procedure of using pronouns in figure 3.6 (page 84). As shown there, the score 3.0 content in a procedural proficiency scale always involves the execution of a mental procedure without any significant errors. Note that in this example, there are two mental procedures listed

4.0	In addition to score 3.0 performance, the student will demonstrate in-depth inferences and applications that go beyond what was taught. For example, the student will: • Revise the use of pronouns that may be presented from other writers and speakers, ensuring that the pronouns agree with the subject.
3.5	In addition to score 3.0 performance, partial success at score 4.0 content
3.0	The student will: • Use pronouns in the correct case (for example, use subjective, objective, and possessive pronouns such as *she, her, hers, he, him,* and *his* in context). • Use reflexive and intensive pronouns (for example, create a sentence with and without an intensive pronoun and explain the difference).
2.5	No major errors or omissions regarding score 2.0 content, and partial success at score 3.0 content
2.0	The student will recognize or recall specific vocabulary (for example, *pronoun, object, subject, objective case, possessive case, subjective case, context*) and perform basic processes, such as: • Explain the difference between the subject and object of a sentence. • Identify objective pronouns in a sentence. • Identify subjective pronouns in a sentence. • Explain when to use possessive pronouns. • Explain when to use an objective pronoun and when to use a subjective pronoun. • Identify compound pronouns in a sentence. The student will recognize or recall specific vocabulary (for example, *intensive pronoun, reflexive pronoun*) and perform basic processes, such as: • Describe the difference between an intensive and reflexive pronoun. • Identify intensive and reflexive pronouns in a text. • Identify the antecedent for an intensive or reflexive pronoun. • Use a reflexive pronoun in a sentence. • Use an intensive pronoun in a sentence.
1.5	Partial success at score 2.0 content, and major errors or omissions regarding score 3.0 content
1.0	With help, partial success at score 2.0 content and score 3.0 content
0.5	With help, partial success at score 2.0 content but not at score 3.0 content
0.0	Even with help, no success

Source: Marzano et al., 2019, p. 37.

FIGURE 3.6: Proficiency scale for using pronouns (grades 7–8).

at the score 3.0 level. This is called *covariance*, and we discuss it later in this chapter (page 90). Briefly, though, when two procedures are sufficiently related that competence at one is associated with competence at another, then they can be included in the same proficiency scale. In this case, the use of subject, object, and possessive pronouns is closely related to the use of reflexive and intensive pronouns.

As figure 3.6 shows, when the score 3.0 section of a proficiency scale includes two elements, the score 2.0 section should have two lists of basic content, one for each of the score 3.0 elements. With procedural knowledge, score 2.0 content has more variation than it does with declarative knowledge. Specifically, there are two kinds of simpler content related to mental procedural knowledge: (1) simple procedures and (2) basic declarative knowledge.

Simple procedures are simple versions of the complex mental procedure stated at the score 3.0 level of a mental procedures proficiency scale. Look at the score 2.0 level of the proficiency scale for using pronouns in figure 3.6; simple procedures related to the score 3.0 mental procedures include the following.

- Identify objective pronouns in a sentence.
- Identify subjective pronouns in a sentence.
- Use a reflexive pronoun in a sentence.
- Use an intensive pronoun in a sentence.

As another example, if a proficiency scale for a mental procedure in mathematics contains the score 3.0 expectation that students will be able to use number lines to order and compare numbers, simple procedures might include the following.

- Plot number pairs on a number line and identify the pair that has the greatest difference (for example, identify that the difference between –78 and –182 is greater than the difference between 5 and –1.45).
- Plot numbers on the number line and identify the largest and the smallest (for example, identify that –0.004 is smaller than 1).

Table 3.7 (page 86) provides additional examples of simple procedures related to score 3.0 mental procedures.

The other type of simpler content related to mental procedures is *basic declarative knowledge*. One of the more interesting aspects of procedural knowledge is that it starts out as declarative knowledge. That is, you have to learn some facts and information about a procedure before you can attempt to perform it. For example, consider the mental procedure of reading a bar graph. Before a student can read a bar graph, they need to learn a basic strategy for the procedure. That basic strategy might be articulated as follows.

TABLE 3.7: Simple Procedures Related to Score 3.0 Mental Procedures

Content Area	Score 3.0 Mental Procedure	Simple Procedures
Reading	Analyze how the connotative meanings of words and phrases impact a text's tone, mood, or theme.	• Identify words that create a formal or informal tone in a text. • Identify words that create a particular emotional mood in a text.
Writing	Support claims and counterclaims with relevant and sufficient evidence.	• Annotate details in a text that relate to a topic or claim. • Identify pieces of textual evidence that support a claim and that support a counterclaim. • Identify one or more sources that support a claim. • Identify one or more sources that support a counterclaim.
Mathematics	Round a given number to the nearest 10 or 100.	• Identify multiples of 10 and 100. • Use a number line to find the nearest multiple of a specified place for a given number. • Use a number line to round up to a given place if the digit in the place immediately to the right of a number is greater than or equal to 5, and round down if the digit is less than or equal to 4. • Identify situations in which rounding might be useful.
Science	Evaluate possible solutions to engineering design problems according to a range of constraints and impacts.	• Identify constraints on possible solutions to an engineering design problem. • Identify potential impacts of a possible solution to an engineering design problem. • Identify how well a possible solution takes constraints into account.
Music	Interpret music by composing and arranging a composition.	• Demonstrate composing in eight measures. • Demonstrate composing in the proper key. • Identify melody in 4/4 time. • Demonstrate following the correct rhythm pattern.
Health	Evaluate a provided food plan for muscle growth over a six-week period.	• Identify caloric needs in a specific situation. • Identify high-protein food sources in a specific situation. • Identify the nutrients most necessary for repairing the body's tissue in a specific situation.

Source: Adapted from Marzano et al., 2019.

1. Determine what the vertical axis means and what the horizontal axis means.
2. Determine the unit of measurement of the vertical axis.
3. Identify the categories that are represented on the horizontal axis.

These three steps, articulated in this way, constitute basic declarative knowledge underlying the mental procedure of reading a bar graph. When the student begins to learn about reading a bar graph, they learn these steps and know them without necessarily being able to perform them. Look at the score 2.0 level of the proficiency scale for using pronouns in figure 3.6 (page 84); basic declarative knowledge related to the score 3.0 mental procedures includes the following.

- Explain the difference between the subject and object of a sentence.
- Describe the difference between an intensive and reflexive pronoun.

Thus, the score 2.0 level of a proficiency scale for mental procedural knowledge should contain some basic declarative knowledge important to the procedure, typically in the form of a description of the basic process involved when the procedure is executed and basic terms and details related to the procedure.

At the score 4.0 level, procedural scales commonly involve executing the procedure with some constraints or in an unusual context. In the proficiency scale for using pronouns in figure 3.6, the sample score 4.0 task requires students to execute the procedure of using pronouns in an unusual context; namely, they must change how another writer or speaker used pronouns to enhance the effectiveness of the message.

Proficiency Scales for Psychomotor Procedural Knowledge

Psychomotor procedures involve skills and processes that are executed physically. For example, using an overhand throw in baseball is a psychomotor skill. Psychomotor procedures are not uniformly found across the various subject areas. However, they do represent a significant amount of the content in subject areas like physical education and the arts. Table 3.8 (page 88) lists examples of psychomotor procedures found in standards.

TABLE 3.8: Examples of Standards Focused on Psychomotor Procedures

Content Area	Grade Levels	Standard
Dance	K–4	Uses locomotor movements (for example, walk, hop, leap, gallop, slide, skip) in different directions (for example, forward, backward, sideward, diagonally, turning)
Physical education	3–6	Uses mature form in balance activities on a variety of apparatuses (for example, balance board, large apparatus, skates)
Music	3–5	Performs independent instrumental parts (for example, simple rhythmic or melodic ostinatos, contrasting rhythmic lines, harmonic progression and chords) while others sing or play contrasting parts
Visual arts	9–12	Applies media, techniques, and processes with sufficient skill, confidence, and sensitivity that one's intentions are carried out in artworks

Source: Adapted from Marzano et al., 2019.

As with mental procedures, the score 3.0 content for psychomotor procedures involves executing the skill without significant error. To illustrate, look at the proficiency scale for the psychomotor procedure of throwing in figure 3.7.

4.0	In addition to score 3.0 performance, the student will demonstrate in-depth inferences and applications that go beyond what was taught. For example, the student will: • Throw with a high level of power and accuracy as needed during games or scrimmages.
3.5	In addition to score 3.0 performance, partial success at score 4.0 content
3.0	The student will: • Throw with proper technique during practice activities. • Throw the ball or apparatus so that it achieves the desired result during practice activities; for example, the student will move toward a teammate, move toward a goal, or move downfield or in the appropriate direction.
2.5	No major errors or omissions regarding score 2.0 content, and partial success at score 3.0 content
2.0	The student will recognize or recall specific vocabulary (for example, *opposition*, *trunk rotation*, *elbow position*, *follow-through*, *accuracy*, *speed*, *power*, *distance*) and perform basic processes, such as: • Throw properly during isolated practice activities. • Demonstrate proper grip of ball or apparatus. • Maintain proper balance during throwing motion. • Use core and lower body strength to generate force.
1.5	Partial success at score 2.0 content, and major errors or omissions regarding score 3.0 content

1.0	With help, partial success at score 2.0 content and score 3.0 content
0.5	With help, partial success at score 2.0 content but not at score 3.0 content
0.0	Even with help, no success

Source: *Marzano et al., 2019, p. 40.*

FIGURE 3.7: Proficiency scale for throwing (grades 6–8).

As with mental procedural knowledge, the score 2.0 content for psychomotor procedures can involve simple procedures as well as basic declarative content. The simple procedures in figure 3.7 include the following.

- Throw properly during isolated practice activities.
- Demonstrate proper grip of ball or apparatus.
- Maintain proper balance during throwing motion.
- Use core and lower body strength to generate force.

The basic declarative knowledge in figure 3.7 involves recognizing or recalling specific vocabulary, such as *accuracy*, *distance*, *elbow position*, *follow-through*, *opposition*, *power*, *speed*, and *trunk rotation*. At the score 4.0 level, the physical skill or process identified at the score 3.0 level is executed with constraints or in an unusual context. In this case, the skill of throwing is executed with a high degree of power and accuracy during games and scrimmages.

To sum up our discussion of proficiency scales for declarative, mental procedural, and psychomotor procedural knowledge, proficiency scales offer a structured way to articulate an explicit knowledge continuum for specific types of knowledge. Declarative proficiency scales often focus on understanding the defining characteristics of a concept or principle (although there are also ten other types of declarative knowledge), while mental procedure and psychomotor procedure proficiency scales deal with the execution of mental and physical skills, respectively.

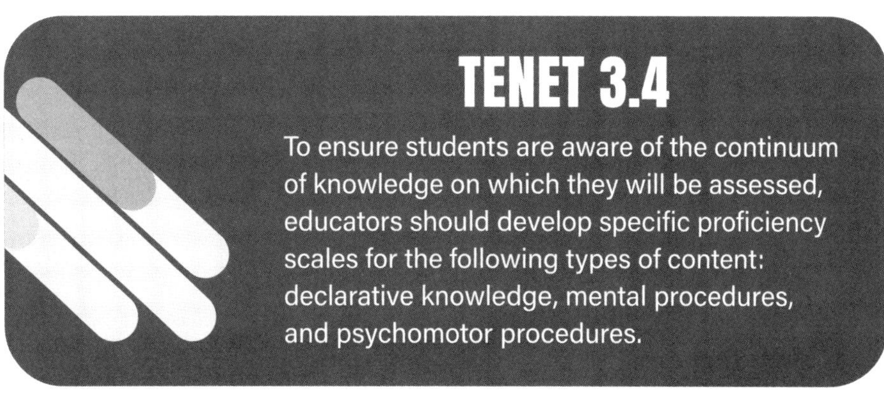

Implications of tenet 3.4 might include the following.

- **Clear learning progressions:** Developing proficiency scales for declarative, mental procedural, and psychomotor procedural knowledge helps students clearly understand the continuum of skills and knowledge they need to master. By breaking down complex knowledge into distinct categories and levels, students can track their progress more effectively, which can increase motivation and provide clearer goals for improvement.
- **Targeted instruction:** When educators design proficiency scales for each type of knowledge, they can tailor their instruction to the specific cognitive and physical processes that students need to learn. This approach ensures that teaching is more focused, allowing students to master foundational skills before moving to more advanced tasks. It also helps educators identify which aspects of knowledge a student may be struggling with, whether it's declarative knowledge, mental procedures, or psychomotor skills.
- **Differentiation of assessment:** By using proficiency scales to assess different types of knowledge (declarative, mental, and psychomotor), educators can create more nuanced and accurate assessments. This differentiation allows for a more comprehensive evaluation of student abilities, highlighting areas of strength and weakness across a range of knowledge types. Additionally, it provides students with a clear understanding of how they will be assessed, reducing anxiety and helping them focus on developing specific skills.

Covariance

One important qualifier to the generalization that all assessments should involve a single dimension is the fact that topics can covary (see Marzano, 2006, 2018, for additional detail on covariance). Simms (2016) explained, "*Covariance* means that two or more elements of knowledge or skill are so closely related that if student performance on one increases, student performance is likely to also increase for the other" (pp. 20–21). To illustrate the point, she highlighted the following three elements:

1. Compare arguments to alternate or opposing arguments.
2. Evaluate the relevance, sufficiency, credibility, and accuracy of evidence for a specific claim.

3. Identify errors in reasoning (i.e., logical errors, fallacies) in an argument. (Simms, 2016, pp. 16–17)

At face value, these statements might be thought of as independent dimensions; you could plausibly assign them each their own measurement topic and write a separate proficiency scale for each. But they can also be legitimately organized under the single measurement topic of analyzing claims, evidence, and reasoning. This is because it is likely that as skill in one element goes up, so too does skill in the other two elements, particularly if these three topics are taught together. These topics, then, are said to covary.

Simms (2016) provided a test as to whether elements truly covary. She explained that covariance can be assumed if all the elements can be integrated into a single task and offered the following task as evidence that the three highlighted elements covary: "Evaluate the argument in a text by deciding if the reasoning is sound, if the claims have sufficient evidence, and if the author appropriately responds to conflicting arguments" (p. 20). Thus, a proficiency scale can include multiple elements at the score 3.0 level if they covary. Figure 3.8 presents a proficiency scale that combines Simms's (2016) highlighted elements into one measurement topic of analyzing claims, evidence, and reasoning. Because the scale has three covarying elements at the score 3.0 level, it also has three sets of basic content at the score 2.0 level. As described previously, one of the indications that elements covary is that they can be combined into a single task at the score 4.0 level, as figure 3.8 shows.

4.0	The student will: • Evaluate the argument in a text by deciding if the reasoning is sound, if the claims have sufficient evidence, and if the author appropriately responds to conflicting arguments (for example, examine the argument in Charles Wilson and Eric Schlosser's book *Chew on This: Everything You Don't Want to Know About Fast Food* and determine how well the authors address opposing arguments that claim that fast food restaurants provide affordable and convenient meals).
3.5	In addition to score 3.0 performance, partial success at score 4.0 content
3.0	The student will: **ACER1—Compare arguments to alternate or opposing arguments** (for example, identify similarities and differences between the claims and evidence provided by two articles featured in *The New York Times'* Room for Debate feature "Taking Sports Out of School"). **ACER2—Evaluate the relevance, sufficiency, credibility, and accuracy of evidence for a specific claim** (for example, read Terra Snider's CNN.com article "Let Kids Sleep Later" and explain why the evidence for her claim that school should start later is or is not sufficient and credible). **ACER3—Identify errors in reasoning (such as logical errors and fallacies) in an argument** (for example, watch a campaign attack ad and identify how the advertisement employs unsound logic to discredit another candidate).

2.5	No major errors or omissions regarding score 2.0 content, and partial success at score 3.0 content
2.0	**ACER1—**The student will recognize or recall specific vocabulary (for example, *argument, backing, claim, evidence, grounds, paragraph, qualifier, reasoning, summarize*) and perform basic processes such as: • Describe the parts of an argument (such as claim, grounds, backing, and qualifier). • Explain the role of grounds, backing, and qualifiers in a claim. • Summarize what each paragraph of an argument seems to be saying. • Annotate a text's central claims and the grounds for the claims. • Annotate the evidence, or backing, given in a text. • Annotate qualifiers in a claim. • Use a graphic organizer to compare the claims and evidence for two arguments. **ACER2—**The student will recognize or recall specific vocabulary (for example, *accurate, cite, claim, credible, evidence, irrelevant, relevant, source, sufficient*) and perform basic processes such as: • List different kinds of evidence that texts can use (such as statistics, quotes, and historical facts). • Describe what makes evidence relevant, sufficient, credible, and accurate. • Outline the evidence for a claim in a text. • Annotate evidence in an argument that cites a source. • Rate the strength of a piece of evidence. **ACER3—**The student will recognize or recall specific vocabulary (for example, *argument, conclusion, fallacy, logic, premise, reasoning, sound, unsound*) and perform basic processes such as: • Describe common fallacies (such as using an overemotional argument, false appeals to authority, and attacking the opponent instead of the argument). • Describe the difference between sound and unsound logic. • Annotate words that indicate a premise (such as *since, because*, and *as an example*). • Annotate words that indicate a conclusion (such as *therefore, consequently*, and *thus*). • Outline the logic of an argument (for example, show which premises lead to which conclusions).
1.5	Partial success at score 2.0 content, and major errors or omissions regarding score 3.0 content
1.0	With help, partial success at score 2.0 content and score 3.0 content
0.5	With help, partial success at score 2.0 content but not at score 3.0 content
0.0	Even with help, no success

Source: Adapted from Simms, 2016.

FIGURE 3.8: Proficiency scale for analyzing claims, evidence, and reasoning (ACER; grade 8).

Proficiency scales with covarying elements, such as the one in figure 3.8, impact assessment design. Specifically, when elements in a proficiency scale covary, teachers do not have to include items for each element on a test and can assign a single score on the proficiency scale for an assessment (as opposed to a score for each element).

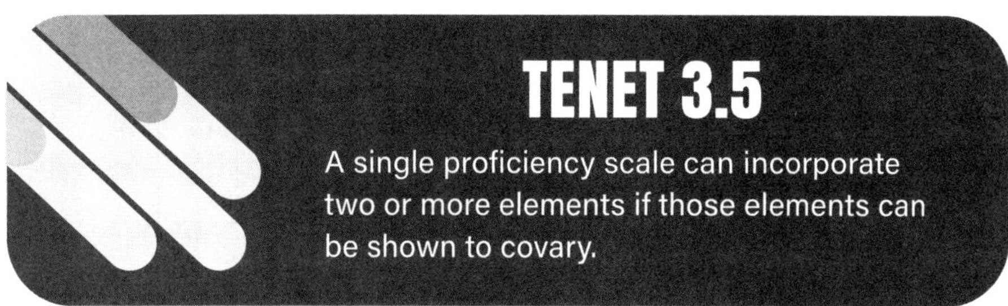

Implications of tenet 3.5 might include the following.

- **Streamlining assessment design:** When elements covary, they can be integrated into a single proficiency scale rather than be assessed separately. This means that educators don't need to create distinct items for each skill or knowledge area on assessments. For instance, instead of designing individual questions for evaluating arguments, evidence, and errors in reasoning, teachers can combine them into one task. This approach can make assessments more efficient while ensuring they accurately reflect students' abilities to synthesize and apply multiple related skills at once.
- **Promoting holistic learning and instruction:** By recognizing that related skills covary, teachers can design lessons that address multiple aspects of a topic simultaneously. In the case of analyzing claims, evidence, and reasoning, a lesson could integrate all three elements, ensuring that as students improve in one area (for example, comparing arguments), they are also likely to improve in others (for example, evaluating evidence and identifying errors in reasoning). This can lead to more cohesive and interconnected learning experiences rather than fragmented instruction.
- **Providing clearer and more meaningful feedback:** When proficiency scales integrate covarying elements, the feedback students receive can be more comprehensive and relevant. Instead of receiving separate scores for each component (for example, claims, evidence, and reasoning), students would get a holistic score that reflects their overall ability to analyze arguments. This simplifies interpretation of performance and provides a clearer understanding of students' progress across related skills, helping both students and teachers focus on areas that need improvement without being bogged down by the complexity of multiple discrete scores.

Misuses of Taxonomies

In *The New Art and Science of Classroom Assessment*, Marzano and colleagues (2019) explained that "taxonomies provide systems that describe different levels of complexity and understanding" (p. 48). Many educators want to use taxonomies when developing proficiency scales, and there are many available, such as the following.

- John B. Biggs and Kevin F. Collis's (1982) Structure of the Observed Learning Outcome (SOLO) taxonomy
- Norman L. Webb's (1999) DOK schema
- Lorin W. Anderson and David Krathwohl's (2001) Taxonomy for Learning, Teaching, and Assessing (the revised Bloom's taxonomy)
- Robert J. Marzano and John S. Kendall's (2007) New Taxonomy of Educational Objectives

Taxonomies can be useful tools when educators use them wisely. Unfortunately, many educators make a serious mistake when using taxonomies to create proficiency scales. The mistake is to mandate that certain levels of every proficiency scale must align with certain levels of a given taxonomy. For example, the revised version of Benjamin Bloom's taxonomy (Anderson & Krathwohl, 2001) articulates six cognitive levels.

1. Create
2. Evaluate
3. Analyze
4. Apply
5. Understand
6. Remember

Thus, educators using the revised version of Bloom's taxonomy for proficiency scale creation might create a template such as the one shown in figure 3.9. Notice that the right column aligns three levels of Bloom's revised taxonomy (analyze, apply, understand) with the score 4.0, 3.0, and 2.0 levels of the proficiency scale. At face value, such a mandate might seem reasonable and even somewhat logical: Shouldn't the target expectation (that is, the score 3.0 content) at least be that students can apply the content they have been taught? Shouldn't we expect students to achieve a higher level of complexity (that is, the score 4.0 content) by analyzing the content?

Proficiency Scale Level		Required Level of Revised Bloom's Taxonomy
4.0	**More complex content**	Analyze
3.5	In addition to score 3.0 performance, partial success at score 4.0 content	
3.0	**Target content**	Apply
2.5	No major errors or omissions regarding score 2.0 content, and partial success at score 3.0 content	
2.0	**Simpler foundational content**	Understand
1.5	Partial success at score 2.0 content, and major errors or omissions regarding score 3.0 content	
1.0	With help, partial success at score 2.0 content and score 3.0 content	
0.5	With help, partial success at score 2.0 content but not at score 3.0 content	
0.0	Even with help, no success	

FIGURE 3.9: Template showing misuse of a taxonomy for proficiency scale creation.

Unfortunately, this reasoning cannot endure a close comparison with the content in state standards; it unravels rather quickly when this logical thread is pulled. To illustrate, consider the following geography expectation for students in grades 3 through 5: "Knows patterns on the landscape produced by physical processes (e.g., the drainage basin of a river system, the ridge-and-valley pattern of the Appalachians, vegetation on the windward and leeward sides of a mountain range)" (McREL, 2014). This statement, extracted directly from standards documents, should be placed at the score 3.0 level of a proficiency scale. And yet it clearly does not involve applying the content, as figure 3.9 mandates. What are teachers to do in such a situation? It is not defensible to require students to apply this knowledge, thus holding them to a higher standard than what the standards documents articulate.

This is why educators should not mandate that certain levels of every proficiency scale align with certain levels of a given taxonomy. Instead, simply preserve the intent of the standards statement and then determine the natural hierarchy of the content. When doing this, it is important to be aware that declarative and procedural knowledge have their own unique hierarchical structures and their own hierarchies of cognitive operations that can be performed on them, as figure 3.10 (page 96) shows.

DECLARATIVE KNOWLEDGE	
Hierarchy	**Cognitive Operations**
Generalizations and principles	*Understanding*
Details	*Recall*
Details	*Recognition*

PROCEDURAL KNOWLEDGE	
Hierarchy	**Cognitive Operations**
Complex processes	*Integrated Execution*
Simple procedures	*Simple Execution*
Details	*Recall*
Details	*Recognition*

Source: Marzano et al., 2019.

FIGURE 3.10: Declarative and procedural knowledge hierarchies.

*Visit **MarzanoResources.com/reproducibles** for a free reproducible version of this figure.*

At the top of the declarative hierarchy are generalizations and principles. *Generalizations* are broad statements about characteristics of groups or types of things. For example, a generalization related to the science topic of natural hazards is:

> *In the last two decades, there has been a dramatic increase in the number of unusually large forest fires, sometimes referred to as megafires.*

Principles are statements of relationships that articulate the interactions between two or more entities. For example, a principle related to natural hazards is:

> *As fire suppression became the norm in forest fire management, smaller fires that would normally thin forests were prevented, allowing forests to become very dense and flammable materials to become overgrown, thus leading to higher risk of fire across larger areas of land.*

Generalizations and principles have details associated with them. *Details* include both factual information and vocabulary terms. For example, the generalization related to the increase in megafires involves the following factual information.

- Housing development in fire-prone areas leads to increased risk of fire from human causes and increased risk to humans themselves from fires.
- Heavy rains and snows caused by La Niña weather patterns increase the growth of annual grasses, which increases fire danger in drought-prone areas.
- The year 2017 was one of the most active years for U.S. wildfires, with more than 8.5 million acres burned.
- Frequent wildfires can change the animal and plant life in certain habitats and allow nonnative, invasive species to thrive. (Marzano et al., 2019, p. 50)

Vocabulary terms for the natural hazards example might include *drought*, *fire suppression*, and *La Niña*.

As figure 3.10 shows, the declarative hierarchy aligns with specific cognitive operations: understanding, recall, and recognition. *Understanding* is the highest level of cognitive operation for declarative knowledge and is usually reserved for generalizations and principles; when a student understands declarative knowledge, they can articulate how generalizations and principles for a specific topic interact with one another. *Recall* usually addresses details; when a student recalls details, they can describe the details that fit within specific generalizations and principles. *Recognition* is the lowest level of cognitive operation for declarative knowledge and means that a student cannot produce the appropriate details for a generalization or principle on their own, but they can recognize such details when presented with them.

At the top of the procedural hierarchy are complex processes. *Complex processes* are large, overarching procedures such as editing a composition for overall logic. As explained earlier in this chapter, all complex processes contain simple procedures. *Simple procedures* are specific strategies and skills, such as examining the transitions between paragraphs and monitoring a composition for a clear beginning, middle, and end. As explained earlier in this chapter, simple procedures are based on declarative knowledge, called *details* in figure 3.10. These *details* include descriptions of simple procedures and vocabulary terms related to simple procedures.

As figure 3.10 shows, the procedural hierarchy is aligned to specific cognitive operations: integrated execution, simple execution, recall, and recognition. *Integrated execution* is at the highest level of cognitive operation for procedural knowledge; at this level, a student can execute a complex process and coordinate the execution, timing, and outputs from the simple procedures with the complex process. *Simple execution* involves the accurate execution of a simple procedure. *Recall* and *recognition* are the lowest levels of cognitive operation for procedural knowledge. *Recall* means that a student can describe the details related to specific simple procedures and complex processes, and *recognition* means that a student cannot produce these details independently but will recognize such details when presented with them.

Given the inherent hierarchical nature of both declarative and procedural knowledge, both types of knowledge have enough complexity to fill the score 2.0 and 3.0 levels of proficiency scales without reverting to other taxonomies that are available to educators. Understanding generalizations and principles usually represents the score 3.0 content for declarative knowledge. Integrated execution of complex processes usually represents the score 3.0 content for procedural knowledge. Score 2.0 content for declarative knowledge typically involves recall and recognition of details, while score 2.0 content for procedural knowledge typically involves simple execution of simple procedures; it can also involve recall and recognition of details. At the score 4.0 level, declarative proficiency scales involve tasks that require students to make inferences and applications beyond what was directly taught. At the score 4.0 level, procedural proficiency scales involve the same basic expectation, except that this usually manifests as executing a procedure under specific conditions or constraints.

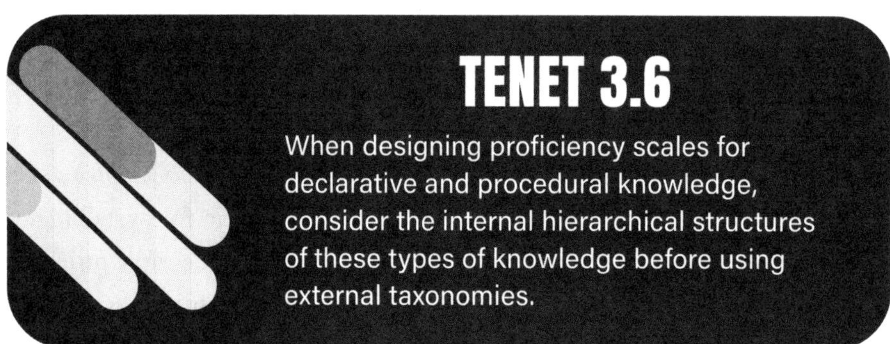

Implications of tenet 3.6 might include the following.

- **Alignment with standards and content:** When designing proficiency scales, educators should focus on the natural progression of skills and knowledge as outlined in curriculum standards rather than strictly aligning proficiency levels to external taxonomies. For instance, if a standard focuses on understanding a concept, the proficiency scale should reflect that understanding at the score 3.0 level, rather than forcing it to fit into a taxonomy level such as *apply* or *analyze*, which may not accurately reflect the nature of the content.
- **Preservation of knowledge complexity:** Declarative and procedural knowledge each have unique hierarchical structures, with declarative knowledge progressing from recognition and recall of details to understanding principles and generalizations. Procedural knowledge, on the other hand, moves from simple execution of simple procedures to the integrated execution of complex processes. Designing proficiency scales with these inherent complexities in

mind allows for a more accurate and meaningful representation of students' learning and skill development, rather than imposing a one-size-fits-all model from an external taxonomy.

Summary

In this chapter, we examined the evolving role of classroom assessments within the broader context of assessment literacy. Historically, the technical literature on assessment has focused predominantly on standardized testing, largely overlooking the importance of classroom assessments. We believe the future of assessment requires a more integrated and nuanced approach, where classroom assessments are grounded in measurement and psychometric principles. As educators move toward more precise, actionable forms of assessment, they will need to understand technical terms like *assessment, test, score, scale*, and *measurement*—and how these terms interconnect to form a cohesive system for evaluating student progress.

Classroom assessments must shift toward a more systematic application of measurement theory, ensuring that assessments not only provide valid inferences about student performance but also align with the continuum of knowledge and skills for each topic being assessed. Unidimensionality is a key concept, suggesting that assessments should measure a single construct at a time to provide clearer, more interpretable results. By using proficiency scales and clear definitions of performance levels, educators can better align assessments with learning goals, track student growth over time, and ensure that classroom assessments reflect true learning progress.

Chapter 4

SCORING CLASSROOM ASSESSMENTS

One might make the case that the traditional method of scoring classroom assessments has been to assign points to items, determine how many of the assigned points an individual testee has acquired, add up the acquired points, divide this sum by the total number of possible points, and then multiply this decimal by one hundred to obtain a percentage score. However, when classroom assessments are based on proficiency scales, the entire processes of assessment design and scoring dramatically change in a number of ways.

Proficiency scales play a pivotal role in expanding the types of assessments that can be effectively used in the classroom. Their clear articulation of the continuum of knowledge and skill for each topic being assessed enables teachers to move beyond traditional pencil-and-paper tests and incorporate a range of assessment methods that provide deeper insights into student learning. Further, proficiency scales transform the scoring and interpretation of classroom assessments. These shifts allow for a more nuanced understanding of student growth and status and provide a clear path for identifying areas where students need further support or enrichment. Proficiency scales also ensure that assessments align with specific learning goals, thus yielding targeted feedback to guide subsequent instruction. This chapter explores these topics, beginning with types of assessments.

Types of Assessments

The use of proficiency scales opens the door for teachers to use multiple types of assessments in addition to traditional pencil-and-paper tests (Marzano, 2018; Marzano et al., 2019). Here, we address several specific types of assessments—including traditional tests—and show how proficiency scales change the way these assessments are scored and interpreted.

Traditional Tests

Traditional tests are historically—and in many places, currently—the most common form of classroom assessment. During a *traditional test*, students record their answers to questions or probes on paper or a computer. Traditional tests usually use selected-response item formats such as multiple choice, alternative choice, multiple selection, matching, fill in the blank, and true or false; they also frequently include short constructed-response items (Marzano et al., 2019).

When proficiency scales are used, a traditional test is constructed and scored with reference to the proficiency scale that corresponds to the test's topic. To illustrate, figure 4.1 depicts a proficiency scale for triangles, while figure 4.2 shows the corresponding test for triangles.

4.0	In addition to score 3.0 performance, the student will demonstrate in-depth inferences and applications that go beyond what was taught. For example, the student will: • Compare the angle sum of triangles to those of other polygons.
3.5	In addition to score 3.0 performance, partial success at score 4.0 content
3.0	The student will: • Use evidence to informally explain relationships among the angles of triangles, including the sum of interior angles and angle-angle similarity.
2.5	No major errors or omissions regarding score 2.0 content, and partial success at score 3.0 content
2.0	The student will recognize or recall specific vocabulary (for example, *angle sum, congruent, corresponding angles, equilateral, exterior angle, interior angle, similarity*) and recognize and recall basic facts, such as: • The measures of the interior angles of a triangle add up to 180 degrees. • When two corresponding angles of two triangles are congruent, the triangles are similar.
1.5	Partial success at score 2.0 content, and major errors or omissions regarding score 3.0 content

1.0	With help, partial success at score 2.0 content and score 3.0 content
0.5	With help, partial success at score 2.0 content but not at score 3.0 content
0.0	Even with help, no success

Source: Adapted from Marzano, 2018.

FIGURE 4.1: Proficiency scale for triangles (grades 7–8).

Section A: Each item is worth five points.

1. When two triangles are congruent: (choose the best answer)
    a. They have the same interior and exterior sum
    b. One has an area twice as large as the other
    c. They tessellate
    d. Their corresponding sides and angles have the same length and measure

2. When two triangles are similar: (choose the best answer)
    a. Their corresponding sides have the same length
    b. Their corresponding angles have the same measure, and their corresponding sides are proportional
    c. Their areas are the same
    d. They have the same perimeter

3. In an equilateral triangle: (choose the best answer)
    a. All three sides have different lengths
    b. All three angles are congruent, and each angle measures 90 degrees
    c. All three sides have the same length, and all three angles are congruent
    d. The perimeter is always twice the length of one side

4. The measures of interior angles of a triangle always add up to ______________.

5. Draw lines between the corresponding angles of the following triangles.

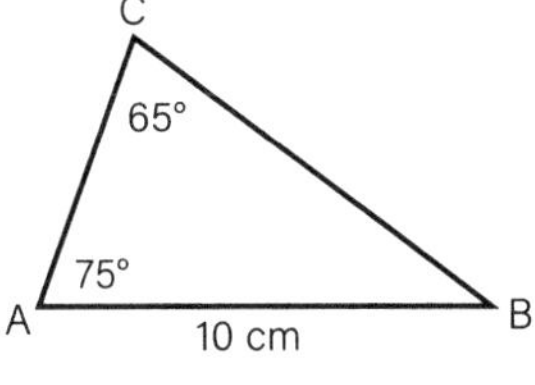

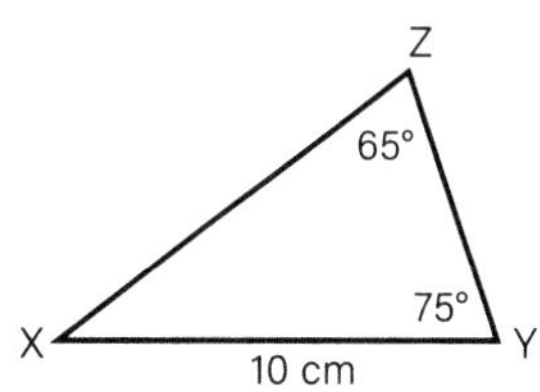

FIGURE 4.2: Traditional test on triangles.

continued →

Section B: Each item is worth ten points.

Determine the unknown angle measure in the following triangle. Explain how you know.

Angle 1: 65°

Angle 2: 45°

Angle 3: ____________

Determine the unknown angle measure in the following triangle. Explain how you know.

Angle 1: 30°

Angle 2: 100°

Angle 3: ____________

Determine the unknown angle measure in the following triangle. Explain how you know.

Angle 1: 52°

Angle 2: 90°

Angle 3: ____________

Section C: Each item is worth twenty points.

Use the following diagram to determine the angle sum of a convex quadrilateral. Explain your thought process.

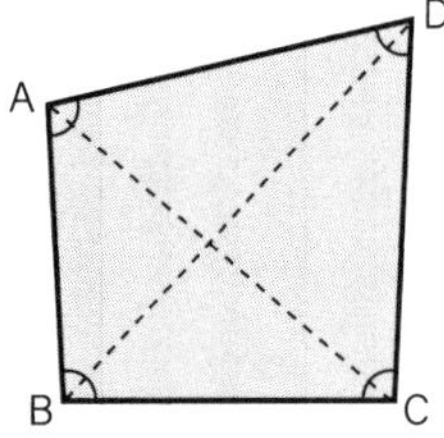

Use the following diagram to determine the angle sum of an octagon. Explain your thought process.

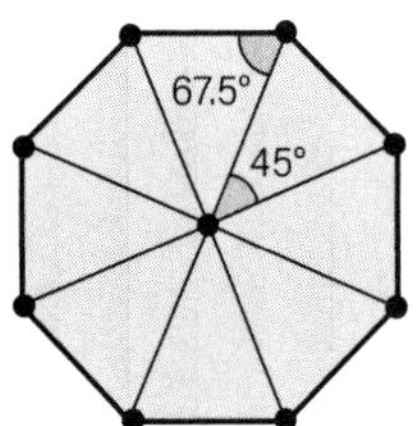

The traditional test in figure 4.2 has three sections. Section A corresponds to the score 2.0 level of the proficiency scale, section B corresponds to the score 3.0 level of the proficiency scale, and section C corresponds to the score 4.0 level of the proficiency scale.

Traditionally, a test like this would be scored by adding up the number of points a student earned and dividing by the total possible points. For example, consider the student whose points obtained per item are shown in the fourth column of figure 4.3. This student earned thirty-seven of ninety-five possible points, for a percentage score of 38.9 percent (equivalent, in many grading systems, to a failing grade). However, when a test is constructed using a proficiency scale, it should not be scored in this way. Instead, we recommend two significantly better options: (1) percentage scores by level and (2) response codes.

Section	Item Number	Possible Points per Item	Points Obtained per Item	Section Percentage
A: Score 2.0 Content	1	5	5	22/25 = 88%
	2	5	4	
	3	5	3	
	4	5	5	
	5	5	5	
	Total	25	22	
B: Score 3.0 Content	6	10	7	15/30 = 50%
	7	10	4	
	8	10	4	
	Total	30	15	
C: Score 4.0 Content	9	20	0	0/40 = 0%
	10	20	0	
	Total	40	0	

Source: Adapted from Marzano, Heflebower, Hoegh, Warrick, & Grift, 2016.

FIGURE 4.3: Percentage scores by level for a traditional test on triangles.

Percentage Scores by Level

Using percentage scores by level involves determining what percentage of available points a student earned *on each section of a test* and using those percentages to assign an appropriate score on a proficiency scale. For example, as shown in the third column of figure 4.3, the test on triangles has twenty-five points available in section A—which addresses the score 2.0 content—and the student earned twenty-two of those points, as the fourth column shows. As the fifth column of figure 4.3 shows, this ratio of 22/25 is converted into a percentage, 88 percent. The first decision a teacher must make is whether this percentage indicates that the student demonstrated an understanding of the score 2.0 content without significant errors or omissions; this decision can often be made by setting a cut score for the section. Assuming the teacher set a cut score of 80 percent for this section, the obtained score of 88 percent would indicate that the student demonstrated adequate competence with the score 2.0 content. At this point, the teacher has determined that the student's score is at least a 2.0.

It is important to acknowledge that we are using the term *cut score* here in a different way than in chapter 2, where it related to the technical characteristics of large-scale assessments. There, we noted that cut scores can involve significant error because educators use them to make important decisions about how students are grouped, what instruction they should receive, and even what instruction they should not receive. Here, we are using the concept of a cut score to make a decision about an individual student's score on a single part of a single test. While it is true that this use of cut scores can also include some error in measurement, that error is localized and relatively inconsequential when compared with the use of cut scores in large-scale assessments.

Next, the teacher considers the student's performance on the score 3.0 content in section B of the test. In our example, figure 4.3 shows that the student earned 50 percent of the available points for section B, indicating that they know only about half of the score 3.0 content. Based on this evidence, the teacher would likely assign a score of 2.5 for the entire test. In effect, the teacher has concluded that the student demonstrated adequate competence on the score 2.0 content and knowledge of about half the score 3.0 content.

Response Codes

In this method, the teacher does not assign points to a student's responses on each item. Rather, the teacher scores each response as correct (C), partially correct (PC), or incorrect (I). If finer distinctions in the quality of student responses are needed—as is often the case with secondary or high school assessment items that might have a wide range of partially correct responses—the additional codes of low partial (LP) and high partial (HP) can be used. Then, the teacher examines the pattern of responses to determine the student's level of proficiency, as figure 4.4 depicts.

As shown in the third column of figure 4.4, the student provided three responses that were completely correct (C) and two responses that were high partial (HP) in their correctness for section A on the score 2.0 content. Thus, the pattern for section A is "High Partial to Correct," as the fourth column of figure 4.4 indicates.

Section	Item Number	Correct, Partially Correct, or Incorrect?	Section Pattern
A: Score 2.0 Content	1	C	High Partial to Correct
	2	HP	
	3	C	
	4	C	
	5	HP	
B: Score 3.0 Content	6	LP	Low Partial
	7	LP	
	8	LP	
C: Score 4.0 Content	9	I	Incorrect
	10	I	
Overall Score			2.25

Source: Adapted from Marzano, 2010.

FIGURE 4.4: Response codes for a traditional test on triangles.

The teacher reexamines the responses from the two items that were high partial and determines that they don't involve any major errors or omissions; thus, the teacher concludes that the student's score is at least a 2.0. Next, the teacher considers the student's responses for section B on the score 3.0 content, which are all low partial (LP). Clearly this pattern does not warrant a score of 3.0, so the teacher next considers a score of 2.5. If the teacher had only used the partially correct (PC) response code, then partial credit on these three items might have led the teacher to assign a score of 2.5. However, since the teacher is using LP and HP response codes, the pattern does not seem to justify a score of 2.5. Therefore, the teacher has two options.

1. **Assign an overall score of 2.0:** This is certainly legitimate, albeit somewhat conservative.
2. **Assign an overall score of 2.25:** This communicates that the student demonstrated knowledge of the score 2.0 content and low partial knowledge of the score 3.0 content.

As shown in the bottom row of figure 4.4, the teacher chose the second option and assigned an overall score of 2.25 to this assessment.

Aberrant Patterns

When examining patterns of responses, a teacher may encounter aberrant patterns. This applies to scoring traditional tests using either points or response codes. An aberrant pattern occurs when a student's responses do not make sense in terms of displaying their level of knowledge on a specific proficiency scale. Consider figure 4.5, which illustrates an aberrant pattern.

Section	Item Number	Correct, High Partial, Low Partial, or Incorrect?	Section Pattern
A: Score 2.0 Content	1	I	Partially Correct
	2	C	
	3	LP	
	4	LP	
	5	LP	
	6	C	
B: Score 3.0 Content	7	C	Correct
	8	C	
C: Score 4.0 Content	9	I	Incorrect
	10	I	

Source: Adapted from Marzano et al., 2019.

FIGURE 4.5: Aberrant pattern of student responses.

Typically, students will have higher scores on items that address score 2.0 content than on items that address the more complex content at the score 3.0 and 4.0 levels. This makes intuitive sense. If the proficiency scale represents a continuum of knowledge, then a learner should have a thorough understanding of the simpler content before they can master the more complex content. But the student responses in figure 4.5 do not follow this logic. The student correctly answered only two of the six questions that address score 2.0 content but correctly answered both questions that address the score 3.0 content.

Although aberrant patterns like this should not occur, they often do. It is important to note that this phenomenon is not specific to classroom assessments. Indeed, aberrant patterns also occur during the development of large-scale assessments, often due to the presence of faulty items. The designers of such tests engage in complex statistical procedures based on item response theory to identify any faulty items on the test and make necessary revisions (for a discussion of item response theory and its related statistical procedures, please see Marzano, 2018). Of course, classroom teachers do not have the luxury of such complex test development procedures. This noted, classroom teachers should examine tests to determine why an aberrant pattern might have occurred. Marzano and colleagues (2019) offered the following possible reasons for aberrant patterns on classroom assessments.

- The questions were poorly written.
- The questions didn't accurately reflect the level of proficiency on the scale.
- The student was rushed or tired or failed to put forth the appropriate effort.
- The student did not understand the question as written.
- The teacher's evaluation of a student response was incorrect. (p. 56)

Marzano and colleagues (2019) also suggested ways of correcting for aberrant patterns. These include the following.

- Ignore the aberrant responses.
- Reclassify aberrant questions to a higher or lower proficiency level based on the response pattern of the entire class.
- Engage in a probing discussion with students to determine the cause of the aberrant pattern and make adjustments accordingly. (p. 56)

In conclusion, while aberrant response patterns can occur due to a variety of factors, it is essential for teachers to carefully analyze and address these discrepancies to ensure accurate assessment and understanding of student proficiency.

Essays and Performance Assessments

Since the earliest educational endeavors, essays have been a common form of assessment. Technically referred to as *extended constructed-response items*, essays require longer responses than *selected-response items* (such as multiple choice, true or false, and matching items) or *short constructed-response items* (which only involve a few sentences or paragraphs). Essays can be scored using proficiency scales. For example, figure 4.6 (page 110) shows an essay assessment designed to be scored using the proficiency scale shown in figure 4.7 (page 110).

What makes a great motivational speech?

To answer this question, please refer to the St. Crispin's Day speech in act 4, scene 3 of Shakespeare's *Henry V* and include the following items in your essay.

- (Score 2.0 content) Identify Henry's emotional plea to motivate his troops (pathos) and spur them into action.
- (Score 3.0 content) Address Henry's credibility as a king of the people as opposed to a tyrant who is forcing his troops into battle (ethos).
- (Score 3.0 content) Demonstrate your understanding of the play's complexity by citing specific evidence to illustrate how Henry's passion (pathos) and desire to put country before self would appeal to the audience's sense of honor, duty to their country, and nationalistic pride.
- (Score 4.0 content) Make a claim about how Henry's speech could compare to political or military leaders from the 20th century and what lessons these more modern figures could learn from his motivational plea.

Source: Adapted from Marzano et al., 2019.

FIGURE 4.6: Essay assessment.

4.0	In addition to score 3.0 performance, the student will demonstrate in-depth inferences and applications that go beyond what was taught. For example, the student will: • Generate and defend a claim about *Henry V*.
3.5	In addition to score 3.0 performance, partial success at score 4.0 content
3.0	The student will: • Understand and exemplify the concepts of ethos and pathos in *Henry V*.
2.5	No major errors or omissions regarding score 2.0 content, and partial success at score 3.0 content
2.0	The student will recognize or recall specific vocabulary (for example, *ethos*, *pathos*) and recognize and recall basic facts, such as: • Identify specific events in *Henry V*.
1.5	Partial success at score 2.0 content, and major errors or omissions regarding score 3.0 content
1.0	With help, partial success at score 2.0 content and score 3.0 content
0.5	With help, partial success at score 2.0 content but not at score 3.0 content
0.0	Even with help, no success

FIGURE 4.7: Proficiency scale for analyzing *Henry V* (grades 9–12).

Note that the essay directions explicitly label which content in the proficiency scale corresponds to each essay prompt. The first prompt focuses on score 2.0 content, the second and third prompts focus on score 3.0 content, and the fourth prompt focuses on score 4.0 content. This represents a new perspective when designing and scoring essay assessments using proficiency scales. Instead of providing one all-encompassing prompt, the teacher includes one or more prompts for the score 2.0, 3.0, and 4.0 levels of a proficiency scale. To use percentage scores by level to score this essay assessment, the teacher assigns ten possible points for each prompt. Figure 4.8 shows one student's scores.

Section	Points Possible	Points Earned	Section Percentage
Score 2.0 Content	10	10	10/10 = 100%
Score 3.0 Content	10	10	18/20 = 90%
	10	8	
Score 4.0 Content	10	6	6/10 = 60%
Overall Score			3.5

Source: Adapted from Marzano et al., 2019.

FIGURE 4.8: Percentage scores by level for an essay assessment on analyzing *Henry V*.

Figure 4.8 shows that the student earned ten of ten possible points for the score 2.0 content (100 percent), eighteen of twenty possible points for the score 3.0 content (90 percent), and six of ten possible points for the score 4.0 content (60 percent). Looking first at the score 2.0 content, the teacher concludes that the student has at least demonstrated competence at the score 2.0 level. Next, the teacher looks at the score 3.0 content. After looking back at the student's essay to confirm that there are no major errors or omissions at the 3.0 level, the teacher concludes that the student has also demonstrated competence at the score 3.0 level. Finally, the teacher looks at the score 4.0 content and concludes that the student has demonstrated competence with some, but not all, of that content. Therefore, the teacher assigns the student a score of 3.5 for this essay assessment.

It is interesting to note that if the student's responses were scored using a traditional points-based approach, which ignores the levels of items on a proficiency scale, the student would have received a score of 85 percent (thirty-four of forty possible points). Such a score equates to a grade of B, whereas a score of 3.5 on a proficiency scale indicates that the student has exhibited competence beyond expectations—a level of performance more commonly associated with a grade of A. In this example, the teacher used percentage scores by level, but the response coding method would have worked just as well and likely yielded the same score of 3.5.

Performance assessments are similar to essays, but they do not necessarily involve an extended written response. Many performance assessments involve oral presentations or participation in structured activities, as the example in figure 4.9 shows.

The Federal Communications Commission (FCC) has released a plan to repeal *net neutrality rules* that were established in 2015. Under the net neutrality rules, the FCC decided to regulate broadband service as a utility, defining and treating it as an essential service, like electricity. There are differing opinions on the need for net neutrality rules.

We have been studying the concepts of free markets and consumer rights. Using what you know about these concepts, take and defend a position on whether the FCC should overturn existing net neutrality rules. As part of this assignment, you will work in teams to prepare a short written description of your position and defend your position in a classroom debate.

- **Task A (score 2.0 content):** Supporters of net neutrality rules say consumers need these protections. Identify consumer rights that net neutrality rules may protect.
- **Task B (score 3.0 content):** Explain how net neutrality rules restrict a free market system.
- **Task C (score 4.0 content):** Identify differing opinions about net neutrality rules. Based on your knowledge of free markets and consumer rights, take and defend a position on whether the FCC should overturn existing net neutrality rules. Write a one-page paper that explains your position and identifies the key points supporting your position. Select one of the key points supporting your position to discuss during the debate.

Source: Adapted from Marzano et al., 2019.

FIGURE 4.9: Performance assessment.

A proficiency scale—with specific expectations at the score 2.0, 3.0, and 4.0 levels—on the topic of the free market system and consumer rights would accompany this performance assessment. Note that the assessment prompts students to engage in three different tasks. If students were asked to complete these tasks in writing only, this performance assessment would be identical to an essay assessment. In this case, each task asks students to respond in writing, but task C also asks students to engage in a debate. While essay assessments request all responses in writing, performance tasks include other forms of student responses.

Probing Discussions

In 1991, Sheila W. Valencia, Anne C. Stallman, Michelle Commeyras, P. David Pearson, and Douglas K. Hartman introduced the assessment strategy of probing discussions; this strategy has been refined and expanded since (Marzano, 2006, 2010, 2018; Marzano et al., 2019). Valencia and colleagues (1991) attempted to measure the amount of information one could gather from a student using four different types of assessment: fill-in-the-blank items, short-answer items, essays, and structured discussions. The structured discussion was the most unusual; in practice, it took the form of a guided review. And it yielded far more information about what a student knew than any other form of assessment.

As Valencia and colleagues (1991) noted, "On average, 66 percent of the topically relevant ideas students gave during interviews were not tested on any of the [other] measures" (p. 226). That is, the other three types of assessment provided only 34 percent of the information that the structured discussion could obtain. While this might seem surprising at first, think about the nature of a structured interview (which we call a *probing discussion*). It is dynamic and offers the teacher questioning and clarification opportunities not available during other assessment types. Examples of this include the following.

- You can ask students to clarify their answers to probes or prompts.
- You can loop back to a previously answered question and ask the student to refine or extend their answer.
- You can ask unplanned questions in response to student answers.

This type of interaction with students not only helps students learn but also sharpens distinctions between what students know and what they do not know (Cusi & Morselli, 2024).

Probing discussions are carried out individually with each student, and they are overtly guided by a specific proficiency scale, which both the teacher and student have in front of them. The teacher begins by asking questions about the score 2.0 content. Such questions are typically simple probes where the teacher asks the student to explain or exemplify specific content at that level. The teacher continues asking questions at the score 2.0 level until it is clear the student understands that content without significant errors or omissions. If the student does not demonstrate such knowledge, the teacher assigns a score of 1.5 or lower depending on the significance of the student's errors or omissions and the type of help the student receives. If the student demonstrates competence at the score 2.0 level, the teacher moves to the score 3.0 content and repeats the process. If the student's responses indicate competence at the score 3.0 level, then the teacher moves on to the score 4.0 content.

Observations

Observations are underutilized but extremely useful; they yield a considerable amount of information about a student. Observations are opportunistic in nature. Teachers don't typically plan for observations, but when they occur and are recognized, the teacher records them. Stated differently, when a teacher happens to see a particular student demonstrate a particular level of performance on a particular proficiency scale, the teacher records that score.

While observations can be used to score any level of content on a proficiency scale, they are most commonly used for score 3.0 and 4.0 content. Figure 4.10 illustrates the proficiency scale for the fourth-grade science topic of animal behaviors.

4.0	In addition to score 3.0 performance, the student demonstrates in-depth inferences and applications that go beyond what was taught.
3.5	In addition to score 3.0 performance, partial success at score 4.0 content
3.0	The student will: **AB—Explain how animals' response to stimuli supports their survival, growth, or reproduction** (for example, explain how an animal responds to danger by running away, becoming very still, or preparing to fight).
2.5	No major errors or omissions regarding score 2.0 content, and partial success at score 3.0 content
2.0	**AB**—The student will recognize or recall specific vocabulary (for example, *response, sense, sense organ, stimulus*) and perform basic processes such as: • Identify the sense organs (internal and external structures) involved in a sense (for example, paws, whiskers, hands, or skin might be involved in an animal's sense of touch). • Explain how information gathered by senses determines an animal's behavior (response to stimulus). • Relate a behavior to how it helps an animal grow, survive, and reproduce in its habitat (for example, electric eels can direct currents of electricity to kill food; animals flee from predators when seeing, hearing, or smelling them; and mating rituals among different organisms help them attract mates). • Explain how a specific animal behavior depends on a specific sense (for example, monkeys communicate with one another by making and hearing sounds). • Explain how a specific animal behavior depends on specific internal or external features (for example, snakes use their tongues to detect vibrations in the air, which allows them to gather information about their surroundings).
1.5	Partial success at score 2.0 content, and major errors or omissions regarding score 3.0 content

1.0	With help, partial success at score 2.0 content and score 3.0 content
0.5	With help, partial success at score 2.0 content but not at score 3.0 content
0.0	Even with help, no success

Source: © 2021 by Marzano Resources. Used with permission.

FIGURE 4.10: Proficiency scale for animal behaviors (AB; grade 4).

Imagine a teacher observes a particular student interacting with other students in a small group activity regarding animal behavior. During that interaction, the student explains how different types of animals respond to danger. They mention different behaviors, including running away, becoming very still, and preparing to fight. In response, the teacher records a score of 3.0 for the student on the animal behaviors topic.

Student-Centered Assessment

Intuitively, it's easy to dismiss the validity and utility of students being involved in the assessment process. It seems that the appropriate place for students is as the subjects of assessments. Additionally, it seems illogical that students could accurately assess themselves. But practices that exclude students from the assessment process are based on misconceptions that John Hattie (2009, 2012, 2015, 2023) highlighted in a series of meta-analytic studies (see also Visible Learning Meta[X™] at www.visiblelearningmetax.com). As of 2023, Hattie had identified over 350 variables that correlated with student achievement; student self-assessment has always been ranked in the top 5 percent of those variables when they are ordered in terms of effect size.

Hattie (2009) defined *student self-assessment* as students being aware of their current levels of performance and making predictions about their future performance. He noted the following:

> Students were very knowledgeable about their chances of success. . . . This shows a remarkably high level of predictability about achievement in the classroom (and should question the necessity of so many tests when students appear to already have much of the information the tests supposedly provide). (p. 44)

Robert J. Marzano, Jennifer S. Norford, Michelle Finn, and Douglas Finn III (2017) proposed the use of the personal tracking matrix as a tool for student self-assessment. A *personal tracking matrix* is derived from a proficiency scale. For example, consider the proficiency scale for solving linear equations through graphing in figure 4.11 (page 116).

4.0	The student will: Test the idea that solving linear equations by graphing is the best solution method for particular situations (for example, list situations in which solving by graphing is the most efficient solution method and situations in which solving algebraically is the most efficient solution method).
3.5	In addition to score 3.0 performance, partial success at score 4.0 content
3.0	The student will: Solve linear equations by graphing (for example, find the point that will satisfy two linear equations by graphing both equations).
2.5	No major errors or omissions regarding score 2.0 content, and partial success at score 3.0 content
2.0	The student will recognize or recall specific vocabulary (for example, *linear equation, slope-intercept form, coordinate plane, intersection point*) and perform basic processes such as: • Convert a linear equation into slope-intercept form. • Graph a linear equation on a coordinate plane. • Determine the intersection point for the graphs of two linear equations. • Verify the point of intersection by inserting the coordinates into each linear equation.
1.5	Partial success at score 2.0 content, and major errors or omissions regarding score 3.0 content
1.0	With help, partial success at score 2.0 content and score 3.0 content
0.5	With help, partial success at score 2.0 content but not at score 3.0 content
0.0	Even with help, no success

Source: Marzano et al., 2017, pp. 83–84.

FIGURE 4.11: Proficiency scale for solving linear equations through graphing (grades 7–8).

Figure 4.12 presents a personal tracking matrix derived from the proficiency scale in figure 4.11. Every statement from the proficiency scale has been transformed into an *I can* statement and given a separate row in the personal tracking matrix. As the third, fourth, and fifth columns of figure 4.12 show, students rate themselves on each of these *I can* statements and—as the sixth column shows—provide evidence for their ratings. The self-rating scale used in a personal tracking matrix has only three levels.

1. I'm still confused about this topic.
2. I've learned some but not all of the topic.
3. I've got this now.

Level	Indicator	My Rating			My Evidence
		I'm still confused about this topic.	I've learned some but not all of the topic.	I've got this now.	
4.0	I can show situations in which solving a linear equation is best done through graphing versus situations in which it is best done algebraically.	X			Practice activity 4
3.0	I can find the point that will satisfy two linear equations by graphing both equations.	X	X		Practice activity 3
2.0	I can verify the point of intersection by inserting the coordinates into each linear equation.	X	X		Practice activity 3
2.0	I can determine the intersection point of the graphs of two linear equations.	X	X	X	Practice activity 2
2.0	I can graph a linear equation on a coordinate plane.	X	X		Practice activity 2
2.0	I can convert a linear equation into its slope-intercept form.	X	X	X	Practice activity 1
2.0	I can provide an explanation of the term *intersection point*.	X	X	X	Online exercise 1 and 2
2.0	I can provide an explanation of the term *coordinate plane*.	X	X	X	Online exercise 1 and 2
2.0	I can provide an explanation of the term *slope-intercept form*.	X	X	X	Online exercise 1 and 2
2.0	I can provide an explanation of the term *linear equation*.	X	X	X	Online exercise 1 and 2

Source: Adapted from Marzano et al., 2017.

FIGURE 4.12: Personal tracking matrix for solving linear equations through graphing.

*Visit **MarzanoResources.com/reproducibles** for a free reproducible version of this figure.*

The student whose self-ratings are shown in the third, fourth, and fifth columns of figure 4.12 has indicated that they are competent on most of the score 2.0 content. The student provided evidence for these ratings by listing online exercises and practice activities in the sixth column. To translate a student's self-ratings on a personal tracking matrix into a score on a proficiency scale, a teacher would first examine the self-ratings and evidence. The example in figure 4.12 probably warrants a score of at least 2.0. However, if the teacher met with the student for an abbreviated probing discussion, they might decide to assign a higher score based on the verbal information the student provides.

By actively involving students in the assessment process using tools like personal tracking matrixes, they become more self-aware of their progress and can engage in meaningful self-reflection. This shift empowers students to take ownership of their learning and provides teachers with timely and accurate data to guide instruction.

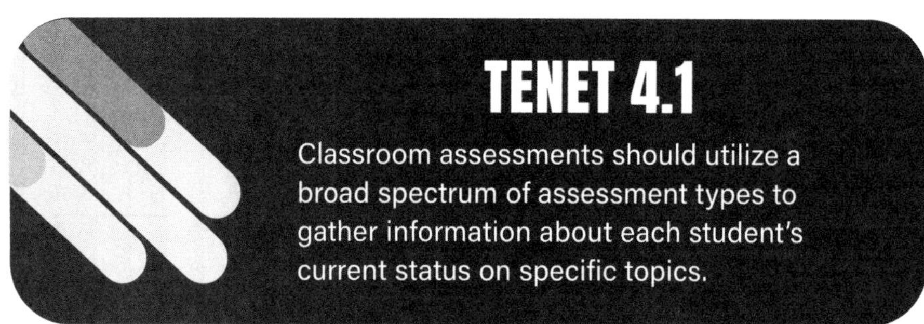

Implications of tenet 4.1 might include the following.

- **Diverse assessment approaches:** There is no single best way to measure what students know and can do in the classroom. When designing assessments, teachers should create multiple ways for students to demonstrate their understanding and consider each source of information when determining a student's understanding relative to the proficiency scale. A written essay does not inherently have a higher level of validity or reliability when compared to an oral presentation or a probing conversation. Teachers should use a variety of assessment methods—such as essays, performance tasks, probing discussions, and observations—so that students can demonstrate their understanding in ways that suit their strengths, whether through written responses, oral presentations, or active participation in discussions.

- **Comprehensive data collection:** Teachers must gather and analyze multiple sources of data when determining student proficiency. This might include traditional assessment forms that produce written artifacts but should also include performance assessments and other assessments that simply result in a score notation (without a written product). This sort of comprehensive data collection ensures a more well-rounded understanding of student progress, rather than relying solely on one type of measure.
- **Ongoing adjustments to instruction:** The use of diverse assessments allows for real-time insights into student learning, enabling teachers to adjust instruction promptly. By continuously tracking student progress using various assessment types, teachers can identify gaps and address them as quickly as possible.

Patterns of Scores

A critical but oft-neglected topic related to classroom assessment literacy is how teachers track and summarize patterns of scores on individual assessments to communicate each student's overall performance on specific topics and content areas. In this section, we describe two methods that teachers might currently use for recordkeeping. The first, tracking scores by assessment type, is inherently problematic, and we do not recommend its continued use. The second, tracking scores by measurement topic, is a much better choice. Besides aligning with our previous recommendations regarding proficiency scales, measurement topic–based recordkeeping also makes far more logical sense than the first option; we recommend it strongly.

Tracking Scores by Assessment Type

Perhaps one of the most enduring—yet unexamined—recordkeeping practices in K–12 education is to track scores by assessment type. Types commonly include quizzes, formal tests, midterms, finals, homework, and so on. Indeed, although the study Susan M. Brookhart and colleagues (2016) conducted did not address recordkeeping per se, their findings highlighted the prevalence of teachers grouping grades by assessment type. To illustrate why this practice is problematic, assume that a seventh-grade mathematics teacher teaches the following topics during a grading period.

- Ratios, Proportions, and Percentages
- Algebraic Thinking
- Integers and Rational Numbers
- Geometry
- Proportional Relationships

As the teacher administers and scores assessments on these topics, the scores on all a student's quizzes, regardless of the topic they address, are recorded in the *quizzes* category; the scores on all formal tests, regardless of the topic they address, are recorded in the *tests* category; and so on. These categories of assessment formats do very little, if anything, to inform students, teachers, and guardians about students' status or growth on specific topics within a given content area. Therefore, we recommend that teachers stop tracking scores by assessment type and begin tracking scores by topic.

Tracking Scores by Measurement Topic

Categorizing scores by measurement topic represents a major shift for most teachers. As explained previously, it requires that they design and score each assessment using the proficiency scale aligned to the assessment topic. Additionally, teachers must select an approach for collecting topic-based assessment scores. Here, we present three options for this endeavor.

The most common protocol for collecting topic-based assessment scores is called *classwide assessments*. In this approach, the teacher simply enters a score for each student in their gradebook after administering and scoring each classwide assessment. For example, during a twenty-day unit (not counting weekends), the students whose scores are shown in figure 4.13 took assessments on days 1, 6, 11, 16, and 20.

Another approach for collecting topic-based assessment scores is called *classwide assessments plus individual assessments*. Here, the teacher administers and enters scores for several classwide assessments and also administers and enters scores for additional assessments with individual students as needed and as opportunity arises. For example, during the twenty-day unit shown in figure 4.14 (page 123), the teacher administered a traditional test for the unit's measurement topic on day 1. Every student received a score on this assessment; this might be considered

	Day of Unit																			
	1	2	3	4	5	6	7	8	9	10	11	12	13	14	15	16	17	18	19	20
Asha	1.0					1.5					2.0					2.0				2.5
Brion	1.5					2.0					3.0					2.5				3.0
Carter	2.0					2.0					3.0					3.0				3.0
Deidre	1.0					2.0					2.5					2.5				2.5
Eric	2.0					2.0					2.5					2.5				3.0

FIGURE 4.13: Classwide assessments.

their *baseline* or *initial score*. Over the next nine days, some—but not all—students received additional scores. Hawar and Imlad received scores on day 3, Fatima received a score on day 5, and Jack received a score on day 6. These scores were generated from individual assessments, such as performance assessments, probing discussions, observations, or student self-ratings. On day 11, the teacher administered another assessment to the entire class and all students received a score. Assessments were again individualized and differentiated during days 12 through 19, with some students receiving additional scores and some not. On day 20, the teacher administered one more classwide assessment and recorded scores for all students.

With this approach, it is important to note that many of the scores recorded in between the classwide assessments can be thought of as opportunistic assessments. As the name implies, *opportunistic assessments* are those that present themselves to teachers on the spur of the moment; they are unplanned assessments. For example, a teacher might walk by a student's desk and have a short discussion with that student about the topic that is the focus of a unit. The teacher turns that conversation into a short probing discussion and subsequently records a score for that student.

Finally, the third approach you might use to collect topic-based assessment scores is called *initial assessment plus individual assessments*. As figure 4.15 (page 124) shows, this is similar to the second approach, except that a classwide assessment is only given on day 1; for the remainder of the unit, students are assessed according to individual needs and as opportunities arise.

In conclusion, tracking scores by measurement topic is a much more effective and informative approach than categorizing scores by assessment type. This method not only provides a clearer picture of each student's progress within specific content areas, but it also aligns more closely with the use of proficiency scales, ensuring that assessments accurately reflect student growth over time. By incorporating both classwide and individual assessments, teachers can gather richer, more individualized data, allowing for timely adjustments to instruction.

	Day of Unit																			
	1	2	3	4	5	6	7	8	9	10	11	12	13	14	15	16	17	18	19	20
Fatima	1.0				1.5						2.0			2.0			2.5			2.5
Gregg	1.5										3.0				3.0			3.5		3.5
Hawar	2.0		2.0								3.0									4.0
Imlad	1.0		1.5								2.5					3.0		3.5		3.5
Jack	2.0					2.5					2.5			3.0			3.5			4.0

FIGURE 4.14: Classwide assessments plus individual assessments.

	Day of Unit																			
	1	2	3	4	5	6	7	8	9	10	11	12	13	14	15	16	17	18	19	20
Kalen	1.0				1.5						2.0			2.0			2.5			2.5
Leona	1.5								3.0						3.0			3.5		
Marci	2.0		2.0							3.0									4.0	
Noah	1.0		1.5				2.5				3.0					3.0		3.5		3.5
Ollie	2.0					2.5					2.5			3.0			3.5		4.0	

FIGURE 4.15: Initial assessment plus individual assessments.

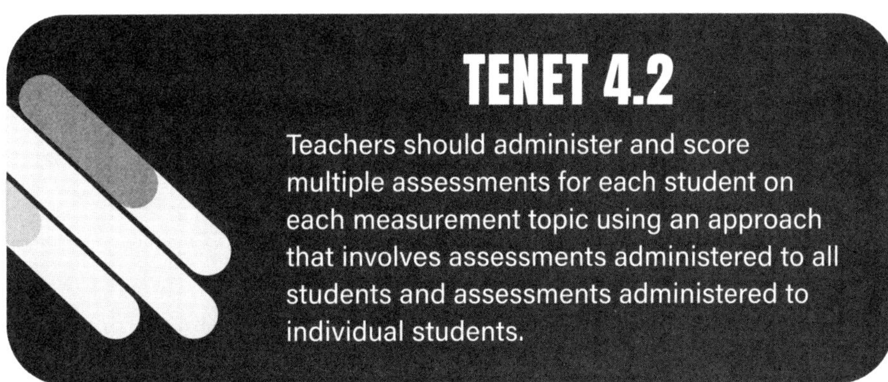

Implications of tenet 4.2 might include the following.

- **Emphasis on differentiation:** Administering both classwide and individualized assessments emphasizes the need to cater to diverse student learning needs. By offering assessments that address both the overall class and the specific needs of individual students, teachers can provide more personalized instruction. This approach allows for better alignment of assessments with students' unique learning paces and styles, fostering a supportive learning environment that prioritizes individual growth and mastery.
- **Encouragement of ongoing evaluation:** The focus on multiple assessments throughout a unit promotes the idea of continuous evaluation, rather than relying on a single final test. Regular assessments enable teachers to track students' progress over time and adjust their teaching strategies accordingly. This ongoing feedback helps students see their development and gives them more opportunities to demonstrate their understanding, reducing reliance on high-stakes testing and promoting a growth-focused mindset.
- **Increased complexity in recordkeeping:** With the implementation of multiple assessments for each student across various topics, recordkeeping becomes more intricate. Teachers must keep track of numerous scores across different assessment types and student progress in various areas. This shift may require adopting new tools or systems for organizing and managing data effectively, such as specialized spreadsheets or learning management systems. It also necessitates a change in how teachers approach grading and data analysis, demanding more thoughtful tracking of student performance over time.

Parallel Assessments

The technical definition of *parallel assessments* indicates two tests that "are assumed to measure the same construct and to have the same means and the same standard deviations" (AERA et al., 2014, p. 221). Stated more simply, a student who takes two parallel assessments, one right after another, should receive precisely the same score on the two tests even though they employed different items. Robert J. Marzano (2018) explained that parallel assessments based on proficiency scales are an "absolute necessity" to track student growth on specific measurement topics (p. 33). As we will explore in the next chapter, parallel assessments are also essential to compute the reliability and validity of classroom assessments.

As noted, the educational measurement literature (Brennan, 2006; Gulliksen, 1950; Horst, 1966; Lindquist, 1951; Linn, 1989; Lord & Novick, 1968; Magnusson, 1967; Thorndike, 1971) has discussed parallel assessments at length. In that literature, psychometricians tend to focus on statistical concepts (such as equal means and variance, dispersion of item difficulties, item covariances, and so on) that are of limited use to the classroom teacher. Nevertheless, classroom teachers can still design effective parallel assessments by creating multiple assessments focused on the same content. Specifically, educators can use a proficiency scale to easily design tests that have sets of items at approximately the same levels of difficulty. For example, various assessments designed for the score 2.0 content on a proficiency scale will include items regarding the same vocabulary and basic information. Assessments designed for the score 3.0 content will include items for the same generalizations, principles, processes, and so on. To design two parallel tests, then, a teacher would ensure identical content for the score 2.0, 3.0, and 4.0 levels but use different types of items or prompts.

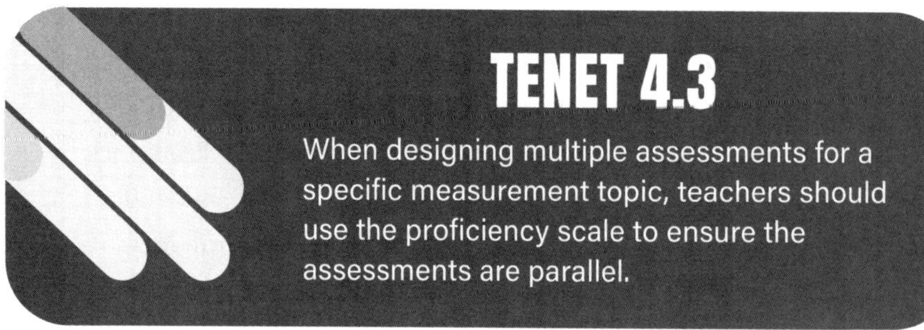

Implications of tenet 4.3 might include the following.

- **Consistency in measurement:** By using proficiency scales to guide the creation of parallel assessments, teachers ensure that the tests measure the same constructs in a consistent manner. This consistency helps ensure that students are assessed on the same content at the same level of difficulty across different assessments, leading to more accurate and reliable comparisons of student performance.
- **Enhanced reliability and validity:** Parallel assessments are crucial for calculating the reliability and validity of classroom assessments. By designing assessments that align with proficiency scales, teachers can ensure that their assessments not only measure what they intend to measure, but that the results are also dependable across different forms of assessment. This, in turn, helps in tracking and supporting student growth over time.
- **Collaboration and efficiency in assessment design:** The process of creating parallel assessments based on proficiency scales can be collaborative. Approaching this task as a team not only makes the process more efficient but also ensures that the assessments are well rounded and comprehensive in measuring the intended content. Additionally, pooling resources (assessment items) allows for a broader range of question types and formats, making the assessments more varied and engaging for students.

Unrecorded Assessments

Thus far in this chapter, we have described how teachers can use proficiency scales to score sets of parallel assessments on specific measurement topics. As they administer and score those assessments, we recommend tracking students' scores by measurement topic. However, before we conclude the chapter, it is important to note that not every assessment administered has to be scored and recorded in a gradebook or other recordkeeping system (Marzano, 2010). Here, we discuss two kinds of unrecorded assessments: instructional feedback and unreliable assessments.

Instructional Feedback

As we will explain in depth in the next chapter, there are two kinds of scores that should be tracked in a gradebook or recordkeeping system: formative scores and summative scores. However, assessments can yield data that are neither formative nor summative scores. For example, instructional feedback from assessments is not entered into a gradebook or recordkeeping system but is a valuable commodity in the K–12 classroom. To further define instructional feedback and preview the concepts of formative and summative scores, table 4.1 compares instructional feedback with formative and summative scores.

TABLE 4.1: Formative and Summative Scores Compared to Instructional Feedback

Formative and Summative Scores	Instructional Feedback
Formative and summative scores can be derived from a variety of types of assessments.	Instructional feedback can be derived from a variety of types of assessments.
Assessments are scored.	Assessments may or may not be scored.
Scores are recorded.	Scores are not recorded.
Scores are used to track student progress.	Because scores are not recorded, they are not part of the formal tracking of students over time, but they do serve to inform the teacher about how both the class and specific students are progressing.
Formative scores are used to generate a summative score.	Instructional feedback is not a formal part of the design of summative scores, but it may help teachers determine the most appropriate summative score for specific students.

Source: Adapted from Marzano, 2010.

As seen in the first row of table 4.1, the same broad spectrum of assessments can generate formative and summative scores and instructional feedback. However, while the assessments used to generate formative and summative scores are always scored, assessments for instructional feedback are only sometimes scored. For example, assessments used for instructional feedback might include the following:

- In response to questions the teacher asks, students hold their thumbs up to signal they know the answer, hold their thumbs down to signal they do not know the answer, and hold their thumbs to the side to signal they are not sure if they know the answer.
- A teacher gives a practice quiz that is scored on the spot by students as the teacher goes through the answers. Each student scores [their] own answers. As the teacher goes over each question, [they ask] students to raise their hands if they feel they need more help with the content. At the end of the activity, each student knows how [they] scored

> on the practice test, and the teacher has a sense of how well the class did. (Marzano, 2010, p. 31)

Both of these examples, despite being quite different, serve as instructional feedback by providing valuable insights into students' knowledge and guiding teachers in adjusting instruction, even though scores are not recorded.

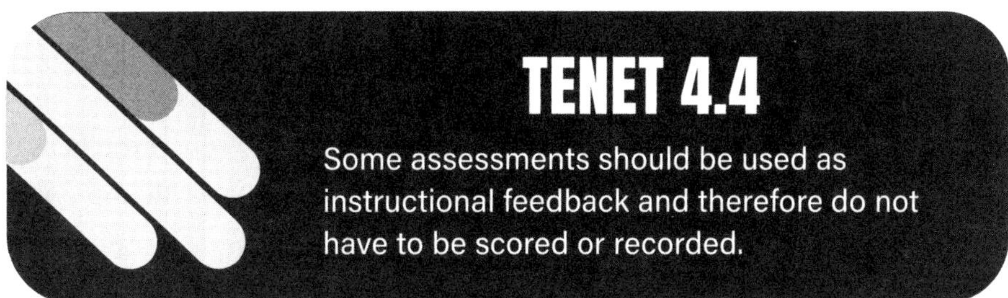

Implications of tenet 4.4 might include the following.

- **Immediate instructional adjustments:** By using assessments as instructional feedback without recording scores, teachers can quickly gauge student understanding and adjust their teaching strategies accordingly to meet students' needs.
- **Informed summative scoring:** Although instructional feedback is not part of formal tracking, it helps teachers make informed decisions when assigning summative scores, ensuring that these scores reflect the most accurate understanding of a student's progress.

Unreliable or Invalid Assessments

The second category of unrecorded assessments involves those assessments that have questionable reliability or validity. We discuss reliability and validity in depth in the next chapter, but for our purposes here, consider the following.

- The *reliability* of an assessment is its level of precision.
- The *validity* of an assessment is the extent to which it actually measures what it purports to measure.

When teachers design and administer their own classroom assessments, some assessments will likely have relatively high reliability and validity, and some will not. When tracking student progress, teachers should record scores from assessments only if they believe the assessments possess high reliability and high validity.

If the teacher doubts the reliability or validity of an assessment, they should not record scores from it. There are a number of indicators that an assessment might not be reliable or valid relative to a specific proficiency scale. These include the following.

- The assessment comes from a textbook or lesson series that is not designed with a proficiency scale in mind.
- The assessment was put together hastily without much attention to the quality of the items.
- The results of the assessment make little sense relative to the teacher's current understanding of students' performance on a specific topic.
- The students report that they were confused by the assessment.

Nevertheless, the information from unreliable or invalid assessments should not be lost. As noted in the previous section, assessments can always be used as instructional feedback. If a teacher administers an assessment and later realizes that it lacks sufficient reliability or validity, they should still examine the results to glean as much information as possible regarding how the class is doing as a whole or how individual students are doing. This information can guide subsequent instruction and the design and administration of subsequent assessments.

For example, during a fourth-grade social studies unit, a teacher administers two assessments on the topic of economic systems. The first assessment, administered on Monday, is carefully designed by the teacher and involves mostly selected-response items and a few short constructed-response items. As she scores each student's responses, the teacher feels like the assessment is providing a fairly accurate indication of each student's current knowledge of economic systems. Therefore, she enters each student's score in her gradebook. On Friday, the teacher administers another assessment on economic systems; this time, it is an essay test. When the teacher designed the test, she thought the prompt was clear about how students should construct their responses. But as she scores the test, the teacher realizes that many of her students have missed the point of what the essay was supposed to be about. As she reexamines the wording of the prompt, the teacher identifies phrases and directions that made the intent of the test ambiguous. Therefore, the teacher finishes scoring the test and decides to discuss it with students at the beginning of the next week. However, she does not enter the scores from this second assessment—the essay test—into her gradebook, since they could be misleading regarding students' current knowledge of economic systems. Thus, the essay test becomes a form of instructional feedback.

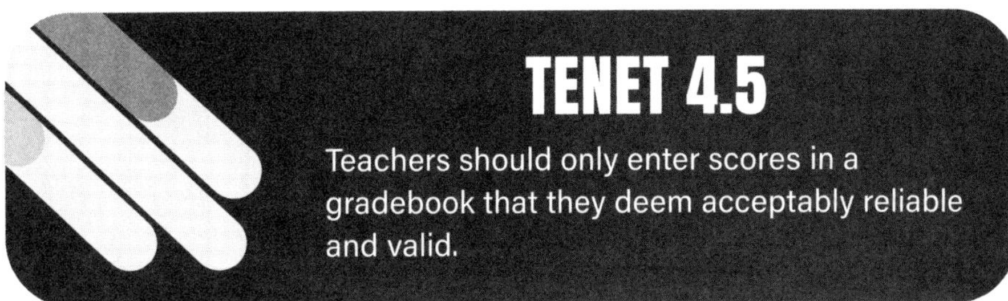

Implications of tenet 4.5 might include the following.

- **Informed gradebook decisions:** Teachers should only record scores from assessments they deem reliable and valid, ensuring that the data accurately reflect student progress and learning outcomes.
- **Ongoing instructional guidance:** Even if an assessment is unreliable or invalid, the feedback gathered from it can still provide valuable insights for improving instruction and guiding future assessments.

Summary

This chapter situated the role of classroom assessments within the broader context of assessment literacy by emphasizing the need for varied, ongoing assessments that align with proficiency scales. Rather than relying on traditional, one-time tests, assessment should be viewed as an ongoing process that allows for timely instructional adjustments. By incorporating diverse methods such as performance tasks, discussions, and self-assessment, teachers can develop a more nuanced understanding of student progress.

The chapter also stressed the importance of tracking student performance by measurement topic, aligning with proficiency scales to offer a clearer picture of student growth. While this approach increases the complexity of recordkeeping, it ultimately supports personalized instruction and fosters continuous evaluation. The use of parallel assessments ensures consistency in measuring student proficiency, and the inclusion of unrecorded assessments further enhances teachers' ability to adjust instruction based on real-time data. These strategies represent a shift toward a more dynamic and accurate approach to classroom assessment.

Chapter 5

AGGREGATING CLASSROOM ASSESSMENT SCORES

Our discussion of classroom assessment in the previous two chapters focused on how to design classroom assessments based on proficiency scales and how to assign scores to individual assessments. However, ultimately, scores from classroom assessments must be aggregated and reported to communicate student status and growth. In this final chapter of part II, we discuss an important aspect of aggregating scores from classroom assessments: aggregating scores *within* measurement topics. In part III—on grading practice—we will discuss another important aspect: aggregating scores *across* measurement topics.

Aggregating scores within a measurement topic means that, at the end of a grading period, the teacher provides a summary score for each student on each measurement topic addressed during that time. There are many ways to do this aggregation; understanding the options requires a complete understanding of the concepts of *formative scores* and *summative scores*. Therefore, we begin this chapter by fully elucidating those terms and differentiating them from the similar-sounding but distinctly different terms *formative assessment* and *summative assessment*.

The Confusing Concept of Formative Assessment

The idea of formative assessment became popular in the early 2000s after Paul Black and Dylan Wiliam (1998a) summarized their conclusions from an analysis of more than 250 studies on formative assessment. They found effect sizes in those studies as high as 0.70 and offered the following recommendations:

> The research reported here shows conclusively that formative assessment does improve learning. The gains in achievement appear to be quite considerable, and as noted earlier, amongst the largest ever reported for educational interventions. As an illustration of just how big these gains are, an effect size of 0.7, if it could be achieved on a nationwide scale, would be equivalent to raising the mathematics attainment score of an "average" country like England, New Zealand or the United States into the "top five" after the Pacific rim countries of Singapore, Korea, Japan and Hong Kong. (p. 61)

As Marzano (2010) explained, an effect size of 0.70 is associated with a 26 percentile point gain in student achievement. Thus, Black and Wiliam were implying that formative assessment in and of itself could dramatically increase students' learning.

Effective, but Not Super Effective

The manner in which Black and Wiliam (1998a) reported their findings captured the attention of U.S. educators. Over the next two decades, formative assessment became a basic component of seemingly every discussion of classroom assessment. According to W. James Popham (2006), "News of Black and Wiliam's conclusions gradually spread into faculty lounges" (p. 86), where it influenced assessment practices ranging from published tests to teacher-designed assessments.

While Black and Wiliam's conclusions seemed reasonable at the time, we think an updated perspective on the research warrants a more conservative conclusion. For example, Black and Wiliam's (1998a) study is sometimes referred to as a meta-analysis. It was not. Black and Wiliam emphasized this by including a section in their study called "No Meta-Analysis," where they explained that while "it might be seen desirable, and indeed might be anticipated as conventional, for a review of this type to attempt a meta-analysis of the quantitative studies that have been reported" (p. 52), the 250 studies they examined were simply too different in terms of nature and purpose to do so. When conducting a meta-analysis, one seeks to compute an average effect size of all the available studies, a summary statistic that takes into account all of the positive, negative, and neutral results in the studies being synthesized. While Black and Wiliam (1998a) certainly conducted a comprehensive analysis of the studies they examined, they did not attempt to compute an average effect size for studies on formative assessment due to their dissimilarity.

Therefore, one must ask, "If they did not compute an average effect size for formative assessment, where did they get the 0.70 effect size they used in their now-famous quote?" In the study, Black and Wiliam (1998a) clearly stated that the 0.70 effect size was simply the largest effect size they found. But they also chose (perhaps inadvisably, given the lack of a meta-analysis) to state that formative assessment "conclusively" (p. 61) improves student learning. Such a claim might be considered unfounded, given the evidence they provided and the lack of any meta-analysis. Unfortunately, educators who read or heard about the study concluded that formative assessment could consistently be expected to produce large positive effects on student learning. This misconception generated a massive movement to train teachers across the United States on various ways to employ formative assessment, even though the effects of this approach had not yet been thoroughly studied.

Fortunately, since the Black and Wiliam (1998a) study, a number of rigorous meta-analyses have been conducted regarding formative assessment. Table 5.1 shows the results of several of these, arranged chronologically.

TABLE 5.1: Meta-Analyses Regarding Formative Assessment

Source	Number of Studies	Number of Effect Sizes	Average Effect Size
Kingston & Nash, 2011	13	42	0.25
Klute, Apthorp, Harlacher, & Reale, 2017	19	30	0.26
Lee, Chung, Zhang, Abedi, & Warschauer, 2020	33	126	0.29
Xuan, Cheung, & Sun, 2022	48	Not reported	0.19
Yao, Amos, Snider, & Brown, 2024	118	258	0.25

Notably, Hattie (2023) reports an average effect size for formative assessment (which he refers to as *formative evaluation*) of 0.40. This is computed from 256 studies involving 905 effect sizes and 138,747 students. Thus, while formative assessment has been shown to have positive effects on student learning, the research indicates that these effects tend to be far more modest than often portrayed.

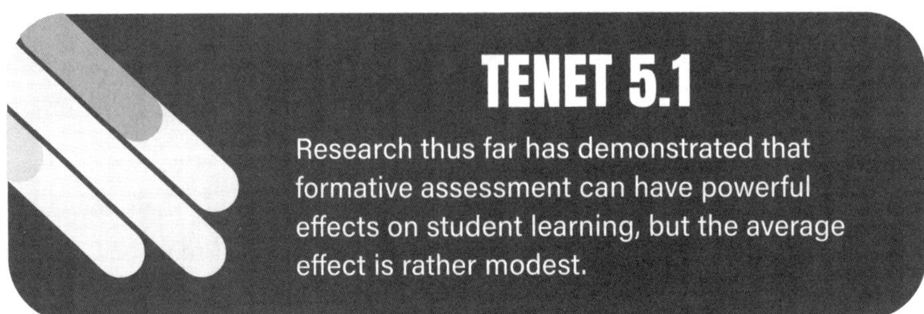

Implications of tenet 5.1 might include the following.

- **The need to manage expectations and implementation:** The discrepancy between early perceptions of formative assessment's effectiveness, as highlighted by Black and Wiliam's influential study, and subsequent meta-analyses underscores the importance of managing expectations among educators. More rigorous meta-analyses following Black and Wiliam's (1998a) study reveal a more modest average effect size, ranging from 0.19 to 0.40. Educators need to be aware of these updated findings to temper expectations and implement formative assessment strategies effectively. This requires a shift from viewing formative assessment as a panacea to understanding it as a valuable, albeit moderately impactful, tool that, when used correctly, can contribute meaningfully to student learning outcomes.
- **Continuous improvement and professional development:** The evolution of research on formative assessment suggests a need for ongoing professional development and refinement of instructional practices. Educators who initially embraced formative assessment based on early claims may benefit from updated knowledge and skills to align their practices with evidence-based insights. This includes understanding how to interpret and apply findings from meta-analyses that provide a clearer picture of formative assessment's effects across different contexts and student populations.

Defined, but Not Clearly Defined

Another aspect that makes the concept of formative assessment confusing (and sometimes misleading) is that researchers and theorists have defined it in a wide variety of ways. Table 5.2 presents a selection of these definitions to illustrate the problem.

TABLE 5.2: Varying Definitions of Formative Assessment

A formative assessment is a practice test.	
Fisher & Frey, 2020	"Providing students with a practice version of an assessment in advance of the 'real' assessment" (p. 84).
Formative assessment provides a snapshot of student knowledge and skill.	
Ayala et al., 2008	"Assessments . . . developed to give a snapshot to students and teachers about what students know and are able to do at a particular time such that this information can be used to close the gap in students' understanding by both teachers and students" (pp. 316–317).
Formative assessment is instructional feedback.	
Heritage, 2008	"Assessment . . . [provides] feedback to teachers and students during the course of learning about the gap between students' current and desired performance so that action can be taken to close the gap" (p. 1).
Lee et al., 2020	"Assessment information comes to a student as instructional feedback to facilitate student learning" (p. 124).
Formative assessment is a set of information-collecting activities.	
Black & Wiliam, 1998b, as cited in Box, Skoog, & Dabbs, 2015	"All those activities undertaken by teachers, and by their students in assessing themselves, which provide information to be used as feedback to modify the teaching and learning activities in which they are engaged. Such assessment becomes 'formative assessment' when the evidence is actually used to adapt the teaching work to meet the needs" (p. 2).
Sato, Wei, & Darling-Hammond, 2008	"Activities undertaken by the teacher and the students as a means of collecting information about the students' understanding or progress and, second, the use of this information to modify teaching and learning activities by the teacher, the students, or both" (p. 672).
Formative assessment is the use of information to adjust learning.	
Black & Wiliam, 2009, as cited in Tetzlaff, Schmiedek, & Brod, 2021, p. 869	"Practice in a classroom is formative to the extent that evidence about student achievement is elicited, interpreted, and used by teachers, learners, or their peers, to make decisions about the next steps in instruction that are likely to be better, or better founded, than the decisions they would have taken in the absence of the evidence that was elicited" (p. 5).

continued →

Decristan et al., 2015	"The repeated use of assessment-based information to recognize and respond to students' needs to enhance learning (see Bell & Cowie, 2001, p. 536)" (p. 1136).
Herman, Osmundson, Dai, Ringstaff, & Timms, 2011	"The use of assessment to 'form' subsequent instruction. . . . Formative assessment involves knowing what the learning goals are, eliciting evidence of student status relative to the goals, and taking action to close any gap between students' current status and the desired goal(s)" (p. 2).
Sato et al., 2008	"The use of . . . information to modify teaching and learning activities by the teacher, the students, or both" (p. 672).
Vanlommel & Schildkamp, 2019	"Using the data about pupils' learning processes to monitor and guide these learning processes" (p. 793).
Formative assessment is a process to facilitate learning.	
Conderman, Pinter, & Young, 2020	"A systematic process teachers use to continuously gather evidence about student learning" (p. 234).
Heritage, 2020	"Three questions that guide the practice for both teachers and students: where are the students going (well-defined learning goals), where are they currently (evidence collected during the course of learning), and how to close the gap between these two (instructional adjustments, feedback, and student involvement)?" (p. 355).
Heritage, Kim, Vendlinski, & Herman, 2008	"A systematic process to continuously gather evidence and provide feedback about learning while instruction is underway. The feedback identifies the gap between a student's current level of learning and a desired learning goal" (p. 1).
Johnson, Sondergeld, & Walton, 2019	"A planned process including a suite of key pedagogical tools used to elicit ongoing evidence of student understanding used by both teachers and students to adjust instruction and procedures within the lesson" (p. 2409).
Klute et al., 2017	"A process that engages teachers and students during instruction in gathering, interpreting, and using evidence about what and how students are learning in order to facilitate further student learning" (p. 1).
Wylie, 2020	"A set of practices or a process where teachers and students gather evidence about learning as it is unfolding and use feedback to modify teaching and learning" (p. 255).
Wylie & Lyon, 2020	"A planned, ongoing process used by all students and teachers during learning and teaching to elicit and use evidence of student learning to improve student understanding of intended disciplinary learning outcomes and support students to become self-directed learners" (pp. 314–315).

As table 5.2 indicates, formative assessment has been variously described as all of the following.

- A practice test
- A snapshot of student knowledge and skill
- Instructional feedback

- A set of information-collecting activities
- The use of information to adjust learning
- A process to facilitate learning

Using one term to describe such a wide range of concepts, activities, and functions impairs the ability of the term *formative assessment* to communicate any meaningful information. Given the equivocal nature of the term *formative assessment* as evidenced by the extant research literature, there is no absolute reference educators can turn to for perfect guidance. In this book, we use the terms *formative* and *summative* specifically and carefully. Districts and schools can and should do the same.

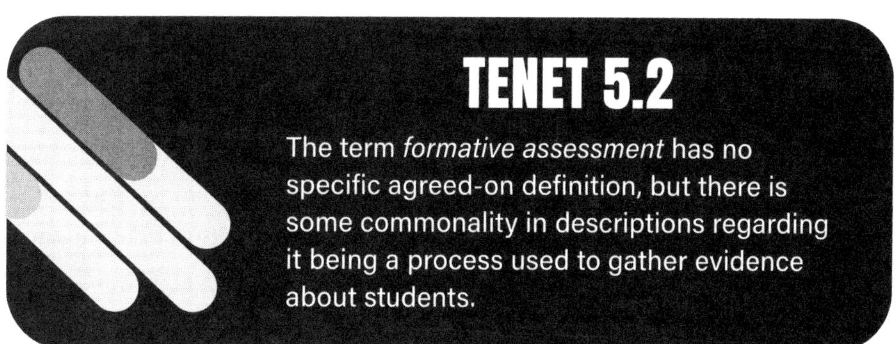

Implications of tenet 5.2 might include the following.

- **Conceptual clarity and communication:** The wide array of definitions associated with formative assessment highlights a lack of consensus within the educational community. This lack of clarity can lead to misunderstandings among educators, policymakers, and stakeholders regarding the purpose and implementation of formative assessment practices. For instance, if one educator interprets formative assessment as primarily involving practice tests, while another views it as a continuous process of gathering evidence to adjust instruction, their instructional practices and expectations for student learning outcomes may differ significantly.
- **Implementation challenges and effectiveness:** The varied definitions pose challenges in effectively implementing formative assessment strategies in educational settings. Educators may struggle to adopt consistent practices when the concept itself is interpreted diversely. This inconsistency can affect the reliability and validity

of assessment data used to guide instructional decisions. Moreover, educators may face difficulty in aligning formative assessment practices with broader educational goals and standards if there is no shared understanding of what constitutes formative assessment.

The Misleading Concept of Summative Assessment

In addition to the confusing research and theory behind formative assessment, the concept has been used in tandem with *summative assessment* to create practices that are detrimental to student learning and accurate reporting. In some schools, educators treat formative assessments as mere practice for summative assessments; formative assessments are practice tests that are not recorded, and only the scores from summative assessments count toward determining proficiency. If a student's score is above a certain cut score on the summative test, they are considered proficient; otherwise, they receive additional instructional support and take another summative assessment.

This approach, however, has a significant flaw, as it fails to account for the inherent error in any test score. All assessments contain some degree of error. The concept of error has been a basic part of measurement theory since the early 1900s (for a discussion, see Marzano, 2018). The place of error in an assessment score is clearly articulated in the following classical test theory equation:

observed score = true score + error

This equation states that the score a student receives on an assessment (called the *observed score*) consists of two parts: the true score and the error score. The *true score* is what the student would have received under ideal conditions (that is, perfect test, perfect administration, student in perfect condition, and so on). But the true score is always contaminated by *error* that makes the observed score either an overestimate or underestimate of the true score. In nontechnical terms, it is accurate to say that one can never know a student's absolute true score or the absolute amount of error associated with an obtained score. But one can compute estimations that provide useful perspectives. For example, as table 5.3 shows, a student's observed score of 70 on an assessment with a high reliability of 0.85 (typical of most large-scale assessments) corresponds to a true score as high as 81 or as low as 59. Error is responsible for a significant margin of error, even on very well-designed assessments.

TABLE 5.3: Reliabilities and 95 Percent Confidence Intervals

Reliability Coefficient	Observed Score on Assessment	Lower Limit	Upper Limit	Range
0.85	70	59	81	22
0.75	70	55	85	30
0.65	70	53	87	34
0.55	70	50	90	40
0.45	70	48	92	44

Note: The standard deviation of this test was 15, and the upper and lower limits have been rounded.
Source: Marzano et al., 2019, p. 3.

Ultimately, no assessment is perfect, and all observed scores contain some amount of error. This means that basing important decisions on a single score from a summative test is not advisable, as the score from that test is imprecise because of error. Using a single test to determine student proficiency overlooks the complexities of learning and fails to account for the continuous nature of student development, making the use of multiple formative scores a more reliable and fair approach, as we describe in the next section.

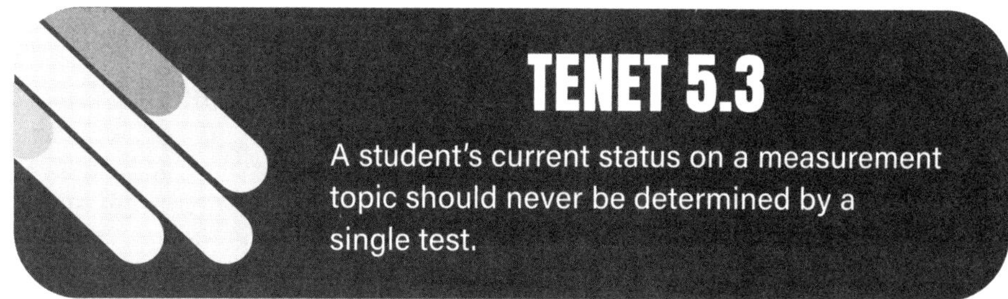

TENET 5.3

A student's current status on a measurement topic should never be determined by a single test.

Implications of tenet 5.3 might include the following.

- **Need for multiple assessments to improve accuracy:** Relying on a single test to determine a student's proficiency is problematic due to the inherent error in any observed score. By using multiple formative assessments over time, teachers can gather more reliable and comprehensive data, leading to a more accurate understanding of a student's true abilities and progress. This approach minimizes the impact of errors or inconsistencies that may arise from any single test, ensuring that student evaluations reflect their true proficiency rather than fluctuations caused by testing conditions or temporary factors.

- **Ongoing assessment for continuous learning:** Tracking student progress across multiple assessments is more accurate than treating learning as a series of discrete, one-time summative evaluations. With this approach, teachers can adjust instruction in real time based on consistent data about a student's performance. By focusing on cumulative patterns of formative scores, teachers are better equipped to support ongoing growth and development, providing a more accurate representation of student proficiency that evolves over time, rather than being locked into a single assessment.

Formative and Summative Scores

A useful perspective for educators is to realize that any given assessment could be considered formative or summative depending on how the information from the assessment is used. Because of the issues with the concepts of formative assessment and summative assessment, Marzano (2010) recommended that educators adopt the terms *formative scores* and *summative scores*, using the terms *formative* and *summative* to label the purpose of scores that are generated from assessments as opposed to the assessments themselves. This is consistent with many of the descriptions in table 5.2 (page 137), which highlight the fact that a formative assessment is not a specific type of test. Rather, it is a process used to gather information about an individual student's knowledge and skill.

To illustrate, recall the discussion about tracking scores by measurement topic in chapter 4 and reconsider the set of scores from classwide plus individual assessments shown in figure 5.1.

Each score for each student represents an assessment on the measurement topic, although not all assessments were applied to every student. The scores in figure 5.1 are all formative scores, including the scores for the last assessment on the twentieth day. This fact cannot be overemphasized, for it means that teachers should always think in terms of collecting a wide array of scores for each student on each measurement topic that come from assessments that are as reliable and valid as possible. They then use these data to generate a summative score for each student on each topic. Even if an assessment was the final test on this measurement topic, it does not represent the student's summative score. Instead, the teacher will use

	Day of Unit																			
	1	2	3	4	5	6	7	8	9	10	11	12	13	14	15	16	17	18	19	20
Fatima	1.0				1.5						2.0			2.0			2.5			2.5
Gregg	1.5										3.0				3.0			3.5		3.5
Hawar	2.0		2.0								3.0									4.0
Imlad	1.0		1.5								2.5					3.0		3.5		3.5
Jack	2.0					2.5					2.5			3.0			3.5			4.0

FIGURE 5.1: Classwide assessments plus individual assessments.

the pattern of scores across the unit to compute a summative score. We describe approaches for computing summative scores in the next section.

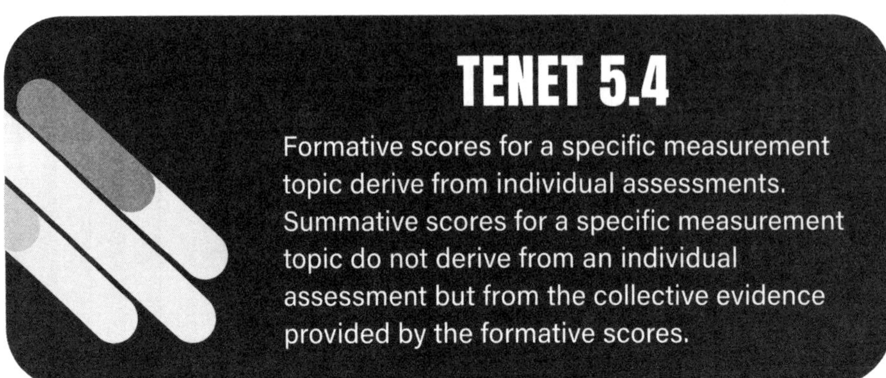

Implications of tenet 5.4 might include the following.

- **Holistic view of student progress:** Rather than placing undue emphasis on any single test, formative scores provide a comprehensive view of a student's learning journey. Teachers can track and analyze patterns of progress over time, allowing for a more accurate picture of student development that reflects continuous learning, rather than judging proficiency based on a single performance.
- **Informed decision making for summative scores:** By basing summative scores on the collective evidence from multiple formative scores, teachers can make more informed and accurate decisions about a student's proficiency. This approach acknowledges that no single test can fully capture a student's understanding, and instead, a summative score is derived from the accumulated data. It allows for more reliable and valid evaluations of student learning, avoiding the potential pitfalls of relying on a single assessment that may not reflect a student's true abilities due to various external factors.

How to Compute a Summative Score

If you use proficiency scales to design and score assessments and track scores from parallel assessments by measurement topic, you will have a set of formative scores for each student for each measurement topic at the end of a grading period.

You can compute a summative score from that set of formative scores in several different ways. Some methods are more accurate than others. We begin our review of these methods with the popular but not very accurate method of averaging.

Averaging and the Decaying Average

Similar to the entrenched practice of tracking scores by assessment type discussed in chapter 4, averaging is an enduring but unexamined practice in education. Many teachers use it for lack of a better option. For example, if a teacher was tracking scores by assessment type, he might summarize a student's performance across the grading period by computing the average of each category of assessment type and then averaging those averages to arrive at a number summarizing the student's performance. For a particular student, the average of all her quiz scores might be 78, the average of all her end-of-unit tests might be 81, and the average of all her assignments might be 86 (assuming all metrics are the percentage of points earned). The teacher computes the average of those averages and reports an overall average of 81.7. While this is an interesting metric, it doesn't provide any useful information about how the student is doing on a particular topic at the end of a grading period. Any useful information was lost when the teacher decided to track scores by assessment type, and averaging is really the only thing you can do with such minimally useful categories.

But what if a teacher is tracking scores by measurement topic? Is averaging an effective method in that case? Not necessarily. Consider Imlad's scores in figure 5.1 (page 143). Over the course of a twenty-day unit for one specific measurement topic, the teacher recorded six scores for Imlad: 1.0, 1.5, 2.5, 3.0, 3.5, and 3.5. Imlad started with a low score of 1.0 and ended with a high score of 3.5. The average of Imlad's six scores is 2.5, but that does not represent his level of knowledge for this measurement topic at the end of the unit, which is the stated purpose and goal of computing a summative score. This is obvious based on the fact that Imlad received progressively higher and higher scores over time, which is the natural consequence of his learning more and more about the topic. In this example, then, using the average is not a good option for computing Imlad's summative score for this measurement topic. This does not mean that the average is never a good option for computing summative scores (we will return to the average in a later section). Rather, the proper generalization is that scores should be aggregated in a way that provides the best estimate of the student's current status relative to a specific measurement topic at the end of a grading period.

In light of this generalization, some teachers opt to use a different type of average that heavily weights more recent scores: the *decaying average*. By this logic, more recent scores are considered to be better indicators of a student's current status and therefore should receive greater weight (Marzano et al., 2019). While variation exists in the formulas teachers use to compute a decaying average, a commonly used one weights the most recent score by 0.65 (or 65 percent) and earlier scores by 0.35 (or 35 percent).

To present a simple example, consider a student, Parker, who has two scores for a measurement topic so far in a unit: 1.5 and 2.0. The traditional average of those two scores is 1.75. But if you weight the more recent score by 65 percent, the decaying average yields a higher number: 1.83.

$$1.5(0.35) + 2.0(0.65) = 1.83$$

If Parker earned another score of 2.5 on the following day, the decaying average would change to 2.27 (higher than the 2.0 traditional average of the three scores).

$$1.83(0.35) + 2.5(0.65) = 2.27$$

Some gradebooks allow for more complex methods of calculating a decaying average, allowing teachers to assign weights to assessments or types of assessments or use a compound exponential decay formula.

Our goal is neither to review all the methods for computing a decaying average nor to explain how to compute decaying averages (if you wish to learn more about the decaying average, please see Marzano et al., 2019). Rather, we simply wish to illustrate that by giving more weight to the most recent score, the decaying average acknowledges that learning occurs over time. This is an admirable acknowledgment. However, the major weakness of the decaying average is that it masks information about previous scores; when using a decaying average, you cannot review each of the scores leading up to the most current score. This is a significant loss; in the next two sections, we review score aggregation methods that preserve this valuable information.

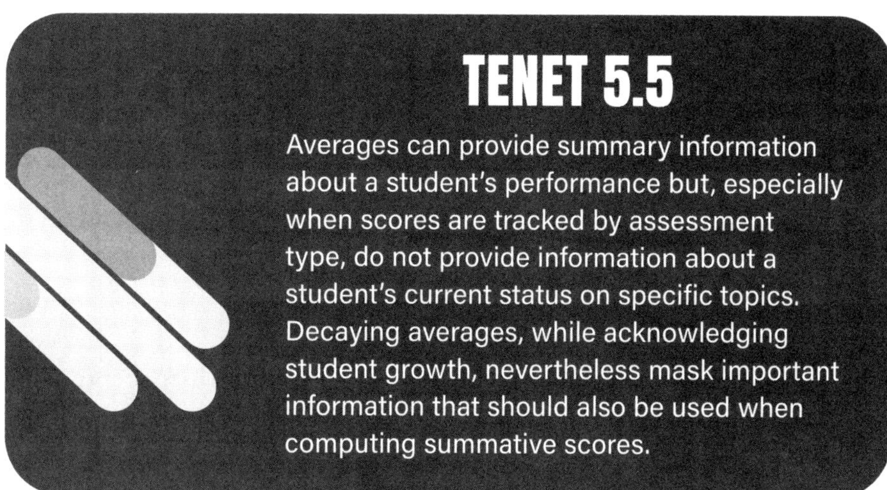

Implications of tenet 5.5 might include the following.

- **The importance of accurate representation of current status:** Averages, particularly when scores are tracked by assessment type, can fail to provide an accurate reflection of a student's current understanding of specific topics. This practice may lead to misinterpretation of student progress, as averages penalize students for poor early performance on assessments and tend to underestimate their current level of knowledge or skill.
- **Potential loss of information about learning:** While decaying averages recognize recent progress by emphasizing more current assessments, they can obscure earlier performance data, which are critical for understanding the full scope of student learning. Teachers may miss key information that reveals earlier struggles or strengths, limiting their ability to fully assess a student's learning trajectory. When calculating summative scores, it's important to consider the complete picture of a student's progress rather than overemphasize recent scores. A more balanced approach that includes earlier performance ensures that summative evaluations are well rounded, offering a fuller understanding of student growth.

Mathematical Model of Best Fit

Marzano (2000, 2006, 2018), independently and with colleagues (Marzano et al., 2019), designed a process for computing a summative score using a set of formative scores tracked by measurement topic. As mentioned earlier in the chapter, the technical term for formative scores is *observed scores*. The process has two steps.

1. Compute trend lines for the set of observed scores using three mathematical models.
    - **Linear:** Assumes that growth occurs in equal increments, represented by a slanted line
    - **Curvilinear:** Assumes that growth occurs quickly at first and slows down over time, represented by a curved line
    - **Arithmetic average:** Assumes that growth does not occur, represented by a horizontal line
2. Compare the trend line for each mathematical model with the student's observed scores to identify the model that best fits the observed scores.

Best fit is a statistical term indicating the trend line with the least amount of error between the scores that the mathematical model predicts (the *predicted scores*) and the observed scores. The following three sections provide detailed examples of how to compute each of the trend lines in step 1. The fourth section, Finding the Best-Fit Model, provides detail on how to compare the trend lines with observed scores, as in step 2.

The Linear Model

Let's begin by considering the linear model. The bars in figure 5.2 show five observed scores a student named Quinley earned for a particular measurement topic: 1.0, 1.5, 1.5, 2.0, and 3.0. The predicted scores from the linear model are represented by the straight line and its scores: 0.9, 1.35, 1.8, 2.25, and 2.7.

The predicted scores correspond to each observed score; that is, the linear model asserts that these are the true scores that the student would have achieved on each assessment if we assume that growth occurs in equal increments (as the linear model does). Clearly, the observed scores are different from the predicted scores. For example, the predicted score for the second assessment is 1.35, whereas the observed score is 1.5. The predicted score for the fourth assessment is 2.25, but the

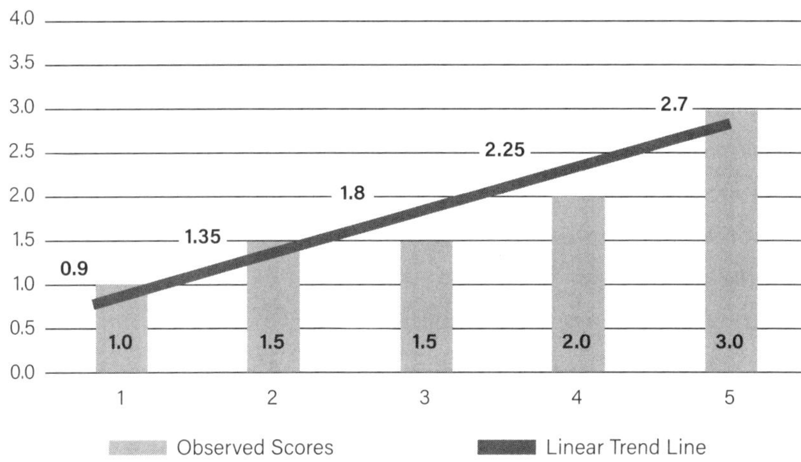

Source: Marzano et al., 2019, p. 83.

FIGURE 5.2: Observed scores and the trend line of predicted scores from the linear model.

observed score is 2.0, and so on. The difference between the observed and predicted scores is assumed to be due to error. Therefore, the linear trend estimates the student's summative score at the end of the grading period to be 2.7.

The Curvilinear Model

Now let's consider the curvilinear model. Figure 5.3 shows Quinley's observed scores (the bars) overlaid with a curved line representing the predicted scores from the curvilinear model: 0.94, 1.50, 1.86, 2.15, and 2.4.

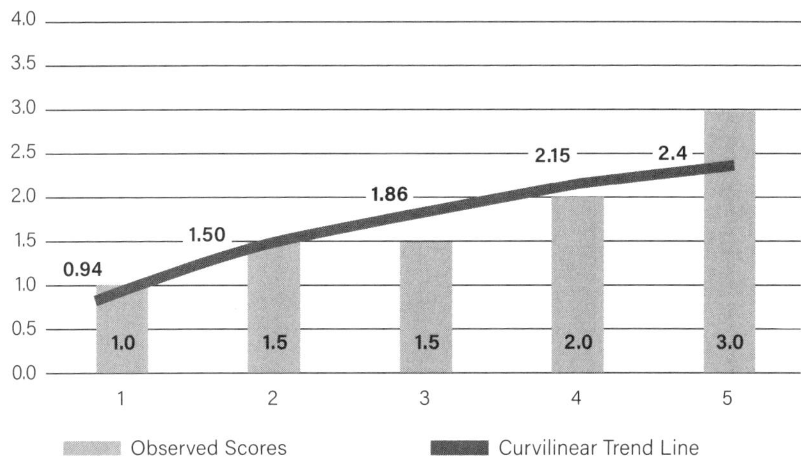

Source: Marzano et al., 2019, p. 84.

FIGURE 5.3: Observed scores and the trend line of predicted scores from the curvilinear model.

Because the curvilinear model is based on a different assumption than the linear model—that growth occurs quickly at first and slows down over time—it predicts different true scores. Notice that the predicted scores from the curvilinear model are larger than those from the linear model for the first three observed scores. However, for the last two observed scores, the predicted scores from the curvilinear model are lower than those from the linear model. This is consistent with the assumption for the curvilinear trend that learning is characterized by big increases early in the learning process that tend to flatten out over time. The curvilinear model estimates the student's summative score at the end of the grading period to be 2.4.

The Arithmetic Average Model

Finally, figure 5.4 shows Quinley's observed scores (the bars) overlaid with a horizontal line representing the predicted scores from the arithmetic average model.

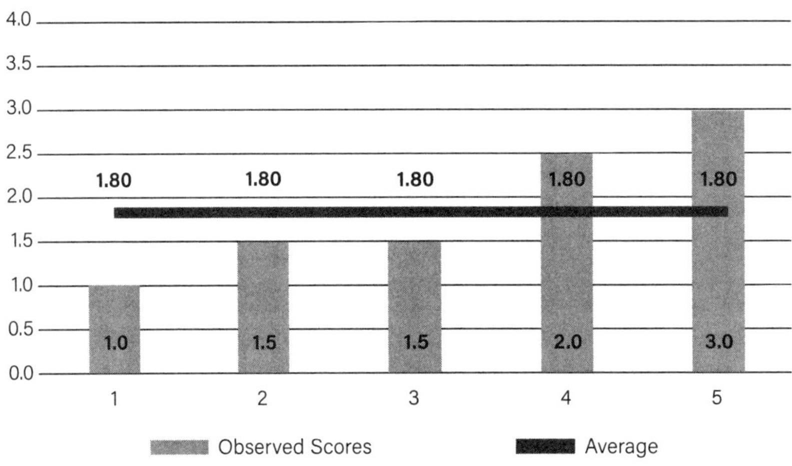

Source: Marzano et al., 2019, p. 85.

FIGURE 5.4: Observed scores and the trend line of predicted scores from the arithmetic average model.

As stated previously, the arithmetic average model assumes that no learning has occurred over time; though this assumption makes little sense, classroom teachers unwittingly invoke it anytime they use the average to estimate a summative score. Although we have made the case that the average should not be used to estimate a summative score from a set of scores tracked by assessment type, there are situations—when scores are tracked by measurement topic—in which the arithmetic average is the model that best fits a set of observed scores. This situation is an aberration in terms of its measurement utility but unfortunately can occur with classroom assessment.

When there is no apparent systematic increase in student learning as depicted by formative scores—for example, if a student scores very high on the first assessment, very low on the second, very high on the third, very low on the fourth, and so on—the arithmetic average model will likely fit the data best. It's useful to make a connection here with the idea of aberrant patterns (see Aberrant Patterns in chapter 4, page 108). When discussed previously, *aberrant pattern* referred to an illogical pattern of item responses from a particular student on a single test. Here, we see an aberrant pattern of scores collected across multiple parallel assessments on a specific measurement topic for a specific student. When this happens, it should send a strong signal to the teacher that something is wrong. The assessments being used might not be sensitive enough to pick up increases in the student's understanding for that particular topic. Or the student is engaged when taking some assessments but not engaged when taking others. When the arithmetic average model seems to be the best fit, it behooves the teacher to look a bit deeper.

Finding the Best-Fit Model

The method of mathematical models produces three different estimates of the student's true summative score at the end of a grading period. In the example with Quinley's scores, those estimates are as follows.

- 2.7 from the linear model
- 2.4 from the curvilinear model
- 1.8 from the arithmetic average model

As stated previously, the best-fit model is the one with the least amount of error between the predicted scores and the observed scores. Said another way, the model whose predicted scores are closest to the observed scores is the best-fit model.

To determine which model's predicted scores are closest to the observed scores, examine the difference (or *error*) between the observed and the predicted true scores. A precision chart such as the one in figure 5.5 (page 152) makes this a fairly straightforward task.

Observed Scores		1.0	1.5	1.5	2.0	3.0	Total Difference or Error	Average Difference or Error
Linear	**Predicted**	0.90	1.35	1.80	2.25	2.70		
	Difference From Observed Score	0.1	0.15	0.3	0.25	0.3	1.1	0.220
Curvilinear	**Predicted**	0.94	1.50	1.86	2.15	2.40		
	Difference From Observed Score	0.06	0	0.36	0.15	0.6	1.17	0.234
Arithmetic Average	**Predicted**	1.80	1.80	1.80	1.80	1.80		
	Difference From Observed Score	0.8	0.3	0.3	0.2	1.2	2.8	0.560

Note: For explicit formulas to create spreadsheet algorithms that compute and evaluate the three mathematical models, please see *Making Classroom Assessments Reliable and Valid* (Marzano, 2018) or visit marzano calc.empowerlearning.net to access an online tool.

Source: Adapted from Marzano et al., 2019.

FIGURE 5.5: Precision chart.

Visit ***MarzanoResources.com/reproducibles*** *for a free reproducible version of this figure.*

The last two columns of the precision chart show the total error and average error associated with each model. By definition, the model with the least amount of overall error is the one that is the most precise. In this case, the linear trend has the least amount of error and would, therefore, be considered the most precise. In more technical terms, the linear trend would be said to fit the data best. Thus, from the perspective of the three mathematical models, the summative score with the least amount of associated error is 2.7, and Quinley's teacher would most likely select this to report as his summative score.

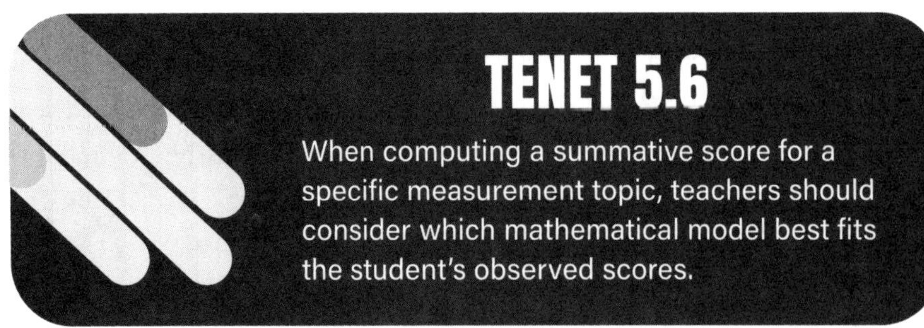

Implications of tenet 5.6 might include the following.

- **Enhanced precision in assessment:** Adopting mathematical models such as linear, curvilinear, or arithmetic average to estimate summative scores enhances precision. By comparing observed scores with predicted scores from different models, you can identify the model that best minimizes error, thereby providing a more accurate estimation of a student's current status for a measurement topic. This approach moves beyond a simple average or even a decaying average, ensuring that summative scores reflect the closest approximation of a student's true score.
- **Insight into learning trajectories:** Utilizing mathematical models helps educators gain insights into students' learning trajectories for specific measurement topics. The models not only quantify growth patterns but also highlight assumptions about how students learn over time. For instance, a curvilinear model indicates rapid initial learning followed by a plateau, whereas a linear model suggests steady, incremental progress.
- **Identification of assessment sensitivity:** When the arithmetic average model emerges as the best fit for a set of observed scores, it signals potential issues with assessment sensitivity or student engagement. This prompts educators to critically examine the assessments used and their alignment with learning objectives. For example, if a student's scores fluctuate widely without a discernible pattern, it may indicate inconsistencies in assessment formats or difficulty levels. By recognizing these patterns through mathematical modeling, teachers can refine assessment practices to ensure they effectively capture and measure student learning outcomes.

Method of Mounting Evidence

While computing and evaluating the predicted scores for various mathematical models against a student's observed scores are sensible ways to estimate a student's summative score, there is an equally sensible way to estimate a student's summative score that does not require mathematical calculations. It is called the *method of mounting evidence*, or the "gradual accumulation of a summative score" (Marzano, 2010, p. 86).

As the name implies, the teacher using this method keeps track of a student's summative score throughout a grading period rather than calculating it at the end of the period. Specifically, as soon as the teacher is relatively certain that the student has achieved *at least* a specific summative score, she records it. This is critical to the accuracy of the method of mounting evidence. Stated differently, a teacher should not enter a proposed summative score unless they believe there is ample evidence to support the accuracy of the proposed score.

This approach is built on the generalization that "a summative score exists only in a particular moment of time" (Marzano et al., 2019, p. 80). If a summative score is a student's current status on a measurement topic, it implies that the student has many summative scores throughout a unit. A teacher using the method of mounting evidence simply makes these explicit in the gradebook.

To illustrate the method of mounting evidence, consider the observed scores for an individual student, Marcus, on a specific measurement topic. During the first week of instruction, the teacher administers a pretest to all students. Marcus receives a score of 1.5. A few days later, the teacher assigns Marcus a score of 2.0 based on a discussion she had with him. A week later, the teacher gives a traditional test to the entire class and assigns Marcus a score of 2.5 on it. At the end of the second week of instruction, the teacher assigns summative scores to students for the measurement topic. Based on Marcus's three scores (1.5, 2.0, and 2.5), she decides she is reasonably sure that Marcus is *at least* at a summative score of 2.0. Even though Marcus has received a score of 2.5, the teacher cannot vouch for this score as a stable current summative score. This logic represents a general parameter of this approach in that the teacher errs on the side of underestimating each student's current summative score. One might say that the teacher continually identifies the minimum current summative score.

Teachers who use the method of mounting evidence will need a recordkeeping system that differs from the traditional gradebook. Figure 5.6 depicts a simple system used by many educators for this purpose.

In figure 5.6, Marcus's observed scores have been entered, along with the date of each score. Notice that nothing was entered in the third column for the first two assessments. This is because the teacher did not decide to assign minimum summative scores until the third assessment. As mentioned previously, it is important that teachers only enter a minimum summative score once they are convinced that the student's true summative score is at least at that level. This is because once

Student: Marcus		
Measurement topic: Equivalent Fractions		
Date	**Observed Score**	**Current Minimum Summative Score**
Jan. 7	1.5	
Jan. 10	2.0	
Jan. 17	2.5	2.0

FIGURE 5.6: Recordkeeping system for the method of mounting evidence.

one has established a current minimum summative score for a student, one need not assess the student anymore at that level. Subsequent assessments need only address score levels higher than the minimum summative score the student has already achieved.

Figure 5.7 (page 156) shows an expanded version of recordkeeping for the method of mounting evidence that accommodates multiple students and multiple measurement topics. This one recordkeeping form will accommodate five different measurement topics. In this case, those five topics all address skills associated with reading comprehension. The teacher's intent might be to address all five during a single grading period, starting with the first topic: determining main idea. The teacher has already started to fill in scores for Marcus, Evie, Maggie, Oakley, and Jasmin.

Marcus's scores (described previously) have been filled in; the small box marked *MSS* is where the teacher enters the student's minimum summative score for each measurement topic, replacing lower scores with higher scores as the teacher feels certain that a higher minimum summative score is justified. In Marcus's case, that minimum summative score was a 2.0. Of note in this example is that the teacher entered scores for every student on two occasions: January 7 and January 17. In this case, the teacher administered an assessment to all students on those two dates. Other than Marcus, three students received second scores in between these two dates. Two other students also received current MSS entries, indicating the teacher believed there was a pattern of scores to justify them. However, two students were not assigned MSS entries—perhaps for lack of scores (in the case of Jasmin) or due to a pattern of scores the teacher did not feel comfortable translating into a minimum summative score (in the case of Oakley).

	Measurement Topic 1: Determining Main Idea	Measurement Topic 2: Determining Words in Context	Measurement Topic 3: Literary Devices	Measurement Topic 4: Author Purpose	Measurement Topic 5: Analyzing Evidence
Marcus	1/7—1.5 1/10—2.0 1/17—2.5 MSS: 2.0	MSS:	MSS:	MSS:	MSS:
Evie	1/7—2.5 1/12—3.0 1/17—3.0 MSS: 3.0	MSS:	MSS:	MSS:	MSS:
Maggie	1/7—2.0 1/14—2.5 1/17—2.0 MSS: 2.0	MSS:	MSS:	MSS:	MSS:
Oakley	1/7—3.0 1/12—2.5 1/17—2.0 MSS:	MSS:	MSS:	MSS:	MSS:
Jasmin	1/7—2.0 1/17—1.5 MSS:	MSS:	MSS:	MSS:	MSS:

FIGURE 5.7: Expanded recordkeeping for method of mounting evidence.

Visit ***MarzanoResources.com/reproducibles*** *for a free reproducible version of this figure.*

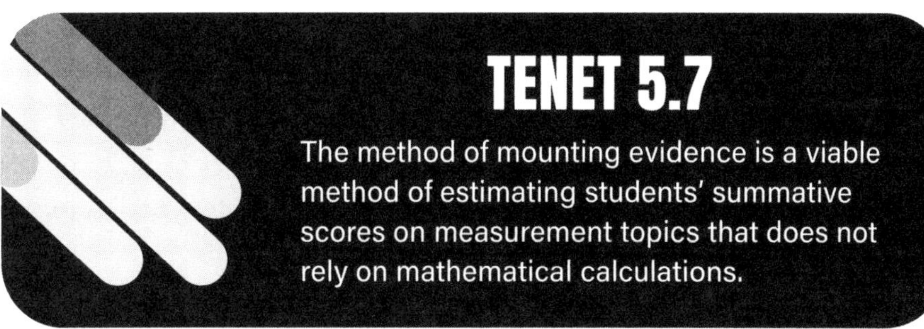

Implications of tenet 5.7 might include the following.

- **Real-time assessment feedback:** The method of mounting evidence allows for continuous and immediate feedback on student progress throughout a grading period. Unlike traditional methods that calculate summative scores at the end of a period, this approach enables teachers to assess and record students' minimum current summative scores as soon as they are reasonably certain of their achievement level. This real-time feedback loop fosters a more dynamic and responsive teaching environment where educators can promptly adjust instructional strategies based on ongoing assessments. It also enhances transparency for students and families by providing clear and updated insights into their students' academic standing on specific measurement topics.
- **Flexible and adaptive grading practices:** The method of mounting evidence encourages educators to adopt a more flexible approach to grading. By focusing on identifying the minimum current summative score, teachers acknowledge that student learning is a continuous process that evolves over time. This approach mitigates the pressure of a single assessment event determining a student's final grade, allowing for a more nuanced evaluation of their progress. It also supports differentiated instruction by guiding teachers to tailor interventions based on students' real-time performance data, rather than relying solely on aggregated scores at the end of a period. As a result, educators can better support diverse learning needs and optimize educational outcomes for all students.

Reporting Metrics

An oft-overlooked detail of generating summative scores concerns how scores will be reported. If you are using a proficiency scale such as the one we recommend and exemplify in this book, students' summative scores will always fall somewhere between 0.0 and 4.0, as figure 5.8 shows.

4.0	In addition to score 3.0 performance, in-depth inferences and applications that go beyond what was taught
3.5	In addition to score 3.0 performance, partial success at score 4.0 content
3.0	No major errors or omissions with score 3.0 content
2.5	No major errors or omissions regarding score 2.0 content, and partial success at score 3.0 content
2.0	No major errors or omissions with score 2.0 content
1.5	Partial success at score 2.0 content, and major errors or omissions regarding score 3.0 content
1.0	With help, partial success at score 2.0 content and score 3.0 content
0.5	With help, partial success at score 2.0 content but not at score 3.0 content
0.0	Even with help, no success at any level

FIGURE 5.8: Proficiency scale with half-point scores.

If you are using the method of mounting evidence, each student's current summative score will be expressed as one of the nine discrete values on the proficiency scale. But if you are using mathematical models, then each student's summative score will likely not exactly align with the nine discrete values on the proficiency scale. For example, the estimates of Quinley's summative score from the section on mathematical model of best fit were as follows.

- 2.7 from the linear model
- 2.4 from the curvilinear model
- 1.8 from the arithmetic average model

Consider the ramifications of rounding these estimates to align with specific scores on the proficiency scale. The first option is to round the scores to the nearest score value on the proficiency scale, as follows.

- **Linear:** 2.7 → 2.5
- **Curvilinear:** 2.4 → 2.5
- **Arithmetic average:** 1.8 → 2.0

This approach obviously masks a great deal of useful information from the mathematical models. The linear and curvilinear estimates present the same summative score of 2.5, and the arithmetic average produces a summative score of 2.0.

Making things even more opaque, some schools round all information to the nearest whole score, as follows.

- **Linear:** 2.7 → 3.0
- **Curvilinear:** 2.4 → 2.0
- **Arithmetic average:** 1.8 → 2.0

Again, a great deal of useful information about the student has been lost in the rounding process.

The second option is to add quarter-point values to the proficiency scale, as figure 5.9 shows, and round each summative score to the nearest quarter-point value, as follows.

- **Linear:** 2.7 → 2.75
- **Curvilinear:** 2.4 → 2.5
- **Arithmetic average:** 1.8 → 1.75

This approach preserves the differences in the estimates computed from the three mathematical models and is more precise than rounding to a whole or half-point score.

4.0	In addition to score 3.0 performance, in-depth inferences and applications that go beyond what was taught
3.75	In addition to score 3.0 performance, partial success of about three-quarters of the content at score 4.0
3.50	In addition to score 3.0 performance, partial success of about one-half of the content at score 4.0
3.25	In addition to score 3.0 performance, partial success of about one-quarter of the content at score 4.0
3.0	No major errors or omissions with score 3.0 content
2.75	No major errors or omissions regarding score 2.0 content, and partial success of about three-quarters of the content at score 3.0
2.5	No major errors or omissions regarding score 2.0 content, and partial success of about one-half of the content at score 3.0
2.25	No major errors or omissions regarding score 2.0 content, and partial success of about one-quarter of the content at score 3.0

FIGURE 5.9: Proficiency scale with quarter-point scores.

continued →

2.0	No major errors or omissions with score 2.0 content
1.75	Partial success of about three-quarters of the score 2.0 content, and major errors or omissions regarding score 3.0 content
1.5	Partial success of about one-half of the score 2.0 content, and major errors or omissions regarding score 3.0 content
1.25	Partial success of about one-quarter of the score 2.0 content, and major errors or omissions regarding score 3.0 content
1.0	With help, partial success at score 2.0 content and score 3.0 content
0.75	With help, partial success of about three-quarters of the score 2.0 content but no success at score 3.0 content
0.5	With help, partial success of about one-half of the score 2.0 content but no success at score 3.0 content
0.25	With help, partial success of about one-quarter of the score 2.0 content but no success at score 3.0 content
0.0	Even with help, no success at any level

It is important to note that the quarter-point version of the proficiency scale could also be used to score individual assessments. However, when teachers are first getting used to scoring individual assessments, we have found that it is better to start with the half-point score version. After teachers have used the quarter-point version to estimate summative scores, they can more easily make the application to individual assessments if they so choose.

The third option is to simply report the raw computed score from the mathematical model. For example, if the best-fit summative score of 2.7 was from the linear model, the score of 2.7 would appear on the report card. While there is no precise description of the meaning of each raw score in this scenario, we have found that educators and non-educators tend to interpret the decimal part of the score as a percentage. For example, a summative score of 2.7 is typically interpreted as *the student has demonstrated understanding of the 2.0 content and 70 percent of the score 3.0 content.* This approach, like the second option, also preserves the differences in the estimates computed from the three mathematical models and is more precise than rounding to a whole-, half-, or quarter-point score.

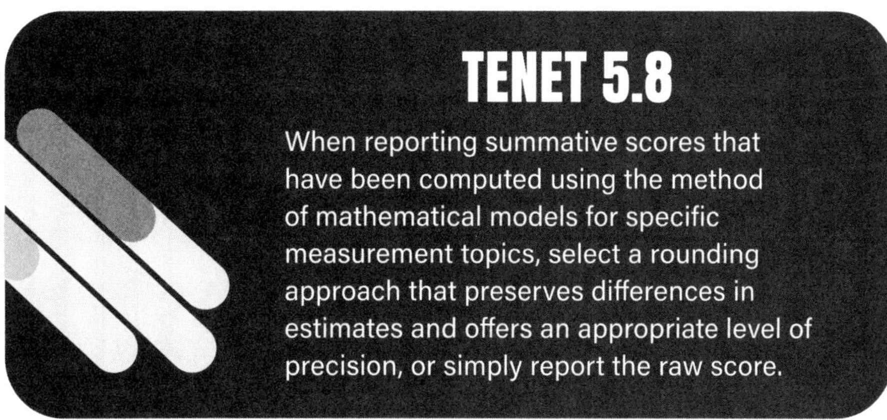

Implications of tenet 5.8 might include the following.

- **Precision and information retention:** The choice to use the rounding approach significantly impacts the precision and informational richness conveyed by summative scores derived from mathematical models. If scores are rounded to the nearest whole or half point on a proficiency scale, nuances between different model estimates can be obscured. Such an approach may simplify reporting but sacrifices detailed differentiation. This simplification might misrepresent the actual differences in student performance as captured by the mathematical models. Thus, educators must weigh the trade-off between simplicity in reporting and the retention of detailed performance distinctions when choosing a rounding method.
- **Clarity and interpretation:** Opting to report raw computed scores directly from the mathematical models provides a level of clarity and transparency in reporting. These scores retain the precise differences calculated by the models, potentially offering more insight into a student's progression and understanding across different measurement topics. Moreover, interpreting the decimal part of these scores as a percentage can provide additional granularity in understanding student achievements. This approach aligns with how educators, students, and families often perceive scores as indicative of partial mastery or progress toward higher levels of proficiency, thereby enhancing the educational utility of reported scores.

Reliability and Validity

Assessment literacy requires that educators have a more detailed understanding of the concepts of reliability and validity, particularly as they relate to classroom assessment scores for individual students. Therefore, we conclude this chapter with a distilled primer on reliability and validity for classroom teachers. For additional information about these important concepts and detailed discussions of how to achieve them in classroom assessment practice, please consult *Making Classroom Assessments Reliable and Valid* (Marzano, 2018).

A Clear View of Reliability

Most educators understand the concept of *reliability* as the accuracy of scores from a test and are aware that it is expressed using the reliability coefficient, a metric that ranges between 0.00 and 1.00. Educators usually assume that if a test has a high reliability coefficient, then the scores from that test are accurate, and if a test has a low reliability coefficient, then the scores may not be accurate. However, educators' general familiarity with reliability and the reliability coefficient does not necessarily indicate that they are aware of their true meanings.

Reliability Coefficient

The reliability coefficient is based on Galton's (1888) correlation coefficient, which you may recall from our review of the sordid history of intelligence testing in the introduction. In 1904, Charles Spearman used the correlation coefficient to hypothesize that the correlation between pairs of similar assessments could be used to estimate how much error existed in each assessment. If two assessments of the same topic have a high correlation approaching 1.0, then the assessments contain relatively little error. Conversely, if two assessments have a low correlation approaching 0.0, then one or both contain a great deal of error. Thus, the correlation coefficient birthed the reliability coefficient. Over time, this correlation between two tests measuring the same content became the accepted definition of reliability.

As the discussion of tenet 5.3 illustrates, large-scale assessments typically have reliabilities at or above 0.85. But Leonard S. Feldt and Robert L. Brennan (1989) cautioned against the practice of judging an assessment from its reliability coefficient:

> Although all such standards are arbitrary, most users believe, with considerable support from textbook authors, that instruments with coefficients lower than .70 are not well suited to individual student evaluations. Although one may quarrel with any standard of this sort, many knowledgeable test

> users adjust their level of confidence in measurement data as a hazy function of the magnitude of the reliability coefficient. (p. 106)

Following these general guidelines, most educators will assume that if a test has a reliability coefficient near 0.90 or above, then the scores for individual students can be highly trusted. Unfortunately, this logic breaks down when one realizes that a reliability coefficient provides information about groups of students, not individual students. According to AERA, APA, and NCME (2014), a reliability coefficient depicts the following:

> The degree to which test scores for a *group* of test takers are consistent over repeated applications of a measurement procedure and hence are inferred to be dependable and consistent for an individual test taker; the degree to which scores are free of random errors of measurement for a given *group*. (pp. 222–223; emphasis added)

For the purposes of this discussion, the critical part of this description of a reliability coefficient is that it tells one how the pattern of scores for groups of students (as opposed to individual students) can be considered precise. This is a foundational awareness educators should cultivate within assessment literacy and is beautifully illustrated by the example in table 5.4.

TABLE 5.4: Repeated Administrations of the Same Test

	Initial Administration	Second Administration A	Second Administration B
Student 1	97	98	82
Student 2	92	90	84
Student 3	86	80	79
Student 4	83	83	72
Student 5	81	79	66
Student 6	80	83	70
Student 7	78	78	66
Student 8	77	74	55
Student 9	70	68	88
Student 10	65	66	78
Correlation With Initial Administration		0.96	0.32

Source: Marzano, 2018, p. 62.

Table 5.4 presents two hypothetical scenarios. The column labeled Initial Administration shows the scores of ten students on a particular test. The columns labeled Second Administration A and Second Administration B represent two separate scenarios in which the same test was given immediately after the first administration, with an important caveat that makes the scenarios hypothetical: The scenarios presuppose that students completely forgot about the first administration of the test before the second administration. While this is clearly impossible, it is a basic assumption of the psychometric theory of reliability. Lee J. Cronbach and Richard J. Shavelson (2004) explained this unusual assumption:

> If, hypothetically, we could apply the instrument twice and on the second occasion have the person unchanged and without memory of his first experience, then the consistency of the two identical measurements would indicate the uncertainty due to measurement error. (p. 394)

Thus, the scores in the Initial Administration (first column) and Second Administration A (second column) columns represent a situation where students receive scores on the second administration that are very similar to what they received on the first administration. As shown in the last row of table 5.4, the correlation between these two sets of scores is 0.96, which is obviously high and is equivalent to the reliability coefficient for this test.

The other scenario begins with the same Initial Administration scores but ends very differently. In the scenario represented by Initial Administration and Second Administration B (third column), students receive very different scores on the two administrations. Thus, the correlation between the two sets of scores is 0.32, which is a very low reliability coefficient. As table 5.4 exemplifies, the reliability coefficient is designed to provide information about the relationship between sets of scores for a group of students, but it is not designed to provide information about the precision of an individual student's score.

Standard Error of Measurement

The fact that the reliability coefficient applies to groups is not to say that one cannot estimate the amount of error in an individual student's score. While acknowledging that "the reliability of a test reveals the effect of measurement error on the observed score of a student cohort," Mohsen Tavakol and Reg Dennick (2011) described that there is a metric that can "calculate the effect of measurement error on the observed score of an individual student" (p. 53). This metric is the *standard error of measurement.* To determine the amount of error in a single score, one must compute the standard error of measurement and then compute an interval of scores in which one is relatively confident the true score falls (Marzano, 2018; Marzano et al., 2019). To illustrate, imagine a test that has a reliability of 0.90 and a standard deviation of 8.0. If you know that a student's observed score on that test is 75, you can compute an interval of scores within which you are 95 percent certain the true score lies. For details about how to compute this interval, consult *Making Classroom Assessments Reliable and Valid* (Marzano, 2018). For this particular test, that interval would be from 70.04 to 79.96. Given the high reliability coefficient of this test, and the fact that you are only 95 percent sure the student's score falls within this range, this is not a very impressive level of accuracy. It is important to note that large-scale assessments use more sophisticated measures of reliability and standard error of measurement, referred to as *item response theory* (for a discussion, see Marzano, 2006).

So how can you address the reliability of your classroom assessments? If you let go of the reliability coefficient—which is reasonable, as it was never meant to be applied to individual students—and simply think of reliability as the process of determining how much error is associated with an individual score (or conversely, which score is associated with the least amount of error), reliability for classroom assessments becomes quite simple.

As shown in How to Compute a Summative Score (page 144), the mathematical model of best fit automatically selects the model with the least amount of error in it (and if you are so inclined, you can compute reliability coefficients for your best-fit scores using the process described in Marzano, 2018). Even better, reliabilities based on the mathematical model of best fit employ information from all observed scores rather than from a single test. Incidentally, this discussion provides another reason to avoid the decaying average: There is no good way to estimate the amount of error associated with the decaying average because it is based on multiple assessments weighted in such a way that reliability cannot be calculated.

Bayesian Statistics

If you use the method of mounting evidence, then you can estimate the error associated with a student's current minimum summative score using Bayesian statistics. This field of statistics is named after Thomas Bayes, an English statistician, philosopher, and clergyman. He is credited with developing Bayes' theorem, which describes how to update probabilities as new evidence becomes available.

Figure 5.10 presents the basic equation for Bayesian statistics and explains the meaning of each element.

$$p(A|B) = \frac{p(B|A)p(A)}{p(B|A)p(A) + p(B|\overline{A})p(\overline{A})}$$

$p(A|B)$ is the probability of event A given event B

$p(A)$ is the probability of event A

$p(B|A)$ is the probability of event B given event A

$p(\overline{A})$ is the probability of event A not occurring, referred to as *NOT A*

$p(B|\overline{A})$ is the probability of event B given *NOT A*

FIGURE 5.10: Basic Bayesian equation and explanation of elements.

While the equation and its elements seem complicated, the equation is used for a simple purpose: to mathematically represent someone's confidence in a conclusion. In 1973, William L. Hays offered a humorous illustration of a situation when being able to mathematically represent your confidence might come in handy. Let's say you were having trouble sleeping one night and went to your medicine cabinet to get a sleeping pill. Now (and this takes a stretch of the imagination), let's say your medicine cabinet has three bottles in it—two with sleeping pills and one with poison—and you grab a bottle without looking and swallow a pill from it. A bit later, you feel sick. You check the internet and find that 80 percent of people who take poison exhibit your symptoms, and 5 percent of people who take sleeping pills exhibit your symptoms. Should you go to the emergency room? What if you could assign a mathematical value to your level of certainty that you took poison?

Leaving aside the common sense solution to this situation (just go to the emergency room and don't waste time on the calculations), Hays (1973) calculated the level of certainty associated with whether or not you took poison, as figure 5.11 shows.

Let's retell that story in a slightly different way to illustrate why Bayesian statistics matters for classroom assessment. Instead of imagining yourself paying attention to your symptoms, imagine you're paying attention to a student's series of observed scores. And instead of trying to figure out if you took poison, you're trying to figure out if you assigned a student the correct minimum summative score. What is the probability that a student would exhibit that particular pattern of scores if their minimum summative score is actually the 3.0 you just assigned?

If B represents your symptoms, A represents the event of taking the poison, and $\overline{A}$ represents the event of taking the sleeping pills, then:

$p(B|A) = 0.80$

$p(B|\overline{A}) = 0.05$

If each bottle had an equal probability of being selected in the dark, then:

$p(A) = 0.33$

$p(\overline{A}) = 0.67$

Substituting these quantities in the basic equation gives:

$$p(A|B) = \frac{(0.80)(0.33)}{(0.80)(0.33) + (0.05)(0.67)} = 0.89$$

Therefore, one can conclude that there is a 0.89 probability that you took poison.

Source: Hays, 1973.

FIGURE 5.11: Using Bayesian statistics to calculate the certainty of an occurrence.

You ask yourself how certain you are that the minimum summative score you assigned is correct. You can assign probabilities to different levels of certainty, as follows.

- Very likely = 0.90
- Likely = 0.70
- Neutral = 0.50
- Unlikely = 0.30
- Very unlikely = 0.10

As Marzano (2018) explained in detail, you can use these values to compute the various components of the Bayesian equation and estimate the probability that the assigned minimum summative score is correct. If you don't want to do the calculations but still want the probability estimate, there are online tools that will crunch the numbers for you (such as www.omnicalculator.com/statistics/bayes-theorem). For a detailed classroom example depicting all estimations and computations, see *Making Classroom Assessments Reliable and Valid* (Marzano, 2018; technical note 3.4, pp. 115–118).

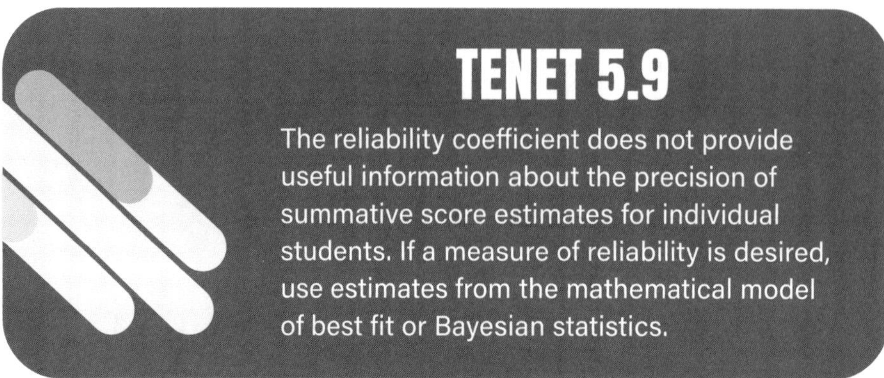

Implications of tenet 5.9 might include the following.

- **Reevaluation of the use of reliability coefficients in classroom assessment:** Educators should recognize that while the reliability coefficient is useful for evaluating group data, it does not accurately reflect the precision of individual student scores. This means that educators should be cautious when relying on reliability coefficients to assess the accuracy of summative scores for individual students, as they may not provide a true picture of a student's performance.
- **Emphasis on alternative methods for precision:** To ensure more accurate estimations of a student's performance, educators may benefit from adopting methods like the mathematical model of best fit or Bayesian statistics. These approaches allow for a more personalized understanding of the amount of error in a student's score, offering a more reliable assessment of individual student progress and learning.
- **Improvement of summative score accuracy:** By using Bayesian statistics or the mathematical model of best fit, teachers can obtain a more precise measurement of a student's true score by accounting for measurement error. These methods provide more nuanced insights into a student's achievement, helping teachers make more informed and confident decisions when assigning summative scores.

A Clear View of Validity

Most K–12 educators define *validity* as the extent to which an assessment measures what it is supposed to measure. If a test is designed to measure students' knowledge of fractions, then it should contain items that involve the various uses of fractions. While this is an accurate generalization about validity, it is important to realize that the concept of validity has evolved over the years into a multifaceted construct.

In 1937, Henry E. Garrett noted that "the fidelity with which [a test] measures what it purports to measure" (p. 324) is the hallmark of its validity. This is the foundational meaning of validity and still the most common interpretation of the concept. But since the 1950s, validity has been thought of as involving three major types: criterion validity, construct validity, and content validity (Messick, 1989). Additionally, since 2000, researchers have added two different perspectives to the discussion of validity: the instrumental perspective and the argument-based perspective (Hathcoat, 2013). Validity in general, and the three different types in particular, looks quite different depending on which perspective is taken. To conclude this chapter, we look at the three types of validity through each of the two perspectives (instrumental and argument based) in relation to classroom assessment.

The Instrumental Perspective

The instrumental perspective focuses on the test itself. This focus on the test has been the traditional approach in measurement theory: A specific test is considered valid to one degree or another. The three major types of validity from this perspective are as follows.

1. *Criterion validity from the instrumental perspective* means that the test in question is highly correlated with another test that is already considered valid (this second test is called the *criterion measure*—thus, criterion validity).
2. *Construct validity from the instrumental perspective* means that the underlying knowledge and skills that are the focus of the test in question can actually be measured using a test. For example, a test about a historical event likely has high construct validity because historical events are fairly concrete. Conversely, a test of students' ability to make complex inductive inferences might have low construct validity because the skill is less concrete. (Psychometricians use a procedure called factor analysis to establish construct validity for large-scale assessments, but such an approach is beyond both the resources of most classroom teachers and the scope of this book.)
3. *Content validity from the instrumental perspective* means that the test addresses the content that it purports to measure. To ensure content

validity in a classroom assessment, simply ensure that the items on the assessment address the content that is the focus of instruction and assessment.

In summary, the instrumental perspective on the three types of validity does not fit well with the recommendations regarding the use of proficiency scales and multiple formative scores to generate a summative score for individual students on specific measurement topics. Given that the instrumental perspective assumes that validity is associated with a specific test, it is not compatible with a system based on multiple formative scores being used to generate a summative score.

The Argument-Based Perspective

Michael T. Kane (1992, 2001, 2009) popularized the argument-based perspective of validity. At its core, the argument-based perspective of validity involves an interpretive argument that "lays out the network of inferences leading from the test scores to the conclusions to be drawn and any decisions to be based on these conclusions" (Kane, 2001, p. 329). In contrast to the instrumental perspective, which assumes validity is associated with a specific test, the argument-based perspective asserts that validity is a function of how the data generated from an assessment or a group of assessments are used to craft an argument regarding a particular student's knowledge or skill. This perspective on validity applies nicely to classroom assessments based on proficiency scales and can encompass multiple assessments of this type. From the argument-based perspective, the three types of validity are as follows.

1. *Criterion validity from the argument-based perspective* means that assessments are valid to the extent that a teacher can use data from them to predict how well students will perform on some type of external test (such as an interim assessment or a year-end assessment).
2. *Construct validity from the argument-based perspective* means that assessments are valid to the extent that a teacher can use data from them to identify specific knowledge and skills that should be directly taught. If you can translate scores from classroom assessments into specific types of instruction for specific students on specific content, then the data generated by the assessments have construct validity.
3. *Content validity from the argument-based perspective* means that assessments are valid to the extent that a teacher can use data from

> them as evidence regarding a student's current knowledge and skill on a specific topic. If you can use the scores to determine what content students know and don't know on a specific progression of knowledge, then the data generated by the assessments have content validity.

In summary, in contrast to the instrumental perspective, the argument-based perspective of validity fits quite well with the concept of multiple formative assessment scores based on proficiency scales being used to generate summative scores. Table 5.5 summarizes the differences between the instrumental and argument-based perspectives of validity relative to the three types of validity.

TABLE 5.5: Comparison of Instrumental and Argument-Based Perspectives of Validity

Validity Type	Instrumental Perspective	Argument-Based Perspective
Criterion Validity	Scores on a specific assessment must be correlated highly with scores on some external assessment of the content already established as valid.	The information a set of assessments provides can be interpreted in terms of how well students might perform on interim and end-of-year assessments.
Construct Validity	Based on statistical analysis, the items on a particular assessment are highly correlated for a particular topic.	The information a set of assessments provides can be interpreted in terms of specific knowledge or skill that can be directly taught.
Content Validity	The scores on a specific assessment clearly measure specific content.	The information a set of assessments provides can be interpreted in terms of students' status on an explicit progression of knowledge.

Source: Adapted from Marzano, 2018.
Visit ***MarzanoResources.com/reproducibles*** *for a free reproducible version of this table.*

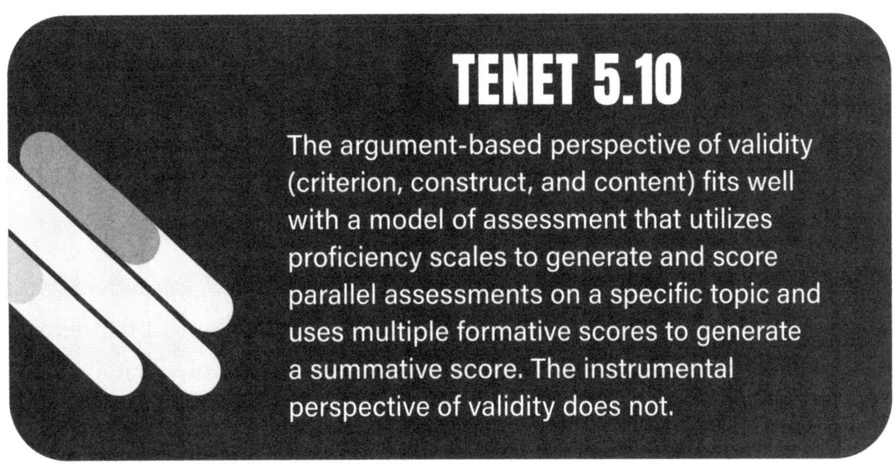

Implications of tenet 5.10 might include the following.

- **Alignment with complex assessment structures:** The argument-based perspective of validity supports the integration of proficiency scales and multiple formative assessments into the assessment process. Unlike the instrumental perspective, which focuses on the validity of a single test instrument, the argument-based perspective emphasizes the interpretive use of assessment data across multiple assessments. This perspective allows educators to construct coherent arguments about students' knowledge and skills based on varied sources of evidence.
- **Support for instructional decision making:** The argument-based perspective emphasizes that validity extends beyond mere test content to encompass how assessment data can inform teaching practices. By adopting this perspective, educators can leverage proficiency scales and formative scores to make informed decisions about curriculum pacing, instructional strategies, and individualized support based on robust evidence of student learning.

Summary

In this chapter, we discussed how classroom assessment scores should be aggregated within measurement topics to effectively communicate student progress and growth. A proper understanding of the distinction between formative and summative assessments and formative and summative scores is critical to any discussion of aggregation. Rather than relying on single assessments, which fail to capture a student's full understanding, formative scores—collected over time—provide a richer, more accurate picture of student growth. By moving away from traditional averages and decaying averages, educators can adopt methods that account for ongoing learning and better reflect a student's current proficiency. Mathematical models, which minimize measurement error, offer a more precise way to compute summative scores based on individual student data.

In addition to refining score aggregation methods, we cautioned against the use of reliability coefficients, which are useful for group-level data but not individual student assessments. Instead, tools like Bayesian statistics or best-fit mathematical models are recommended to provide more reliable estimates of a student's actual performance. This chapter also challenged traditional notions of validity, promoting the argument-based perspective that aligns with proficiency scales and multiple formative scores. This comprehensive approach fosters a more equitable, accurate, and growth-oriented system of classroom assessment.

PART III
Grading Practice

Chapter 6

GRADING SYSTEMS

At the beginning of chapter 5, we made a distinction between two ways teachers should aggregate scores. One is to aggregate scores *within* specific measurement topics. As the discussion in chapter 5 indicates, this type of aggregation should produce an estimate of a student's summative score that contains the least amount of error. The second way to aggregate scores is *across* measurement topics, which we address in this chapter. When aggregating scores across measurement topics, teachers combine the summative scores on various measurement topics to form an overall score. This overall score is commonly reported as a grade.

The Problem With Overall Grades

Many treatments of assessment in education do not include a discussion of grading, yet it has been used as a measure of student knowledge and skill for over a century. Indeed, in their research review "A Century of Grading Research," Brookhart and colleagues (2016) referred to grades as "the most common educational measure" (p. 803). While the term *grade* can refer to a score on a particular assessment, here we define grades as "composite measures of student performance on student report cards" (Brookhart et al., 2016, p. 804).

Brookhart and colleagues (2016) explained that during the 19th century, educators reported student progress to families orally, with little standardization regarding the content of these reports. The practice of using oral reports was eventually replaced by written narratives that were more amenable to standardization. The beginning of the 20th century saw the use of the one-hundred-point scale on report cards, but the overall letter grade gradually replaced the one-hundred-point scale. While the overall letter grade initially employed a nine-point scale (A+, A–, B+, B–, C+, C–, D+, D–, and F), it slowly devolved to the five-point scale (A, B, C, D, F) that "remains the most prevalent grading scale in schools in the U.S. today" (Brookhart et al., 2016, p. 820).

One of Brookhart and colleagues' (2016) more important findings was that educators have thought of a grade as something that is earned, particularly in the 20th century. Although this perspective became less prominent over time, one can make the case that this belief is still at least a tacit part of grading protocols in many American school systems. While one might not find it specifically stated in the grading policies of a school or district, it can be found in many of the components included in a grade that do not deal with academic content (Hough, 2023; Leap Scholar, 2025; Suzuki, Hong, Ober, & Cheng, 2022). These components include factors such as work completion, behavior, attitudes, attendance, and so on. While these are certainly important areas of student development, they deal with students' compliance regarding school norms as opposed to what they know and can do regarding academic content. That is, they require students to *earn* a grade by exhibiting specific attitudes and behaviors. This invalidates the overall grade as a measure of students' knowledge and skill.

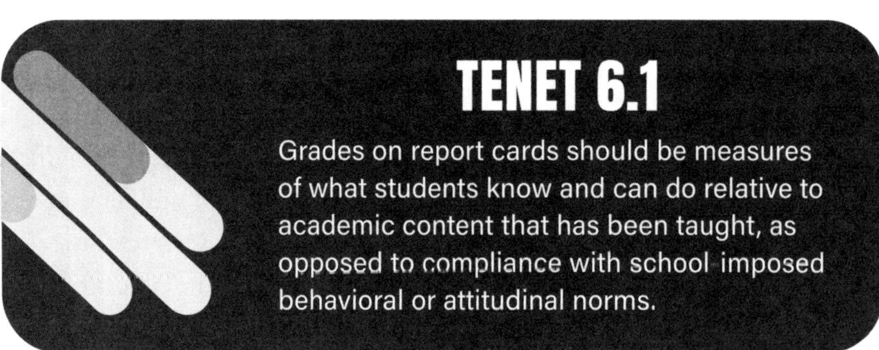

Implications of tenet 6.1 might include the following.

- **Increased focus on academic achievement:** By ensuring that grades accurately reflect students' academic progress, educators can help shift the focus away from nonacademic factors like attendance or behavior. This leads to more meaningful assessments of what students actually know and can do in relation to the content they have learned. As a result, grades become a more valid and reliable measure of academic achievement, providing clearer insights into a student's strengths and areas for improvement.

- **Separation of academic and behavioral assessment:** Separating behavioral factors from academic grading means that schools may need to reconsider their grading practices. Practices such as deducting points for late work, giving bonus points, or using zeros for incomplete tasks can undermine the accuracy of grades as representations of academic skills. Educators, schools, and districts will need to develop more nuanced approaches to reporting behavioral skills to ensure that grades remain focused on academic content.
- **A more equitable approach:** Emphasizing grading that reflects only academic performance rather than compliance with behavioral expectations can lead to a more equitable grading system. Students who may struggle with behaviors but excel academically would not be penalized for factors outside of their control, like home life or learning difficulties, thus providing a more accurate picture of their knowledge and abilities. This could promote fairness and inclusivity in how students are assessed and ensure that grades are a true reflection of their academic progress.

Nonacademic Skills

Brookhart and colleagues (2016) found that much of the grading research from the 20th century dealt with the question "What do grades mean?" That question is still relevant and is essentially a construct validity question. Recall from chapter 5 that construct validity (from the argument-based perspective) signals the extent that scores translate from classroom assessments into specific types of instruction for specific students on specific content.

Unfortunately, Brookhart and colleagues (2016) found that grades commonly included many factors other than students' level of knowledge and skill regarding academic content, a situation they refer to as "'hodgepodge' grading" (p. 826). It is certainly legitimate for a school or district to seek to develop students' knowledge and skill in areas that are not considered academic content. However, the scores in these areas should not be mixed with scores on academic content. When a school or district mixes scores on nonacademic factors with scores on academic knowledge and skill, it engages in hodgepodge grading. The solution is to ensure that aggregation across topics stays within the general domain of each topic.

There are many domains that schools and districts might report on in addition to academic content. Many of them have their roots in the 1980s K–12 education movement to enhance students' thinking and reasoning abilities, and several of these domains were defined in the book *Dimensions of Thinking* (Marzano et al., 1988). Here, we briefly summarize some of those important domains: traditional metacognitive skills, metacognitive life skills, cognitive analysis skills, and knowledge application skills.

Traditional Metacognitive Skills

Traditional metacognitive skills are commonly thought of as high-level thinking skills. This is because such skills involve thinking about one's own thinking and, therefore, apply to a wide variety of activities. Table 6.1 lists traditional metacognitive skills.

TABLE 6.1: Traditional Metacognitive Skills

Metacognitive Skill	Description
Staying focused when answers and solutions are not immediately apparent	This skill helps students overcome obstacles and stay focused when challenges arise. It also helps students to recognize how much effort they are putting into accomplishing a specific task.
Pushing the limits of one's knowledge and skills	This skill helps students set goals and engage in tasks that are personally challenging. When using this skill, students will strive to learn more and accomplish more.
Generating and pursuing one's own standards for performance	This skill enables students to envision and articulate criteria for what a successful project will look like.
Seeking incremental steps	This skill helps students take on complex tasks using small incremental steps so they do not become overwhelmed by the task as a whole.
Seeking accuracy	This skill helps students vet sources of information for reliability and verify information by consulting multiple sources known to be reliable.
Seeking clarity	This skill helps students identify points of confusion when they are learning new information. This allows students to independently seek a deeper understanding.

Metacognitive Skill	Description
Resisting impulsivity	When faced with a desire to form a quick conclusion, this skill helps students refrain from doing so until they can gather more relevant information prior to taking action.
Seeking cohesion and coherence	When students are creating something with a number of interacting parts, this skill helps them monitor the relationships between what they are currently doing and the overall intent of the project in which they are engaged.
Setting goals and making plans	This skill helps students set short- and long-term goals, create timelines or blueprints, monitor progress, and make necessary adjustments.
Growth mindset thinking	This skill helps students take on challenging tasks with an attitude that helps them succeed, even when confronted by major obstacles.

Source: © 2017 by Marzano Resources. Adapted with permission.

Metacognitive Life Skills

Metacognitive life skills—or simply *life skills*—are those actions and behaviors that help students become productive members of their school and classroom communities. Again, they are metacognitive in nature because each skill involves students analyzing their actions and their thinking relative to these specific areas. Table 6.2 lists four life skills, but schools and districts could add other such skills as they deem necessary.

TABLE 6.2: Metacognitive Life Skills

Life Skill	Description
Participation	Participation involves the set of decisions and actions that helps students add to group discussions and engage actively in questioning and answering questions.
Work completion	Work completion involves the set of decisions and actions that helps students manage their workload and complete tasks efficiently and effectively.
Behavior	Behavior involves the set of decisions and actions that helps students follow classroom rules and norms designed to create an efficient and orderly learning environment for all.
Working in groups	Working in groups involves the set of decisions and actions that helps students function as productive and supportive members of groups designed to enhance the learning of the students within those groups.

Source: © 2017 by Marzano Resources. Adapted with permission.

Cognitive Analysis Skills

Cognitive analysis skills are those that people use to unpack and examine knowledge and skills they are learning with the ultimate outcome of developing deeper understanding and skill. Table 6.3 presents eight cognitive analysis skills.

TABLE 6.3: Cognitive Analysis Skills

Cognitive Analysis Skill	Description
Comparing	Comparing is the process of determining similarities and differences between elements or concepts.
Analogical reasoning	Analogical reasoning is the process of determining how one set of elements or concepts is related to another set of elements or concepts.
Classifying	Classifying is the process of using definable attributes to organize concepts or elements into categories or related subcategories.
Analyzing perspectives	Analyzing perspectives is the process of analyzing one's own perspective and the reasoning supporting it and contrasting that with a different perspective and the reasoning supporting it.
Constructing support	Constructing support is the process of formulating a claim and then developing a well-constructed argument that supports it.
Analyzing errors in reasoning	Analyzing errors in reasoning is the process of recognizing logical fallacies or errors in information generated by others or oneself.
Analyzing inferences	Analyzing inferences is the process of identifying the inferences one makes automatically and unconsciously as well as the inferences one makes during conscious reasoning.
Generating mental images	Generating mental images is the process of creating images that represent information and procedures.

Source: © 2017 by Marzano Resources. Adapted with permission.

Knowledge Application Skills

Knowledge application skills are akin to cognitive analysis skills in that they promote deeper understanding and higher levels of skill. Additionally, they are typically employed when using knowledge in unique situations. Table 6.4 lists six knowledge application skills.

TABLE 6.4: Knowledge Application Skills

Knowledge Application Skill	Description
Decision making	Decision making is the process of generating and applying criteria to select between alternatives that appear equal.
Problem solving	Problem solving is the process of overcoming obstacles or constraints to achieve a goal.
Invention	Invention is the act of creating a new process or product that meets a specific identified need. In a sense, it might be likened to problem solving in that it addresses a specific need. However, problem solving is limited in duration.
Experimental inquiry	Experimental inquiry is the process of generating a hypothesis about a physical or psychological phenomenon and then testing the hypothesis.
Investigation	Investigation is the process of identifying and then resolving differences of opinion or contradictory information about concepts, historical events, or future possible events.
Systems analysis	Systems analysis is the process of describing and analyzing the parts of a system, with particular emphasis on the relationships among the parts.

Source: © 2017 by Marzano Resources. Adapted with permission.

Assessment for Nonacademic Skills

Like with academic content, proficiency scales can guide instruction and student assessment in the skills in the various domains discussed here. For example, figure 6.1 shows a proficiency scale for the cognitive analysis skill of comparing at the middle school level.

4.0	The student will: • Describe how the comparison process can be made more rigorous or informative.
3.5	In addition to score 3.0 performance, partial success at score 4.0 content
3.0	The student will: **COM—Independently execute a comparison process that involves selection of items, characteristics, and self-analysis.**
2.5	No major errors or omissions regarding score 2.0 content, and partial success at score 3.0 content

FIGURE 6.1: Proficiency scale for comparing (COM; grades 6–8). continued →

2.0	**COM**—The student will perform basic processes such as: • Describe a comparison process that involves selection of items, characteristics, and self-analysis (for example, [1] select the items you wish to compare and the method you will use to record and organize your ideas [such as a Venn diagram, comparison matrix, double-bubble diagram], [2] identify the general focus of what you want to learn about the items, [3] identify characteristics that will provide you with the most information about your focus for learning, [4] gather and record information about how the items are similar and different for each characteristic, [5] summarize what you have learned from the comparison task and identify questions about the items that are still unanswered for you).
1.5	Partial success at score 2.0 content, and major errors or omissions regarding score 3.0 content
1.0	With help, partial success at score 2.0 content and score 3.0 content
0.5	With help, partial success at score 2.0 content but not at score 3.0 content
0.0	Even with help, no success

Source: © 2021 by Marzano Resources. Used with permission.

Rather than assessing nonacademic skills by asking questions (or using similar techniques), it is better to design structured situations where students can demonstrate these skills as they engage in academic tasks. For example, figure 6.2 shows sample assessment tasks for comparing at the middle school level.

4.0	After students have completed a complex comparison task, ask them to describe how the task could have been made more rigorous or informative. Student suggestions should include concrete ways to make the characteristics on which items are compared more detailed and nuanced.
3.0	Present students with a comparison task that involves self-analysis and for which they must execute all parts of the process, such as identifying the items to be compared, identifying the characteristics on which the items are compared, and summarizing what they have learned through the process. The characteristics on which items are compared should add to a deeper understanding of one or both items. Students should be able to describe new insights they have gained as a result of the process.
2.0	Ask students to describe the comparison process they used. The process should include specific steps such as: (1) select the items you wish to compare and the method you will use to record and organize your ideas (such as a Venn diagram, comparison matrix, or double-bubble diagram); (2) identify the general focus of what you want to learn about the items; (3) identify characteristics that will provide you with the most information about your focus for learning; (4) gather and record information about how the items are similar and different for each characteristic; (5) summarize what you have learned from the comparison task and identify questions about the items that are still unanswered for you. Students should be able to describe what each step entails.

Source: © 2017 by Marzano Resources. Adapted with permission.

FIGURE 6.2: Assessment tasks for comparing (grades 6–8).

Assessment tasks such as those shown in figure 6.2 allow students to demonstrate competence at the score 2.0, 3.0, and 4.0 levels for nonacademic skills such as comparing. At the score 2.0 level, students describe the process associated with the target skill. At the score 3.0 level, students demonstrate the process. At the score 4.0 level, students explain how the process could be made more rigorous and informative.

In sum, measurement topics in the nonacademic domains can be scored in the same way as measurement topics in the academic domains. Relative to the issue of hodgepodge grading, a viable solution is to aggregate summative scores only within their own domains. To illustrate, during an eight-week grading period, a middle school science teacher addressed and generated summative scores for six science topics, three traditional metacognitive skills, four metacognitive life skills, two cognitive analysis skills, and two knowledge application skills. Figure 6.3 reports the summative scores and their average for each domain. To preserve clarity, the average for each domain would be reported separately on the student's report card.

Domain	Topic	Summative Score for Each Topic	Average of Summative Scores
Science	Weather and Climate	2.5	2.92
	The Solar System	3.0	
	Cells and Microorganisms	2.5	
	Body Systems	3.0	
	Forces and Motion	3.0	
	Energy	3.5	
Traditional Metacognitive Skills	Seeking Accuracy	3.0	2.67
	Seeking Clarity	2.5	
	Resisting Impulsivity	2.5	

FIGURE 6.3: Aggregating summative scores within domains. continued →

Metacognitive Life Skills	Participation	3.0	3.25
	Work Completion	4.0	
	Working in Groups	3.0	
	Behavior	3.0	
Cognitive Analysis Skills	Comparing	2.5	2.5
	Classifying	2.5	
Knowledge Application Skills	Investigation	3.0	3.0
	Systems Analysis	3.0	

Visit ***MarzanoResources.com/reproducibles*** *for a free reproducible version of this figure.*

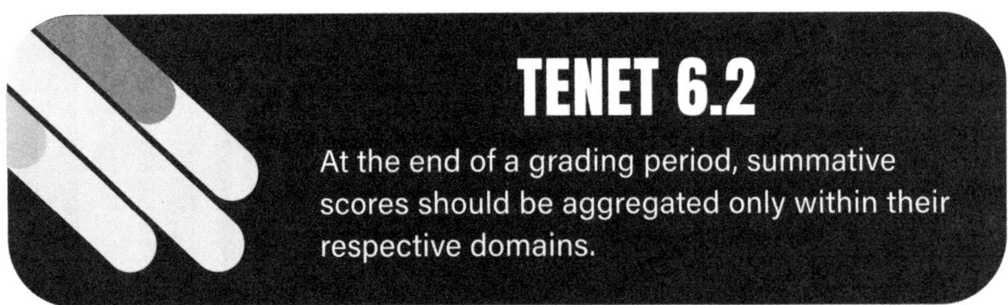

Implications of tenet 6.2 might include the following.

- **Changes in reporting practices:** Schools will need to shift their grading systems and report card formats to reflect scores for each domain, rather than providing a single, holistic grade. This could involve restructuring the layout of report cards to separate academic content from nonacademic skills.
- **Collaboration with vendors for technical solutions:** To implement this change, schools will need to collaborate with software vendors or

seek creative solutions to redesign their report cards and transcripts in a way that aligns with this approach. The necessary adjustments may not be straightforward and could require technical innovation, particularly in systems not currently designed to handle multiple domains (academic versus nonacademic) separately.

- **Impacts on transcripts and long-term reporting:** The shift to domain-specific grading will raise questions about how this change affects high school transcripts, which typically present a single grade per subject area. Schools will need to decide whether to list scores for each domain (resulting in potentially lengthy transcripts) while balancing higher education and employment stakeholders' desire for concise summarization of student performance.

Grade Conversions

As mentioned several times so far, Brookhart and colleagues (2016) found that overall grades are still the most common educational measure. These overall grades are likely expressed using the letters *A*, *B*, *C*, *D*, and *F*. To facilitate these reporting conventions, schools and districts might opt to convert aggregated summative scores for specific domains to overall grades. Even if a school or district has made a conceptual shift to focusing reporting on the more precise level of measurement topics, it might still wish to report the traditional letter grade or percentage score, if for no other reason than families are so used to seeing them.

Converting grades might seem simple, but it is not. Traditional assessment, scoring, and grading practices are based on percentages of items answered correctly and the resulting number of points earned. We have demonstrated the errors and misconceptions that arise from such approaches. Ultimately, the problem is that traditional practices provide little, if any, information about what students know about specific content. In contrast, proficiency scale scores provide concrete information about students' knowledge and skill relative to specific content.

Recall that a typical proficiency scale has nine values, ranging from 0.0 to 4.0 in half-point increments. Each value of the scale has a specific definition in terms of knowledge and skill regarding a specific measurement topic. Therefore, if a teacher assigns a score of 3.0 to a student regarding a specific measurement topic, it means that the student has exhibited knowledge of the target content for that measurement topic. If a teacher assigns a score of 1.0 to a student, it means that, with help, the student has partial success with some of the score 2.0 and 3.0 content. Stated differently, even a score of 1.0 indicates that a student has some knowledge of the score 2.0 and 3.0 content but requires some help to demonstrate that partial knowledge.

The values on a proficiency scale have different meanings than the values associated with the percentage method or the point method. For example, traditional point and percentage approaches would likely translate a score of 1.0 out of a total score of 4.0 as an indication that a student knows only 25 percent of the content. This is very different from the proficiency scale descriptor for a score of 1.0: "With help, partial success at score 2.0 content and score 3.0 content." Because of these differences, translating the aggregated summative score in a given domain into a traditional grade must be done very thoughtfully. For example, consider the conversion chart in table 6.5.

Table 6.5 presents a system to translate scores on proficiency scales into traditional letter grades (A, B, C, D, and F) and percentage scores (1–100). This conversion system could apply to an average score aggregated from a set of summative scores across measurement topics within the same domain. For example, consider the average summative score of 2.92 shown in figure 6.3 (page 185) for the six science summative scores of 2.5, 3.0, 2.5, 3.0, 3.0, 3.5. Using the conversion chart in table 6.5, this score would be assigned a letter grade of B and a percentage score of 88. Knowing that 2.92 represents the average score or central tendency for the set of six summative proficiency scale scores, one can conclude that the student's typical performance across the measurement topics was to demonstrate mastery of the score 2.0 content and the vast majority of the score 3.0 content. This provides the student, their family, teachers, and administrators with significant and meaningful information about the student's performance on those six measurement topics.

A critical issue when designing a conversion system is determining the cut score for each letter grade. Consider the following implications of the system shown in table 6.5.

- **The letter grade of A starts at the average score of 3.00:** This indicates that the central tendency for the scores that were averaged is mastery of the score 2.0 and the score 3.0 content.
- **The letter grade of B starts at the average score of 2.50:** This indicates that the central tendency for the scores that were averaged is mastery of the 2.0 content and partial mastery of about half of the score 3.0 content.

TABLE 6.5: Conversion Chart

Scale Score	Percentage	Grade	Scale Score	Percentage	Grade	Scale Score	Percentage	Grade	Scale Score	Percentage	Grade
4.00	100	A	2.25 to 2.29	75	C	1.30 to 1.31	50	F	0.73 to 0.75	25	F
3.90 to 3.99	99	A	2.20 to 2.24	74	C	1.28 to 1.29	49	F	0.70 to 0.72	24	F
3.80 to 3.89	98	A	2.15 to 2.19	73	C	1.26 to 1.27	48	F	0.67 to 0.69	23	F
3.70 to 3.79	97	A	2.10 to 2.14	72	C	1.24 to 1.25	47	F	0.64 to 0.66	22	F
3.60 to 3.69	96	A	2.05 to 2.09	71	C	1.22 to 1.23	46	F	0.61 to 0.63	21	F
3.50 to 3.59	95	A	2.00 to 2.04	70	C	1.20 to 1.21	45	F	0.58 to 0.60	20	F
3.40 to 3.49	94	A	1.95 to 1.99	69	D	1.18 to 1.19	44	F	0.55 to 0.57	19	F
3.30 to 3.39	93	A	1.90 to 1.94	68	D	1.16 to 1.17	43	F	0.52 to 0.54	18	F
3.20 to 3.29	92	A	1.85 to 1.89	67	D	1.14 to 1.15	42	F	0.49 to 0.51	17	F
3.10 to 3.19	91	A	1.80 to 1.84	66	D	1.12 to 1.13	41	F	0.46 to 0.48	16	F
3.00 to 3.09	90	A	1.75 to 1.79	65	D	1.10 to 1.11	40	F	0.43 to 0.45	15	F
2.95 to 2.99	89	B	1.70 to 1.74	64	D	1.08 to 1.09	39	F	0.40 to 0.42	14	F
2.90 to 2.94	88	B	1.65 to 1.69	63	D	1.06 to 1.07	38	F	0.37 to 0.39	13	F
2.85 to 2.89	87	B	1.60 to 1.64	62	D	1.04 to 1.05	37	F	0.34 to 0.36	12	F
2.80 to 2.84	86	B	1.55 to 1.59	61	D	1.02 to 1.03	36	F	0.31 to 0.33	11	F
2.75 to 2.79	85	B	1.50 to 1.54	60	D	1.00 to 1.01	35	F	0.28 to 0.30	10	F
2.70 to 2.74	84	B	1.48 to 1.49	59	F	0.98 to 0.99	34	F	0.25 to 0.27	9	F
2.65 to 2.69	83	B	1.46 to 1.47	58	F	0.96 to 0.97	33	F	0.22 to 0.24	8	F
2.60 to 2.64	82	B	1.44 to 1.45	57	F	0.94 to 0.95	32	F	0.19 to 0.21	7	F
2.55 to 2.59	81	B	1.42 to 1.43	56	F	0.91 to 0.93	31	F	0.16 to 0.18	6	F
2.50 to 2.54	80	B	1.40 to 1.41	55	F	0.88 to 0.90	30	F	0.13 to 0.15	5	F
2.45 to 2.49	79	C	1.38 to 1.39	54	F	0.85 to 0.87	29	F	0.10 to 0.12	4	F
2.40 to 2.44	78	C	1.36 to 1.37	53	F	0.82 to 0.84	28	F	0.07 to 0.09	3	F
2.35 to 2.39	77	C	1.34 to 1.35	52	F	0.79 to 0.81	27	F	0.04 to 0.06	2	F
2.30 to 2.34	76	C	1.32 to 1.33	51	F	0.76 to 0.78	26	F	0.01 to 0.03	1	F

Source: Marzano, 2018, pp. 100–101.

- **The letter grade of C starts at the average score of 2.00:** This indicates that the central tendency for the scores that were averaged is mastery of the score 2.0 content but no evidence of competence with the score 3.0 content.
- **The letter grade of D starts at the average score of 1.50:** This indicates that the central tendency for the scores that were averaged is partial success at the score 2.0 content and major errors or omissions regarding score 3.0 content.
- **The letter grade of F denotes any average score below the 1.50 level:** This indicates that the student requires help to demonstrate any success with any of the content.

Thus, when proficiency scales are used as the method of providing information on report cards, every letter grade has a relatively precise meaning.

It is important to note that the decisions about cut scores for grades should be local decisions that reflect the values of all constituents. For example, some schools have established an average cut score of 3.25 for the start of the A letter grade. This communicates that the central tendency of the summative scores must indicate more than competence at the 3.0 level of the scale. Other schools have determined that the letter grade of D should start at the average score of 0.50. This means that students would receive a score of at least a D if their average score indicated that, with help, they have partial success at the 2.0 level. In effect, this cut score communicates that any learning demonstrated with help deserves a letter grade of at least a D. Still another option we have observed is that the letter grade of A starts at the average score of 3.00, but an average score of 3.50 or higher receives the distinction of "with honors."

Finally, it is important to note that the conversion chart includes percentage scores that go along with each letter grade. In general, percentage scores are intended to provide guidance about how percentage scores on a specific assessment should be translated into a letter grade (Brookhart et al., 2016). There is no universally accepted system for this. However, it is highly popular to start the letter grade of A at the percentage score of 90, the letter grade of B at the percentage score of 80, the letter grade of C at the percentage score of 70, and the letter grade of D at the percentage score of 60. This is frequently referred to as the ten-point grading system. This notwithstanding, there is sometimes a great deal of discussion regarding where to start the letter grade of D, with some educators arguing strongly for the percentage score to be much higher than 60.

No matter what issue is being debated regarding grading, using proficiency scale values as a reference point helps guide deliberations. For example, if the average of a set of summative scores is 1.01 (let's say), this means that the student's typical performance on the measurement topics was that, with help, the student exhibited partial success with the score 2.0 content but not the score 3.0 content. The question, then, facing school policymakers is what letter grade should be used to represent this performance. Does partial success at the 2.0 level truly represent a letter grade of F, or is the letter grade of D more appropriate? Again, questions like this can only be answered at the local level, but proficiency scales provide a clearer reference point regarding students' knowledge and skill than do simple percentages that have no overt reference to specific knowledge and skill.

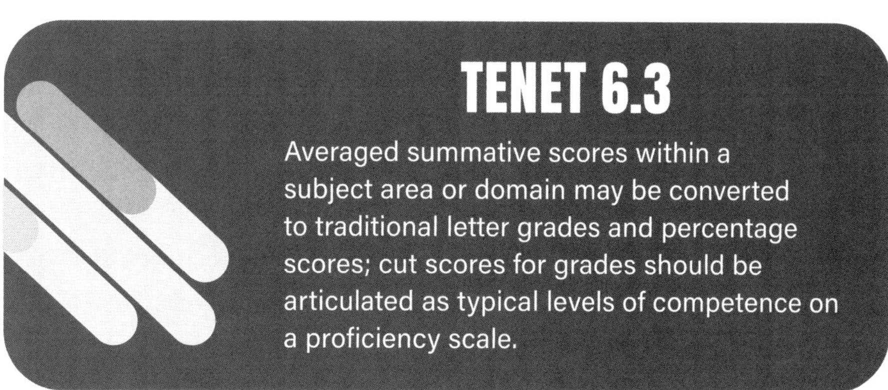

Implications of tenet 6.3 might include the following.

- **Need for collaboration and consensus on grading values:** Converting proficiency scale scores to traditional grades requires careful thought and collaboration. Schools should work together to create a conversion chart that aligns with the values and expectations of the school community. This can serve as a foundation for creating a shared philosophy of grading that ensures all stakeholders (students, teachers, families) understand the meaning of grades. This effort to reach consensus enhances the transparency and fairness of grading practices, as it reflects a unified approach to assessing and representing student learning.
- **Validity and reliability of grading practices:** Converting proficiency scale scores to traditional grades works effectively only when teachers first determine a summative score based on the

proficiency scale. If educators continue to rely on traditional point or percentage systems and try to map them onto the proficiency scale, they risk losing the integrity and accuracy of the assessment. The proficiency scale provides specific information about a student's content knowledge, whereas the traditional percentage-based system is more general and may not capture the nuanced understanding a proficiency scale offers. Therefore, any attempt to force-fit a points or percentage system into proficiency scale–based grading undermines the system's reliability and meaning.

Conjunctive Approach

The examples presented thus far have used a simple average to aggregate summative scores across topics; this is called a *compensatory approach* because, when computing an average, higher scores compensate for lower scores (Kifer, 1994; Marzano, 2006, 2010). Notwithstanding the usefulness of a compensatory approach in providing a sense of the central tendency in a set of scores, there are alternative options for aggregating summative scores across topics within a domain, such as the approach we present in this section: the conjunctive approach.

At a basic level, a *conjunctive approach* does not combine the summative scores across topics in some arithmetic manner. Rather, it is based on decision rules for sets of summative scores. A given decision rule will designate which sets of summative scores must have certain values to be awarded a given grade. The conjunctive approach (Plake, Hambleton, & Jaeger, 1997) was first applied to grading by Marzano in 2006 and developed over the subsequent decades (Marzano, 2010, 2018; Marzano et al., 2017). Marzano and colleagues (2017) illustrated the conjunctive approach using the nine mathematics measurement topics shown in the first column of figure 6.4.

The measurement topics in the first column of figure 6.4 were introduced during the first grading period of a school year. The second column identifies the extent that the content in each topic's proficiency scale was addressed during the grading period.

Measurement Topic	Exposure to Content	Criteria for Letter Grade of A
Decimals	Complete	3.0 or above
Fractions	Just started score 3.0 content	2.5 or above
Area	Score 2.0 content only	2.0 or above
Volume	Score 2.0 content only	2.0 or above
Multiplication	Complete	3.0 or above
Division	Complete	3.0 or above
Ordered Pairs and Coordinate Systems	Score 2.0 content only	2.0 or above
Addition and Subtraction	Complete	3.0 or above
Perimeter	Just started score 3.0 content	2.5 or above

Source: Adapted from Marzano et al., 2017.

FIGURE 6.4: Scoring criteria for a grade of A for first trimester.

- *Complete* means the teacher taught the content at all levels of the scale, and every student had the opportunity to demonstrate competence at each level of the scale.
- *Score 2.0 content only* means the teacher taught the score 2.0 content only, and students have not had the opportunity to demonstrate competence beyond the score 2.0 level.
- *Just started score 3.0 content* means the teacher taught all of the score 2.0 content but only some of the score 3.0 content; students are not expected to demonstrate proficiency at the score 3.0 level yet.

These gradations of coverage across measurement topics occur fairly frequently in schools; some topics take longer than a single grading period to adequately address. So, how do you aggregate summative scores across these measurement topics to arrive at an overall grade? Using a compensatory approach such as averaging will provide a skewed view: Five of the nine topics in figure 6.4 have not been completely taught. If students have not had the opportunity to learn the score 3.0 content, they will likely receive summative scores less than 3.0, making the grade of A unreachable for many students, even if they have learned well all that was taught.

The solution to this problem is found in the third column of figure 6.4, labeled *criteria for letter grade of A*. These are the cut scores necessary to receive a letter grade of A.

- For the four topics that were completely covered during the grading period, students must obtain a proficiency scale score of 3.0 or above to be in the A category.
- For the three topics where the teacher addressed only the 2.0 content, students must have a score of 2.0 or higher to be in the A category.
- For the two topics where the teacher has just started to address the score 3.0 content, students must have a score of 2.5 or higher to be in the A category.

To effectively employ this version of the conjunctive approach, you will need to create similar criteria charts for the other letter grades of B, C, D, and F. For example, figure 6.5 shows a criteria chart for a letter grade of B using the same scenario as figure 6.4.

Measurement Topic	Exposure to Content	Criteria for Letter Grade of B
Decimals	Complete	2.5 or above
Fractions	Just started score 3.0 content	2.0 or above
Area	Score 2.0 content only	1.5 or above
Volume	Score 2.0 content only	1.5 or above
Multiplication	Complete	2.5 or above
Division	Complete	2.5 or above
Ordered Pairs and Coordinate Systems	Score 2.0 content only	1.5 or above
Addition and Subtraction	Complete	2.5 or above
Perimeter	Just started score 3.0 content	2.0 or above

Source: Adapted from Marzano et al., 2017.

FIGURE 6.5: Scoring criteria for a grade of B for first trimester.

The approach described thus far and illustrated by figure 6.4 and figure 6.5 is just one version of a conjunctive approach. An alternative version of the conjunctive approach does not focus on specific measurement topics or the extent that they have been covered, as shown in table 6.6. This manifestation of the conjunctive approach simply provides an alternative way to summarize student performance by focusing on the pattern of summative scores across a set of measurement topics within a domain.

TABLE 6.6: Conjunctive Approach That Does Not Focus on Specific Measurement Topics

Grade	Score Pattern
A	No topic score below 2.5 and the majority at 3.0 or above
B	No topic score below 2.0 and the majority at 2.5 or above
C	No topic score below 1.5 and the majority at 2.0 or above
D	No topic score below 1.0 and the majority at 1.5 or above
F	Some topic scores below 1.0 or the majority not above 1.5

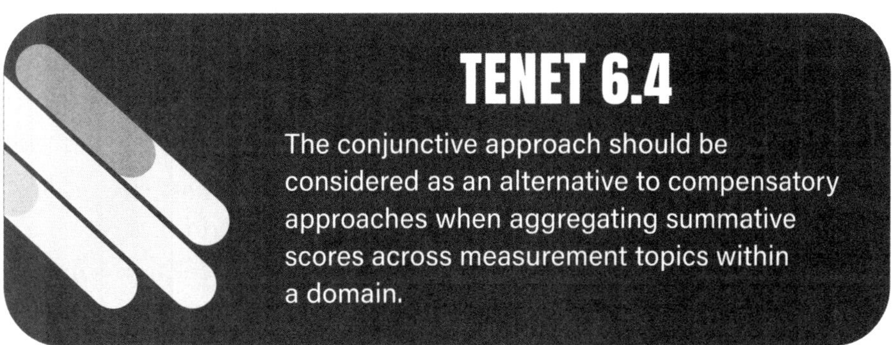

Implications of tenet 6.4 might include the following.

- **Clarity in grading expectations:** Schools will need to develop a clear and consistent system for implementing the conjunctive approach. Unlike compensatory approaches where higher scores can offset lower ones, the conjunctive approach emphasizes meeting certain criteria in all areas. To be successful, schools must communicate a conjunctive grading system effectively to families and students, especially when it comes to transitioning from traditional grading systems.
- **Differentiated expectations across grading periods:** When a conjunctive approach incorporates varying levels of content exposure (for example, some topics being fully taught, while others are just

beginning), expectations for proficiency can shift across grading periods. For example, families may question why a 2.0 might be sufficient for an A in one grading period but not the next, when more content has been covered. This potential confusion requires careful explanation and ongoing communication.

Validation Studies

Once procedures are in place for aggregating summative scores across topics and computing overall grades, schools and districts should validate the accuracy of those overall grades by computing yearly correlations between them and one or more criterion measures. Ideally, the measure used as the criterion should be the assessment that is considered the most valid indicator of students' achievement on the content that was directly taught. Theoretically, a school can select any measure that fits this description, but in most cases, schools select the end-of-year state test. There are obvious reasons for this choice: Schools are commonly evaluated by state departments of education according to students' performance on these assessments. When end-of-year state tests serve as the criterion measure, then the correlations computed yearly can be considered a validity check for the proficiency scales that the school uses. Recall from the discussion in chapter 5 that this is a type of criterion validity: Assessments are valid to the extent that a teacher can use data from them to predict how well students will perform on some type of external test.

Brookhart and colleagues (2016) found that, in general, correlations between traditional grades and external assessments like state tests are about 0.50: "Across 100 years of research, teacher-assigned grades typically correlate about .5 with standardized measures of achievement" (p. 822). But the types of grades recommended in part II of this book are not traditional grades; rather than being computed using points and percentages (as traditional grades are), we recommend assigning grades based on standards for performance derived from state standards. Following Thomas R. Guskey and Jane M. Bailey (2001), we will use the term *standards-based grades* to denote these grades in the following discussion.

A grading system that assigns scores to students by standard should correlate better with state tests (also based on standards) than a traditional grading system; nevertheless, findings have been mixed. While Brookhart and colleagues (2016) found that standards-based grades correlated with external assessments at about the same level as traditional grades, one of the studies in their synthesis—by Aimee Howley, Patricia S. Kusimo, and Laurel Parrott (2000)—found a much higher correlation for standards-based grades (0.71). Erin Lehman, David De Jong, and Mark Baron (2018) also reported substantially higher correlations with external tests for standards-based grades than for traditional grades.

Relative to our proposed methodology, it is important to note that these studies of standards-based grades (Howley et al., 2000; Lehman et al., 2018) did not necessarily use the approach recommended in this book. Whereas we recommend a very specific type of proficiency scale, many schools and districts use their own versions of a scale. Not all of these versions constitute effective measurement devices, and thus, their use detracts from the correlation between their grading system and criterion measures. For example, figure 6.6 shows a scale that is ineffective as a measurement device.

Level	Description
Advanced	The student demonstrates knowledge and skill above grade-level expectations.
Proficient	The student demonstrates knowledge and skill at grade-level expectations.
Progressing	The student demonstrates partial knowledge and skill at grade-level expectations.
Beginning	The student demonstrates partial knowledge and skill at grade-level expectations only with help.

Source: Marzano et al., 2019, p. 28.

FIGURE 6.6: Generic scale used for all measurement topics.

The most obvious problem with this scale is that it provides no guidance to the teacher or the students about what is expected at the various levels of the scale. Consequently, each teacher independently determines the exact content that demonstrates a score of proficient on the scale, undermining consistency across classrooms and threatening the scale's validity and predictive power relative to other criterion measures. The use of ineffective scales such as the one in figure 6.6 may also help to explain the mixed research findings on correlations between standards-based grading and criterion measures. Given that not all scales used in schools have the same level of utility or accuracy as measurement devices, the following comments apply specifically to the use of the type of proficiency scale described in this book.

A growing number of studies have emerged that indicate strong relationships between the type of proficiency scale we recommend and large-scale assessments (Haystead, 2016; Haystead & Marzano, 2022; Lehman et al., 2018; Marzano & Haystead, 2023; Rains, 2020). For example, table 6.7 (page 198) shows the relationship in one district between proficiency scale scores and state test results for third-grade mathematics. As the first column of table 6.7 shows, thirteen proficiency scales—each representing one measurement topic—were addressed in third-grade mathematics. The second column shows how many students had mastered (score 3.0 or above) the number of measurement topics in the first column. The third column shows the percentage of students who mastered a particular number of proficiency scales and also received a score of proficient or above on the state test.

TABLE 6.7: Relationship Between Students' Scores on Proficiency Scales and Scores on the State Test

Measurement Topics Mastered	Number of Students	Percent Proficient or Above
0	12	0
1	2	0
2	6	0
3	13	0
4	8	0
5	13	23
6	29	21
7	12	42
8	29	52
9	29	76
10	29	48
11	40	80
12	44	84
13	227	96

Source: Adapted from Haystead, 2016.

To interpret table 6.7, consider the twelve students in the first row who did not receive a score of 3.0 or above on any of the thirteen measurement topics; none of these twelve students demonstrated proficiency on the state test. In contrast, consider the 227 students in the last row who received a score of 3.0 on all thirteen measurement topics; 96 percent of those 227 students also demonstrated proficiency on the state test.

In general, table 6.7 indicates that once students have mastered at least five proficiency scales, they begin to demonstrate scores of proficient or above on the state test. The more proficiency scales students master, the higher the odds are that they will receive a score of proficient or above on the state test.

Using data from the same district, Cameron L. Rains (2020) reported correlations between the percentage of students mastering different numbers of measurement topics and the percentage of those same students receiving a score of proficient or above on the state test. Using the 2016 state assessment data for language arts, Rains computed correlations that ranged from 0.93 to 0.98 across grades 3 through 5. In mathematics, the correlations ranged from 0.95 to 0.98. Of course, these correlations are significantly larger than the average correlation of 0.50 reported by Brookhart and colleagues (2016).

While a school or district could reasonably consider these large correlations between measurement topics and scores on a state test sufficient evidence to keep using its measurement topics and the proficiency scales that accompany them, a much stronger and more useful approach is to conduct yearly studies of the relationship between students' scores on proficiency scales and their scores on state tests or other appropriate criterion measure. The following process can be used for these studies.

1. Determine the number of students who have demonstrated mastery on proficiency scales for differing numbers of measurement topics, ranging from zero through the total number of measurement topics addressed during the school year.
2. For each group of students who mastered a specific number of measurement topics, determine the percentage who received scores of proficient or higher on the criterion test.
3. Compute a correlation between these two quantities. If that correlation is large, then consider the current version of measurement topics and their proficiency scales as valid and useful tools.
4. If the correlation is low, then consider that as evidence that changes must be made in the proficiency scales or the way teachers are using them to assess students.

Of course, a central issue in this endeavor is determining what is a large correlation and what is not. The research described in this section provides some guidance to this end. Specifically, correlations should be at least 0.50 to align with the historical relationship between grading practices and external tests. Our recommendation is that the correlations should be much higher, ideally approaching or exceeding 0.90.

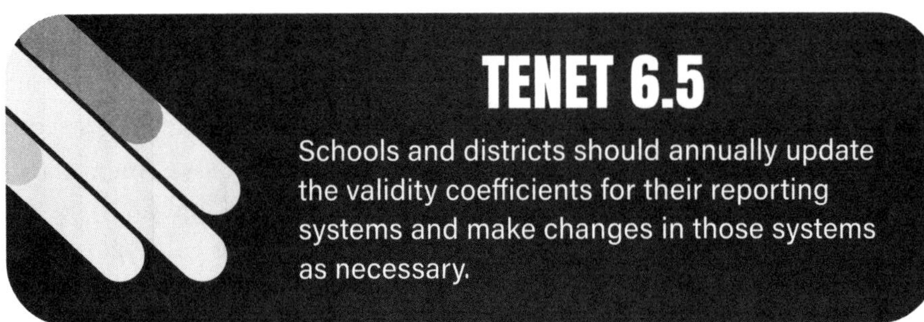

TENET 6.5

Schools and districts should annually update the validity coefficients for their reporting systems and make changes in those systems as necessary.

Implications of tenet 6.5 might include the following.

- **Ongoing evaluation and refinement of grading systems:** Schools and districts must commit to regularly assessing the validity of their grading systems by comparing student performance on proficiency scales with external criterion measures, such as state assessments. This continuous evaluation ensures that grading systems remain accurate and aligned with actual student achievement. Low correlation between the proficiency scales and state tests signals that revisions are necessary, whether through refining the proficiency scales or adjusting instructional practices. This process encourages a culture of improvement and responsiveness to data, ensuring that grading systems evolve to reflect student performance more accurately.
- **Increased accountability for grading practices:** By regularly updating validity coefficients and adjusting grading systems as needed, schools and districts will be held accountable for ensuring that their grading practices are valid and reliable indicators of student achievement. The focus on high correlation between internal measures (like proficiency scales) and external criterion measures (like state assessments) promotes transparency in how grades are assigned and provides external validation for the grading process.
- **Improved decision making for educational stakeholders:** Continuous validation of grading systems through updated validity

coefficients allows teachers, administrators, and policymakers to make more informed decisions about curriculum, instruction, and assessment strategies. High correlations between proficiency scales and state test performance provide confidence that the grading system is accurately measuring student achievement. Conversely, if correlations are low, the data can guide decisions on revising the grading practices, leading to better-aligned teaching methods and more effective learning outcomes for students.

Summary

In this chapter, we emphasized that grades should reflect what students know and can do academically, rather than being influenced by nonacademic factors like behavior or attendance. To create a more valid and equitable grading system, we recommend separating academic achievement from nonacademic skills. We also advocate for thoughtful mapping of proficiency scale–based aggregated scores to letter grades to accurately reflect students' understanding, with schools collaborating to define consistent and transparent grade cutoffs.

We also introduced the conjunctive approach to grading, which ensures that students meet specific criteria for each topic, rather than allowing higher scores to compensate for lower ones. This approach requires clear communication and consistency, as grading expectations may shift depending on the extent of content coverage. Finally, we highlight the importance of continuously validating grading systems by comparing student performance on proficiency scales with external measures, such as state tests. This ongoing validation ensures that our grading practices remain accurate, aligned with student achievement, and effective in supporting educational decisions. As we move into the next chapter, you will see how these grading systems set the foundation for understanding and implementing competency-based education, where mastery and progress take center stage in student learning.

Chapter 7

COMPETENCY-BASED SYSTEMS

Aligning grading practices with external measures of student proficiency leads logically to an examination of competency-based education, which requires accurate and valid measurements of students' knowledge and skill. Competency-based education is not a new idea (Marzano, Zima, & Simms, 2025). From competency-based education's experimental roots in the early 20th century until 2024—when all fifty states in the United States provided options for schools to offer competency-based approaches (Stanford, 2024)—K–12 schools have been incorporating practices that allow students to advance based on mastery of content rather than seat time.

While there are many different versions of competency-based education and many characteristics that describe it, two seem to be a part of every version.

1. Students can improve previously assigned scores.
2. Students can work ahead on content that has not yet been addressed in class.

These two characteristics require adjustments to grading practices. Here, we begin by considering adjustments required when students are simply allowed to improve previously assigned scores (but are not allowed to work on content not yet addressed in class). Then, we add the variable of working ahead in a subsequent section.

Improving Scores

A competency-based approach that allows students to improve previously assigned scores is probably the easiest to implement. To illustrate, consider a fourth-grade class whose social studies curriculum involves eighteen measurement topics. The teacher sequences these eighteen proficiency scales to create eighteen units over the course of the school year; each unit will last two weeks. After the first unit, students' summative scores for the measurement topic taught during that unit vary: Some students have demonstrated proficiency (score 3.0), some students have demonstrated proficiency beyond the learning target (scores 3.5 and 4.0), and some students have not yet demonstrated proficiency (scores 2.5 and below).

When the teacher begins the next unit on a different topic, those students with summative scores of 2.5 or below will be behind in the quest to show mastery of all eighteen measurement topics by the end of the year. To address this issue, the teacher provides time for students to increase their scores on previous topics. This could be as little as fifteen to twenty minutes several times a week or as much as multiple class periods each week. This ensures that every student has ample opportunity to demonstrate proficiency for all eighteen measurement topics.

When students are allowed to improve their scores, it becomes increasingly likely that all students will eventually achieve a score of 3.0 or above for each of the measurement topics, ideally by the end of the year. If the school converts these scores to letter grades using one of the conversion options described in chapter 6 (Grade Conversions, page 187; where 3.0 is the cut point for an A), then most students will earn a grade of A. This may confuse families who are used to traditional systems, where grades are used to differentiate achievement and compare students to one another. Although we encourage educating all members of the school community on the approach to grades described in this book, which emphasizes measuring and communicating individual student learning, temporarily preserving some differentiation among grades by using an alternative conversion scale may smooth the transition.

As briefly mentioned in chapter 6, the cut score for each letter grade can be set at any level as long as those levels have a strong logic. Therefore, to differentiate students' achievement, a competency-based school might raise the cut score for an

A to 3.25 or 3.5. Students who want to achieve a grade of A would have multiple opportunities to increase their scores to the 3.5 and 4.0 levels to meet their goal.

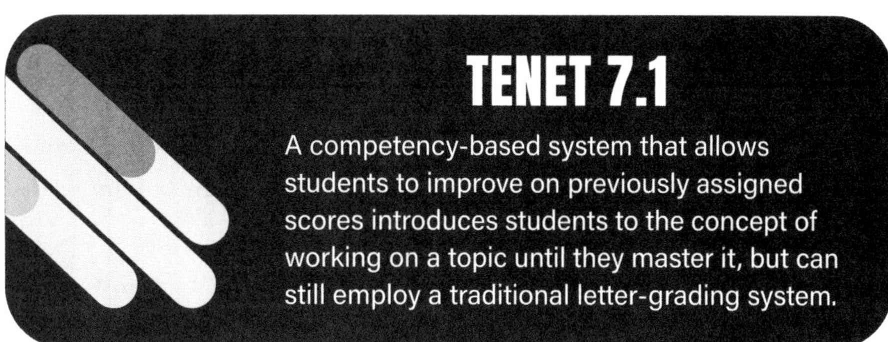

Implications of tenet 7.1 might include the following.

- **Increased opportunities for mastery:** Allowing students to improve their scores ensures that learning is seen as a continuous process where students have multiple opportunities to demonstrate mastery, thus promoting a growth mindset and reducing the pressure of having to perform perfectly on the first attempt.
- **Differentiation of achievement:** By adjusting the cut scores for letter grades, schools can maintain a level of differentiation among students, ensuring that higher levels of mastery are recognized and incentivized, which provides more meaningful distinctions in achievement.
- **Flexibility and responsiveness to individual learning needs:** This approach enables teachers to be more responsive to individual student needs, offering tailored support to those who need it while maintaining the expectation that all students can achieve mastery by the end of the course.

Working Ahead

Now we add the second characteristic of competency-based systems—students can work ahead on content that has not yet been addressed in class—to the first characteristic of improving previously assigned scores. This second characteristic requires that the school has a well-articulated vertical alignment of measurement topics. For example, in a science class at the seventh-grade level, a measurement topic addresses how gravitational forces between the Earth and the moon create tides. At the eighth-grade level, a measurement topic addresses how gravity affects objects in the solar system. While the eighth-grade version addresses the same general topic (gravity) as the seventh-grade version, the eighth-grade version requires a deeper understanding of gravity and its implications than the seventh-grade version. With measurement topics vertically aligned across grade levels, students can work on advanced topics that have not been addressed in class but are related to topics that have been addressed.

To understand how working ahead affects grading, consider a seventh-grade student. In science, he is working on ten measurement topics: Seven topics are at the seventh-grade level and three are at the eighth-grade level. He receives an unweighted summative score for each topic at the end of the grading period, as shown in the third column of figure 7.1.

Measurement Topic	Grade Level	Unweighted Summative Score	Weighted Summative Score
Topic 1	7	3.0	3.0
Topic 2	7	3.5	3.5
Topic 3	7	4.0	4.0
Topic 4	7	3.0	3.0
Topic 5	7	2.5	2.5
Topic 6	7	3.0	3.0
Topic 7	7	4.0	4.0
Topic 8	8	1.5	4.5
Topic 9	8	1.0	4.0
Topic 10	8	0.5	3.5
Total		26	35
Average		2.6	3.5

Source: © 2021 by Robert J. Marzano.

FIGURE 7.1: Grading when a student works ahead.

The third column of figure 7.1 shows that the student received much higher summative scores for the seventh-grade topics than for the eighth-grade topics. This makes sense because the student has only recently started working on these more difficult, higher-level topics. The simple average for these ten scores is 2.6, which translates to a letter grade of B using the conversion chart in table 6.5 (page 189). However, if the student's scores on the eighth-grade topics are weighted as shown in the fourth column of figure 7.1 (to account for them being above the student's grade level), the weighted average is 3.5, which translates to a letter grade of A.

As shown so far in this chapter, the ability for students to work ahead on content not yet addressed in class and to improve previously assigned scores affects grading practices. When this flexibility is incorporated into a competency-based system, traditional letter grades can be used while still maintaining the focus on mastery and individual progress.

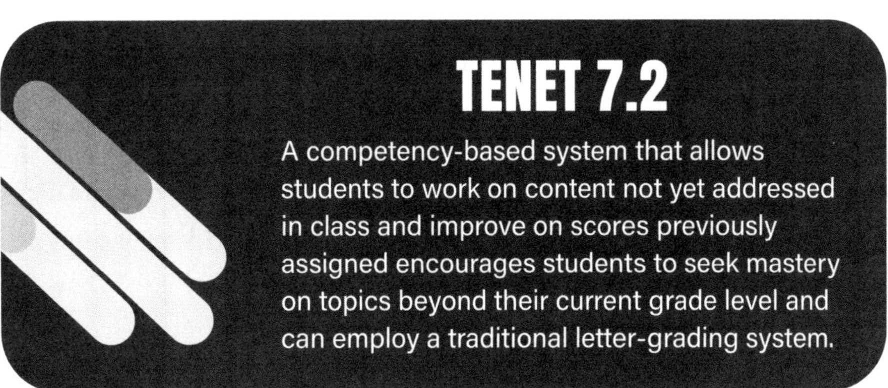

Implications of tenet 7.2 might include the following.

- **Encouragement of advanced learning:** Allowing students to work ahead on content not yet covered in class promotes intellectual curiosity and provides motivated students the opportunity to challenge themselves by exploring advanced material, fostering a deeper understanding of the subject matter.
- **Differentiated learning paths:** This approach acknowledges that students have varying paces and abilities, enabling them to progress through content at their own rate. It ensures that students who are ready for more challenging material can continue their learning without being held back by the pacing of the rest of the class.
- **Flexible and fair grading:** By employing a weighted grading system for advanced topics, schools can fairly measure students who work

ahead without penalizing them for tackling more difficult material. This ensures that students are rewarded for taking initiative and engaging with more complex content while maintaining the integrity of the grading system.

The changes in grading that accompany a competency-based system also extend to the various formats for report cards.

Reporting by Grade Levels and Courses

One of the unique aspects of competency-based systems is that they can report a student's status and growth both for the content they are working on in their current year of schooling and also the content they have addressed since they entered the competency-based system. To illustrate, consider the competency-based report card in figure 7.2. It shows the grade level a student is currently working on for each subject area, denoted by the number of completed measurement topics at that level expressed as a proportion, such as "4 of 32." For example, in mathematics, the placement of this proportion in the fifth-grade row means that the student is working on fifth-grade mathematics content and has demonstrated proficiency (that is, achieved a score of at least 3.0) on four of the thirty-two topics.

Figure 7.2 also shows scores for grade levels the student has already completed. Once a level is complete, the proportion of topics mastered is no longer reported (since it would be meaningless at that point) and performance at the completed level is denoted by the labels "3.0 Proficient" or "4.0 Honors." The first label, 3.0 Proficient, means that the student received a score of 3.0 or higher on all measurement topics at that level, but the majority of scores were 3.0. The second label, 4.0 Honors, means that the student received a score of 3.0 or higher on all measurement topics at that level, but the majority of scores were 4.0. This convention employs the same overall logic as the conjunctive approach to grading, introduced in chapter 6 (Conjunctive Approach, page 192). The basic idea here is that even though all students have exhibited a proficiency score of at least 3.0, differentiation between students can still be acknowledged by creating a conjunctive rule that sorts students into two groups. "Proficient" applies to students who have all summative scores above 3.0, and the majority of those scores are 3.0. "Honors" applies to students who have all summative scores above 3.0, and the majority of scores are 4.0.

Grade	Art	Career Literacy	Mathematics	Personal and Social Skills	Language Arts	Science	Social Studies	Technology
8								
7								
6								
5			4 of 32					
4		7 of 11	3.0 Proficient		7 of 31	2 of 23		
3		3.0 Proficient	4.0 Honors	2 of 6	3.0 Proficient			
2	9 of 10	3.0 Proficient	3.0 Proficient	3.0 Proficient	4.0 Honors	3.0 Proficient	2 of 15	7 of 8
1	3.0 Proficient	3.0 Proficient	4.0 Honors	3.0 Proficient	3.0 Proficient	3.0 Proficient	3.0 Proficient	4.0 Honors
K	3.0 Proficient	3.0 Proficient	4.0 Honors	3.0 Proficient	3.0 Proficient	3.0 Proficient	3.0 Proficient	3.0 Proficient

Source: Adapted from Marzano, 2010.

FIGURE 7.2: Competency-based report card for grades K–8.

Alternatively, completed levels might report the average score across all measurement topics at that level. For example, instead of an overall score of 4.0 for third-grade mathematics, the student whose report card is shown in figure 7.2 might have received a score of 3.68. In all cases, this average score would be at least 3.0, since students in a competency-based system must obtain at least a score of 3.0 before progressing to the next level of content.

The system shown in figure 7.2 works well up through eighth grade. However, at the high school level, courses typically take the place of grade levels, necessitating a course-based approach to reporting, as shown in figure 7.3. As in grades K–8, high school students must demonstrate proficiency on all the measurement topics for a course to receive credit for that course. If the majority of a student's scores are 3.0, then the final score of 3.0 Proficient is reported; if the majority of a student's scores are 4.0, then the final score of 4.0 Honors is reported. Again, as an alternative, the average of all measurement topic scores could be entered as the final score for a course.

Subject Area	Course	Score
Mathematics	Calculus	
	Geometry	
	Algebra II	12 of 24
	Algebra I	3.0 Proficient
Science	AP Environmental Science	
	Physics	
	Chemistry	6 of 22
	Biology	3.0 Proficient
Social Studies	Economics	
	World History	11 of 21
	U.S. History	4.0 Honors
	Geography	3.0 Proficient
Language Arts	Shakespeare	
	Ancient Literature	13 of 22
	European Literature	3.0 Proficient
	U.S. Literature	3.0 Proficient

Art	Orchestra	
	Performing Arts	9 of 21
	Painting	3.0 Proficient
Technology	Web Design	
	Computer Science Analysis and Design	17 of 22
	Foundations of Computer Science	4.0 Honors

Source: Adapted from Marzano, 2010.

FIGURE 7.3: Competency-based report card for high school.

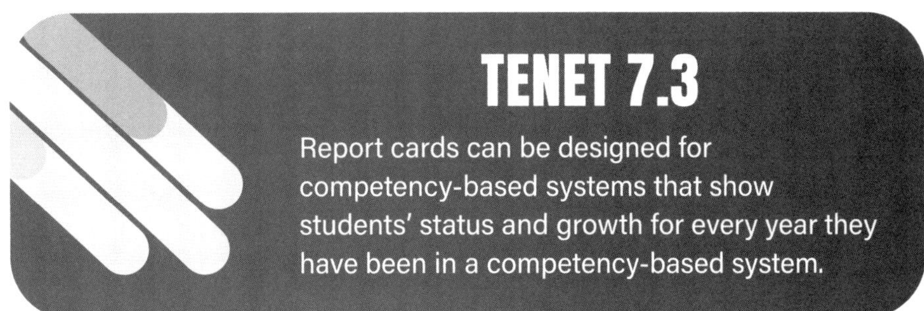

Implications of tenet 7.3 might include the following.

- **Holistic tracking of student progress:** This system allows for the continuous monitoring of a student's academic development over time, offering insights not only into their current proficiency but also how their learning has accumulated and built across grade levels and subjects.
- **Clear communication of mastery:** By reporting proficiency levels and scores for each measurement topic at both current and past grade levels, students, families, and educators can easily identify areas of strength and opportunities for growth, ensuring transparency and clarity in how student achievement is evaluated.
- **Adaptability for different educational stages:** The system seamlessly transitions from grade-level reporting in K–8 to course-based reporting in high school, allowing for consistent tracking of student mastery across different stages of the educational journey while maintaining alignment with competency-based principles.

Reporting on Pace

A unique aspect of competency-based systems is that they can report the pace at which a student is progressing through the curriculum. Keeping track of student pace provides a constant early warning system regarding those students who might be falling behind in specific subject areas or specific topics within subject areas. Jeni Gotto, Oliver Grenham, Brian J. Kosena, Robert J. Marzano, and Pamela Swanson (2025) described one metric for pace reporting called the *grade-level equivalent* (GLE). The GLE indicates a student's position on the learning continuum, from prekindergarten to grade 12, and each student has a GLE for each content area. For example, a GLE of 2.5 in mathematics indicates that a student has demonstrated proficiency on all of the mathematics measurement topics for second grade and half of the mathematics measurement topics for third grade. Teachers and administrators monitor GLE scores for each student to determine whether they are on track to graduate in an appropriate amount of time.

Another approach is the elementary report card format that includes a pace metric that Marzano and colleagues (2017) suggested. As shown in the top row of figure 7.4, Jimmy Kaufman is in the fourth grade chronologically. The report card depicts Jimmy's status for eight subject areas: (1) mathematics, (2) language arts, (3) science, (4) social studies, (5) physical education, (6) health, (7) world languages, and (8) visual and performing arts. Directly below each subject area is listed the grade level Jimmy is working on for that subject area. For mathematics, health, world languages, and visual and performing arts, Jimmy is working at the fourth-grade level. For language arts and social studies, Jimmy is working at the third-grade level. And for science and physical education, Jimmy is working at the fifth-grade level.

For each subject area, the report card in figure 7.4 also indicates the number of measurement topics that make up the specified level and how many of the measurement topics the student has mastered. There are also three icons in the report: (1) a trophy, (2) a speedometer, and (3) a light bulb. The trophy highlights how many measurement topics the student has mastered, the speedometer explains the extent to which the student is on pace, and the light bulb highlights how many measurement topics the student mastered at the score 4.0 level.

This level of reporting detail can be embedded in middle school report cards and, theoretically, in high school report cards. However, secondary educators tend to maintain more traditional-looking report cards.

Jimmy Kaufman		Grade Level: 4 Report Date: March 14, 2025	
Mathematics Grade 4 Ten measurement topics, seven complete	Student has mastered 70 percent of this year's learning!	Language Arts Grade 3 Seven measurement topics, four complete	Student has mastered 57 percent of this year's learning!
	On pace		Trending to complete this year on pace, but one level below
	Zero of ten learning targets demonstrated at score 4.0		Four of seven learning targets demonstrated at score 4.0
Science Grade 5 Five measurement topics, three complete	Student has mastered 60 percent of this year's learning!	Social Studies Grade 3 Four measurement topics, three complete	Student has mastered 75 percent of this year's learning!
	On pace		Trending to complete this year ahead of schedule, but one level below
	Zero of five learning targets demonstrated at score 4.0		One of four learning targets demonstrated at score 4.0
Physical Education Grade 5 Seven measurement topics, six complete	Student has mastered 86 percent of this year's learning!	Health Grade 4 Seven measurement topics, four complete	Student has mastered 57 percent of this year's learning!
	Trending to complete this year one month ahead of schedule		On pace
	Three of seven learning targets demonstrated at score 4.0		Two of seven learning targets demonstrated at score 4.0
World Languages Grade 4 Four measurement topics, two complete	Student has mastered 50 percent of this year's learning!	Visual and Performing Arts Grade 4 Six measurement topics, four complete	Student has mastered 67 percent of this year's learning!
	Trending to complete this year two weeks behind schedule		On pace
	Two of four learning targets demonstrated at score 4.0		Zero of six learning targets demonstrated at score 4.0

Source: Adapted from Marzano et al., 2017.

FIGURE 7.4: Report card that includes pace.

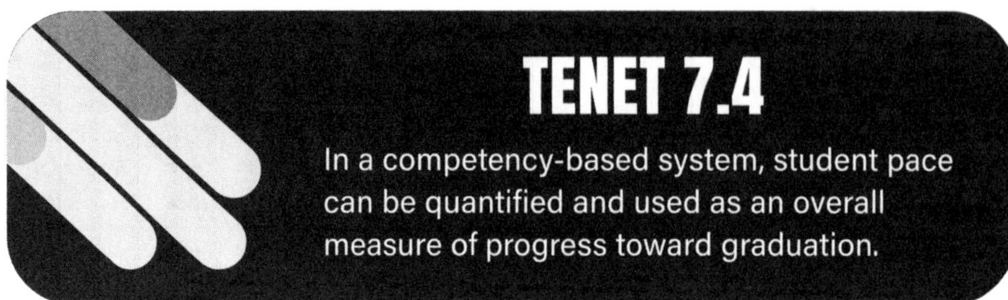

Implications of tenet 7.4 might include the following.

- **Individualized progress monitoring:** Quantifying student pace through metrics like GLE allows for more personalized tracking of a student's academic journey. This helps educators identify students who are ahead or behind and provide targeted support to ensure they stay on track for graduation.
- **Enhanced communication with stakeholders:** The inclusion of pace metrics on report cards offers a clearer picture of a student's academic trajectory, helping families and administrators understand not just what a student has mastered but also the rate at which they are progressing. This can foster more informed conversations about educational strategies and interventions.
- **Flexible learning pathways:** By reporting on pace, competency-based systems offer greater flexibility, allowing students to progress at their own speed through the curriculum. This can support differentiated learning experiences, where students who master content more quickly can advance, while others receive the time they need to fully grasp concepts before moving forward.

Summary

In this chapter, we focused on competency-based education, a system that emphasizes mastering content rather than spending a set amount of time in class. Effective competency-based implementation requires adjustments to grading practices; this ensures that students can demonstrate proficiency over time and that their achievements are accurately differentiated. Competency-based systems also utilize innovative methods of reporting student progress. Tools such as grade-level equivalents and detailed report cards that track mastery across all content areas allow for more personalized progress tracking. This approach not only supports individualized learning paths but also enhances communication with stakeholders. By integrating pace as a measure of academic progress, competency-based education ensures that all students have the opportunity to stay on track for graduation while receiving the support they need. In the upcoming epilogue, we'll bring all three parts of the book together, providing guidance about how you can use the tenets presented throughout the book to improve your assessment literacy.

Epilogue

APPLYING THE TENETS OF ASSESSMENT LITERACY

This book has cut a broad swath through previous assumptions about assessments. Each chapter presented tenets that together define an equitable, classroom-centered paradigm of assessment literacy. In all, there are forty-three tenets articulated in the preceding chapters, as shown in table E.1 (page 218). These tenets challenge traditional assumptions about assessments in K–12 education, urging educators and school systems to adopt more nuanced approaches. Along with each of the forty-three tenets, we articulated implications for educators. Thus, even in their raw form, the tenets provide insights and guidance relative to the role of assessment in K–12 schooling.

TABLE E.1: Tenets of Assessment Literacy

Chapter	Tenets
Introduction: Revisiting Assessment Practices	**Tenet I.1:** Systems used to classify students in K–12 education should be used only after a thorough examination of the potential negative effects on each individual student.
Chapter 1: The Influence of Large-Scale Assessments	**Tenet 1.1:** Large-scale assessments were introduced to American K–12 education in the late 19th century and have grown to encompass several types and purposes. Nevertheless, measurement experts increasingly emphasize the limitations of large-scale assessments, especially when measuring general cognitive skills. **Tenet 1.2:** Interim assessments are designed to complement year-end assessments. They can serve a number of functions, including guiding instruction, evaluating students, and predicting how well students will perform on year-end assessments. However, they only provide a limited amount of data and cannot be used for all purposes.
Chapter 2: Technical Characteristics of Large-Scale Assessments	**Tenet 2.1:** Large-scale assessments should represent only one piece of information when making decisions about students, and they should never be the primary piece of information. **Tenet 2.2:** Large-scale assessments measure only a sample of the important content in a given subject area. **Tenet 2.3:** Large-scale assessments are not necessarily aligned with state or local standards. **Tenet 2.4:** Large-scale assessments are not necessarily comparable to one another. **Tenet 2.5:** Students should receive information and experiences that make them familiar with the nature and formats of the large-scale assessments they will take. **Tenet 2.6:** Large-scale assessment scores for students who are not fully engaged in taking the test are typically underestimates of the students' actual knowledge and skill. **Tenet 2.7:** A single score on a test should always be interpreted from the perspective that it might contain significant error. **Tenet 2.8:** Cut scores should be considered cautiously when making decisions about individual students. **Tenet 2.9:** Subscores in isolation should not be used to make decisions about student placement for instruction. **Tenet 2.10:** Educators should provide enough accommodations to ensure that each student's performance on an assessment is the most accurate estimate possible of the student's true status.
Chapter 3: Rethinking Classroom Assessments	**Tenet 3.1:** A single score on an assessment should represent a single construct or dimension. **Tenet 3.2:** Using points and percentages to score assessments without explicit reference to a continuum of knowledge and skill can be highly misleading in terms of the status of individual students.

Chapter	Tenets
	Tenet 3.3: Proficiency scales should be used to explicitly articulate the continuum of knowledge and skill for specific measurement topics and explicitly guide the measurement process. **Tenet 3.4:** To ensure students are aware of the continuum of knowledge on which they will be assessed, educators should develop specific proficiency scales for the following types of content: declarative knowledge, mental procedures, and psychomotor procedures. **Tenet 3.5:** A single proficiency scale can incorporate two or more elements if those elements can be shown to covary. **Tenet 3.6:** When designing proficiency scales for declarative and procedural knowledge, consider the internal hierarchical structures of these types of knowledge before using external taxonomies.
Chapter 4: Scoring Classroom Assessments	**Tenet 4.1:** Classroom assessments should utilize a broad spectrum of assessment types to gather information about each student's current status on specific topics. **Tenet 4.2:** Teachers should administer and score multiple assessments for each student on each measurement topic using an approach that involves assessments administered to all students and assessments administered to individual students. **Tenet 4.3:** When designing multiple assessments for a specific measurement topic, teachers should use the proficiency scale to ensure the assessments are parallel. **Tenet 4.4:** Some assessments should be used as instructional feedback and therefore do not have to be scored or recorded. **Tenet 4.5:** Teachers should only enter scores in a gradebook that they deem acceptably reliable and valid.
Chapter 5: Aggregating Classroom Assessment Scores	**Tenet 5.1:** Research thus far has demonstrated that formative assessment can have powerful effects on student learning, but the average effect is rather modest. **Tenet 5.2:** The term *formative assessment* has no specific agreed-on definition, but there is some commonality in descriptions regarding it being a process used to gather evidence about students. **Tenet 5.3:** A student's current status on a measurement topic should never be determined by a single test. **Tenet 5.4:** Formative scores for a specific measurement topic derive from individual assessments. Summative scores for a specific measurement topic do not derive from an individual assessment but from the collective evidence provided by the formative scores. **Tenet 5.5:** Averages can provide summary information about a student's performance but, especially when scores are tracked by assessment type, do not provide information about a student's current status on specific topics. Decaying averages, while acknowledging student growth, nevertheless mask important information that should also be used when computing summative scores. **Tenet 5.6:** When computing a summative score for a specific measurement topic, teachers should consider which mathematical model best fits the student's observed scores.

continued →

Chapter	Tenets
Chapter 5: Aggregating Classroom Assessment Scores	**Tenet 5.7:** The method of mounting evidence is a viable method of estimating students' summative scores on measurement topics that does not rely on mathematical calculations. **Tenet 5.8:** When reporting summative scores that have been computed using the method of mathematical models for specific measurement topics, select a rounding approach that preserves differences in estimates and offers an appropriate level of precision, or simply report the raw score. **Tenet 5.9:** The reliability coefficient does not provide useful information about the precision of summative score estimates for individual students. If a measure of reliability is desired, use estimates from the mathematical model of best fit or Bayesian statistics. **Tenet 5.10:** The argument-based perspective of validity (criterion, construct, and content) fits well with a model of assessment that utilizes proficiency scales to generate and score parallel assessments on a specific topic and uses multiple formative scores to generate a summative score. The instrumental perspective of validity does not.
Chapter 6: Grading Systems	**Tenet 6.1:** Grades on report cards should be measures of what students know and can do relative to academic content that has been taught, as opposed to compliance with school-imposed behavioral or attitudinal norms. **Tenet 6.2:** At the end of a grading period, summative scores should be aggregated only within their respective domains. **Tenet 6.3:** Averaged summative scores within a subject area or domain may be converted to traditional letter grades and percentage scores; cut scores for grades should be articulated as typical levels of competence on a proficiency scale. **Tenet 6.4:** The conjunctive approach should be considered as an alternative to compensatory approaches when aggregating summative scores across measurement topics within a domain. **Tenet 6.5:** Schools and districts should annually update the validity coefficients for their reporting systems and make changes in those systems as necessary.
Chapter 7: Competency-Based Systems	**Tenet 7.1:** A competency-based system that allows students to improve on previously assigned scores introduces students to the concept of working on a topic until they master it, but can still employ a traditional letter-grading system. **Tenet 7.2:** A competency-based system that allows students to work on content not yet addressed in class and improve on scores previously assigned encourages students to seek mastery on topics beyond their current grade level and can employ a traditional letter-grading system. **Tenet 7.3:** Report cards can be designed for competency-based systems that show students' status and growth for every year they have been in a competency-based system. **Tenet 7.4:** In a competency-based system, student pace can be quantified and used as an overall measure of progress toward graduation.

Visit ***MarzanoResources.com/reproducibles*** *for a free reproducible version of this table.*

We designed these tenets to inspire and guide schools and districts to engage in critical reflection, rather than simply following prescribed practices. Beyond this, we encourage educators to translate the tenets into a series of actionable questions that reveal assumptions and beliefs about the appropriate uses of assessments and help them evaluate their current assessment systems. Not every tenet needs to be translated into a specific question; rather, the information in multiple tenets might be best expressed in a single question. Also, some tenets don't lend themselves to explicit questions. The following figures present sample questions for each of this book's parts: large-scale assessments (figure E.1), classroom assessments (figure E.2, page 222), and grading practice (figure E.3, page 223). These questions utilize a Likert-type continuum that ranges from the traditional perspective on assessment (represented by 1 on the Likert scale) to the assessment-literate perspective described in this book (represented by 5 on the Likert scale). Schools and districts should feel free to design their own questions from the tenets that provide the most useful information for them, though we recommend employing the Likert scale.

	1	2	3	4	5	
We should place a great deal of emphasis on the scores of individual students on large-scale assessments and communicate to students the importance of receiving high scores on such assessments.						We should consider scores on large-scale assessments as one small piece of information about students and have a process for helping students realize that their score on any type of large-scale assessment is not necessarily an accurate indication of what they know and are able to do.
We should trust that if students learn the content in the curriculum we teach, that knowledge will transfer to them performing well on large-scale assessments.						We should ensure we know the specific content included in the large-scale assessments students take and make sure that all students have the opportunity to learn that specific content.
We should not teach test-specific thinking skills because it is an inappropriate form of "teaching to the test."						We should be aware of the test-specific thinking required on large-scale assessments our students take and make sure students practice those test-specific types of thinking.

FIGURE E.1: Sample Likert questions for large-scale assessment tenets. continued →

	1	2	3	4	5	
We should not be concerned about the context in which students take a test, since it has little to do with their performance on the test.						We should make sure we are aware of all those factors that can artificially inhibit a student's performance on a large-scale assessment and make accommodations to mitigate those factors.
We should not try to motivate students to perform well on large-scale assessments, since they have little to do with their performance.						We should try to motivate students to do well on large-scale assessments, since their level of motivation has a profound influence on the scores they receive.

Visit ***MarzanoResources.com/reproducibles*** *for a free reproducible version of this figure.*

	1	2	3	4	5	
Teachers should design their own assessments in which they independently assign points to items.						Teachers should design their own assessments but use a clearly defined continuum of knowledge and skills to do so, and assign points to items based on the level of knowledge and skill for each item.
Teachers should use percentages and points to score classroom assessments at their own discretion.						Teachers should use percentages and points to score classroom assessments only if they can be interpreted in terms of a specific continuum of knowledge and skill.
Teachers should assign a single score to each assessment regardless of the content addressed in the test.						Teachers should ensure that any score assigned to an assessment represents a single dimension only. If a test covers more than one dimension, a single score should be assigned to each dimension.
Proficiency scales are not necessary because the state standards and the curriculum in the textbooks used in the school or district adequately define the important content.						Proficiency scales should be designed for all important subject matter content at every grade and course level for the school or district.
There should be no single reference point for the assessments designed in the school or district.						Proficiency scales should be the reference point for designing and scoring all assessments.

	1	2	3	4	5	
Teachers should primarily use traditional forced-choice and short constructed-response assessments to determine what students know and can do.						Teachers should use a wide array of types of classroom assessments to determine what students know and can do.
A summative score for a specific student on a specific topic should be computed from a specific summative test.						A summative score for a specific student on a specific topic should be derived from multiple parallel assessments using a well-articulated system for estimating a true summative score.
Teachers should enter all scores assigned to students without exception.						Teachers should ensure that any score or grade entered into a gradebook is judged to have acceptable reliability and validity.
The reliability of classroom assessments should be computed using the same reliability coefficients used for large-scale assessments.						The reliability of classroom assessments should be determined using methods that estimate the aggregate error across parallel assessments.
The validity of classroom assessments should be determined using the same methods employed with large-scale assessments.						The validity of classroom assessments should be determined using argument-based approaches.

FIGURE E.2: Sample Likert questions for classroom assessment tenets.

*Visit **MarzanoResources.com/reproducibles** for a free reproducible version of this figure.*

	1	2	3	4	5	
At the end of a grading period, summative scores across all domains should be aggregated into a single overall score.						At the end of a grading period, summative scores should be aggregated only within their respective domains and not across domains.
Translating summative scores into traditional letter grades should be done by computing an average summative score on all measurement topics addressed during the grading period.						Translating summative scores into traditional letter grades should take into account how much of the content in proficiency scales has been directly addressed in class.

FIGURE E.3: Sample Likert questions for grading practice tenets. continued →

	1	2	3	4	5	
If a competency-based system is being used, then traditional letter grades cannot be generated.						If a competency-based system is being used, then overall letter grades should be computed using a weighting system for scores on topics that have not been addressed in class.
If a competency-based system archives information about students' scores across the years, then this information should not be translated into a metric of student learning.						If a competency-based system keeps track of students' scores across the years each student has been in the system, then student pace should be computed as a measure of overall student learning.

*Visit **MarzanoResources.com/reproducibles** for a free reproducible version of this figure.*

As noted, the statements in the left column of each figure (denoted by 1) represent a traditional perspective regarding assessments. The statements in the right column of each figure (denoted by 5) represent the perspective on assessment literacy described in this book. Also note that each item has a middle score of 3. A response of 3 would represent the belief that the best option is to use some components of both perspectives.

Various constituent groups, such as teachers, administrators, families, and students, within a school or district can respond to the items in figures E.1, E.2, and E.3. The aggregate results from these responses can be used to determine tendencies in assumptions and beliefs. At least two types of comparisons are important to make with the data from these constituent groups.

One comparison is between what different constituent groups believe the school or district should be doing. For example, it is common for students, teachers, and administrators to perceive the benefits of grading approaches that do not mix academic content scores across different domains into an overall grade. In contrast, families might be in favor of an overall grade that combines scores across different domains. Discovering and disclosing situations like this can be beneficial to a school or district, since those actions frame issues that must be resolved before policies are changed.

Another important type of comparison is between what constituent groups believe should be done with assessments and the way the school or district is currently using them. For example, it might be the case that almost all constituent groups want students to be well prepared for large-scale assessments, but the school or district currently does nothing to this end. This finding would point to the need for a new initiative in the school or district.

By comparing responses from various groups, schools can identify areas of alignment or discrepancy in their assessment practices. We recommend using this feedback to inform changes and better align assessment practices with the principles outlined in the tenets. Ultimately, the goal is to create a more thoughtful, reflective approach to assessment that supports student learning and development.

As you explore assessment literacy, it is important to recognize that changing the way we view and utilize assessments in K–12 education is a journey; it will not happen overnight. The tenets we present in this book serve as guideposts; they are designed to help you gradually shift from traditional practices that limit the potential of your students to an inclusive, reflective, and dynamic model that promotes their full academic and personal growth.

Throughout these chapters, we have explored the historical context and evolving role of assessments, from large-scale assessments that impact entire systems to classroom-based measures that shape daily learning. We have highlighted the need for assessments that do more than rank and sort students; assessment should support learning and provide meaningful insights into student progress. As you have discovered, the tenets emphasize the importance of using assessments not as tools for exclusion or reinforcement of biases but as instruments for supporting every student's unique learning journey.

Now, it is time to act. The insights we present in this book are not just theoretical. They demand action, reflection, and change. The questions raised in this epilogue exploring the assumptions we hold about assessments and how they impact our students are an invitation to rethink how we approach assessment, grading, and reporting. We urge you to actively engage with tenet-driven questions, collaborate across teams, and implement practices that challenge outdated paradigms. Whether it's reconsidering how you classify students, refining your use of proficiency scales, or developing grading systems that better reflect student growth and mastery, we ask you to take the first steps toward creating an educational system that values learning over labels and progress over performance.

References and Resources

Achieve, Inc. (2006, June 5). *An alignment analysis of Washington State's College Readiness Mathematics Standards with various local placement tests.* Author. Accessed at https://files.eric.ed.gov/fulltext/ED500440.pdf on October 27, 2025.

American Educational Research Association, American Psychological Association, & National Council on Measurement in Education. (1999). *Standards for educational and psychological testing.* American Educational Research Association.

American Educational Research Association, American Psychological Association, & National Council on Measurement in Education. (2014). *Standards for educational and psychological testing.* American Educational Research Association.

Anderson, L. W., & Krathwohl, D. R. (Eds.). (2001). *A taxonomy for learning, teaching, and assessing: A revision of Bloom's taxonomy of educational objectives.* Longman.

Angoff, W. H. (1971). Scales, norms, and equivalent scores. In R. L. Thorndike (Ed.), *Educational measurement* (2nd ed., pp. 508–600). American Council on Education.

Ayala, C. C., Shavelson, R. J., Ruiz-Primo, M. A., Brandon, P. R., Yin, Y., Furtak, E. M., et al. (2008). From formal embedded assessments to reflective lessons: The development of formative assessment studies. *Applied Measurement in Education, 21*(4), 315–334.

Baker, E. L., Chung, G. K. W. K., & Cai, L. (2016). Assessment gaze, refraction, and blur: The course of achievement testing in the past 100 years. *Review of Research in Education, 40*(1), 94–142. https://doi.org/10.3102/0091732X16679806

Berman, A. I., Haertel, E. H., & Pellegrino, J. W. (2020). Introduction: Framing the issues. In A. I. Berman, E. H. Haertel, & J. W. Pellegrino (Eds.), *Comparability of large-scale educational assessments: Issues and recommendations* (pp. 9–24). National Academy of Education.

Biggs, J. B., & Collis, K. F. (1982). *Evaluating the quality of learning: The SOLO taxonomy (structure of the observed learning outcome)*. Academic Press.

Binet, A., & Simon, T. (1916). The development of intelligence in the child (E. S. Kite, Trans.). In A. Binet & T. Simon, *The development of intelligence in children (The Binet-Simon Scale)* (pp. 182–273). Williams & Wilkins. https://doi.org/10.1037/11069-004 (Original work published 1908)

Black, P., & Wiliam, D. (1998a). Assessment and classroom learning. *Assessment in Education: Principles, Policy and Practice*, *5*(1), 7–74. https://doi.org/10.1080/0969595980050102

Black, P., & Wiliam, D. (1998b). *Inside the black box: Raising standards through classroom assessment*. Nelson.

Black, P., & Wiliam, D. (2009). Developing the theory of formative assessment. *Educational Assessment, Evaluation and Accountability*, *21*(1), 5–31.

Borgonovi, F. (2022). Is the literacy achievement of teenage boys poorer than that of teenage girls, or do estimates of gender gaps depend on the test? A comparison of PISA and PIAAC. *Journal of Educational Psychology*, *114*(2), 239–256. https://doi.org/10.1037/edu0000659

Box, C., Skoog, G., & Dabbs, J. M. (2015). A case study of teacher personal practice assessment theories and complexities of implementing formative assessment. *American Educational Research Journal*, *52*(5), 956–983.

Brennan, R. L. (Ed.). (2006). *Educational measurement* (4th ed.). Rowman & Littlefield.

Brigham, C. C. (1923). *A study of American intelligence*. Princeton University Press.

Brookhart, S. M., Guskey, T. R., Bowers, A. J., McMillan, J. H., Smith, J. K., Smith, L. F., et al. (2016). A century of grading research: Meaning and value in the most common educational measure. *Review of Educational Research*, *86*(4), 803–848. https://doi.org/10.3102/0034654316672069

Burstein, L. (1983). A word about this issue. *Journal of Educational Measurement*, *20*(2), 99–101.

Buzick, H. M., Casabianca, J. M., & Gholson, M. L. (2023). Personalizing large-scale assessment in practice. *Educational Measurement: Issues and Practice*, *42*(2), 5–11. https://doi.org/10.1111/emip.12551

Camara, W. J., Mattern, K., Croft, M., Vispoel, S., & Nichols, P. (2019). A validity argument in support of the use of college admissions test scores for federal accountability. *Educational Measurement: Issues and Practice*, *38*(4), 12–26.

Camina, E., & Güell, F. (2017). The neuroanatomical, neurophysiological and psychological basis of memory: Current models and their origins. *Frontiers in Pharmacology*, *8*, Article 438.

Cartagena, S., & Pike, L. (2022). Defying deficit thinking: Clearing the path to inclusion for students of all abilities. In R. D. Williams (Ed.), *Handbook of research on challenging deficit thinking for exceptional education improvement* (pp. 101–126). IGI Global. https://doi.org/10.4018/978-1-7998-8860-4.ch005

Cizek, G. J. (2007). Formative classroom assessment and large-scale assessment: Implications for future research and development. In J. H. McMillan (Ed.), *Formative classroom assessment: Theory into practice* (pp. 99–115). Teachers College Press.

Conderman, G., Pinter, E., & Young, N. (2020). Formative assessment methods for middle level classrooms. *The Clearing House: A Journal of Educational Strategies, Issues and Ideas, 93*(5), 233–240.

Crane, E. (2010). *Building an interim assessment system: A workbook for school districts.* Council of Chief State School Officers. Accessed at https://files.eric.ed.gov/fulltext/ED528642.pdf on October 28, 2025.

Cronbach, L. J., & Shavelson, R. J. (2004). My current thoughts on coefficient alpha and successor procedures. *Educational and Psychological Measurement*, *64*(3), 391–418.

Cusi, A., & Morselli, F. (2024). The key-roles of the expert during classroom discussions aimed at fostering formative assessment processes through the use of digital technologies. *ZDM—Mathematics Education*, *56*(4), 741–755. https://doi.org/10.1007/s11858-024-01572-0

Decristan, J., Klieme, E., Kunter, M., Hochweber, J., Büttner, G., Fauth, B., et al. (2015). Embedded formative assessment and classroom process quality: How do they interact in promoting science understanding? *American Educational Research Journal*, *52*(6), 1133–1159.

Dee, T. S., & Jacob, B. A. (2010). The impact of No Child Left Behind on students, teachers, and schools. *Brookings Papers on Economic Activity*, 149–207.

DePascale, C., & Gong, B. (2020). Comparability of individual students' scores on the "same test." In A. I. Berman, E. H. Haertel, & J. W. Pellegrino (Eds.), *Comparability of large-scale educational assessments: Issues and recommendations* (pp. 25–48). National Academy of Education.

Downing, S. M., & Haladyna, T. M. (Eds.). (2006). *Handbook of test development.* Routledge. https://doi.org/10.4324/9780203874776

Erwin, B., Brown, D., & Mann, S. (2023, May 3). *50-state comparison: High school graduation requirements.* Accessed at www.ecs.org/50-state-comparison-high-school-graduation-requirements-2023 on April 4, 2025.

Everson, H. T., & Forte, E. (2020). Introduction to special section: Issues and advances in standard setting methods. *Educational Measurement: Issues and Practice, 39*(1), 7. https://doi.org/10.1111/emip.12324

Every Student Succeeds Act, 20 U.S.C. § 6301 (2015). Accessed at www.congress.gov/bill/114th-congress/senate-bill/1177 on April 4, 2025.

Feldt, L. S., & Brennan, R. L. (1989). Reliability. In R. L. Linn (Ed.), *Educational measurement* (3rd ed., pp. 105–146). American Council on Education.

Fisher, D., & Frey, N. (2020, March). The power of practice assessments. *Educational Leadership, 77*(6), 84–85.

Galton, F. (1883). *Inquiries into human faculty and its development.* Macmillan.

Galton, F. (1888). Co-relations and their measurement, chiefly from anthropometric data. *Proceedings of the Royal Society of London, 45*, 135–145.

Galton, F. (1889). *Natural inheritance.* Macmillan.

Gardner, H. (1993). *Multiple intelligences: The theory in practice.* Basic Books.

Garrett, H. E. (1937). *Statistics in psychology and education* (2nd ed.). Longmans, Green.

Gotto, J., Grenham, O., Kosena, B. J., Marzano, R. J., & Swanson, P. (2025). *Pioneers of personalized education: Westminster Public Schools and the pursuit of competency-based learning.* Marzano Resources.

Gulliksen, H. (1950). *Theory of mental tests.* Wiley.

Guskey, T. R., & Bailey, J. M. (2001). *Developing grading and reporting systems for student learning.* Corwin Press.

Haladyna, T. M. (1994). *Developing and validating multiple-choice test items.* Erlbaum.

Haladyna, T. M., & Downing, S. M. (2004). Construct-irrelevant variance in high-stakes testing. *Educational Measurement: Issues and Practice, 23*(1), 17–27. https://doi.org/10.1111/j.1745-3992.2004.tb00149.x

Haladyna, T. M., & Rodriguez, M. C. (2013). *Developing and validating test items.* Routledge.

Hathcoat, J. D. (2013). Validity semantics in educational and psychological assessment. *Practical Assessment, Research and Evaluation, 18*(9).

Hattie, J. (2009). *Visible learning: A synthesis of over 800 meta-analyses relating to achievement.* Routledge.

Hattie, J. (2012). *Visible learning for teachers: Maximizing impact on learning.* Routledge.

Hattie, J. (2015). The applicability of visible learning to higher education. *Scholarship of Teaching and Learning in Psychology, 1*(1), 79–91. https://doi.org/10.1037/stl0000021

Hattie, J. (2023). *Visible learning: The sequel—A synthesis of over 2,100 meta-analyses relating to achievement.* Routledge.

Hattie, J. (2024, November). *Formative evaluation.* Accessed at www.visiblelearningmetax.com/influences/view/formative_evaluation on May 24, 2025.

Hays, W. L. (1973). *Statistics for the social sciences* (2nd ed.). Holt, Rinehart and Winston.

Haystead, M. W. (2016, January). *An analysis of the relationship between essential learning mastery and mathematics achievement in grades 3 and 4.* Marzano Resources. Accessed at www.marzanoresources.com/clark-pleasant-istep-ela-math-exec-summary.html on March 1, 2025.

Haystead, M. W., & Marzano, R. J. (2022). *A validity study of GLEs as predictors of student performance on external assessments: Preliminary analysis.* Marzano Academies.

Heritage, M. (2008). *Learning progressions: Supporting instruction and formative assessment.* Council of Chief State School Officers. Accessed at www.michiganassessmentconsortium.org/wp-content/uploads/Learning-Progressions.pdf on October 28, 2025.

Heritage, M. (2020). Getting the emphasis right: Formative assessment through professional learning. *Educational Assessment, 25*(4), 355–358.

Heritage, M., Kim, J., Vendlinski, T. P., & Herman, J. L. (2008, August). *From evidence to action: A seamless process in formative assessment?* (CRESST Report No. 741). National Center for Research on Evaluation, Standards, and Student Testing. Accessed at https://cresst.org/wp-content/uploads/R741.pdf on September 8, 2025.

Herman, J. (2017). *Interim assessments in brief.* WestEd, Center on Standards and Assessment Implementation. Accessed at https://csaa.wested.org/resource/interim-assessments-in-brief on July 14, 2025.

Herman, J., Osmundson, E., Dai, Y., Ringstaff, C., & Timms, M. (2011, November). *Relationships between teacher knowledge, assessment practice, and learning—Chicken, egg, or omelet?* (CRESST Report No. 809). National Center for Research on Evaluation, Standards, and Student Testing. Accessed at https://files.eric.ed.gov/fulltext/ED527530.pdf on October 28, 2025.

Horst, P. (1966). *Psychological measurement and prediction.* Wadsworth.

Hough, L. (2023, Spring/Summer). The problem with grading. *Harvard Ed.*, (171), 38–47.

Howley, A., Kusimo, P. S., & Parrott, L. (2000). Grading and the ethos of effort. *Learning Environments Research, 3*(3), 229–246. https://doi.org/10.1023/A:1011469327430

Jensen, A. R. (1980). *Bias in mental testing.* Free Press.

Johnson, C. C., Sondergeld, T. A., & Walton, J. B. (2019). A study of the implementation of formative assessment in three large urban districts. *American Educational Research Journal, 56*(6), 2408–2438.

Kaestle, C. (2013). *Testing policy in the United States: A historical perspective.* The Gordon Commission on the Future of Assessment in Education. Accessed at https://ets.org/Media/Research/pdf/kaestle_testing_policy_us_historical_perspective.pdf on April 4, 2025.

Kamin, L. J. (1977). The politics of IQ. In P. L. Houts (Ed.), *The myth of measurability* (pp. 45–65). Hart.

Kane, M. T. (1992). An argument-based approach to validity. *Psychological Bulletin, 112*(3), 527–535.

Kane, M. T. (2001). Current concerns in validity theory. *Journal of Educational Measurement, 38*(4), 319–342.

Kane, M. T. (2009). Validating the interpretations and uses of test scores. In R. W. Lissitz (Ed.), *The concept of validity: Revisions, new directions, and applications* (pp. 39–64). Information Age.

Kendall, J. S., & Marzano, R. J. (2000). *Content knowledge: A compendium of standards and benchmarks for K–12 education* (3rd ed.). ASCD.

Kifer, E. (1994). Development of Kentucky's Instructional Results Information System (KIRIS). In T. R. Guskey (Ed.), *High stakes performance assessment: Perspectives on Kentucky's educational reform* (pp. 7–18). Corwin Press.

Kingston, N., & Nash, B. (2011). Formative assessment: A meta-analysis and a call for research. *Educational Measurement: Issues and Practice, 30*(4), 28–37.

Klute, M., Apthorp, H., Harlacher, J., & Reale, M. (2017, February). *Formative assessment and elementary school student academic achievement: A review of the evidence* (REL Report No. 2017–259). National Center for Education Evaluation and Regional Assistance & Regional Educational Laboratory Central. Accessed at https://ies.ed.gov/rel-central/2025/01/other-21 on October 28, 2025.

Latham, H. (1877). *On the action of examinations considered as a means of selection.* Deighton, Bell.

Lawrence, C. R. (2011). *The eugenics record office at Cold Spring Harbor Laboratory (1910–1939).* Embryo Project Encyclopedia. Accessed at https://hdl.handle.net/10776/2091 on April 4, 2025.

Leap Scholar. (2025, September 26). *USA grading system in 2025: A comprehensive guide* [Blog post]. Accessed at https://leapscholar.com/blog/usa-grading-system-understanding-us-grading-gpa-marking on October 28, 2025.

Lee, H., Chung, H. Q., Zhang, Y., Abedi, J., & Warschauer, M. (2020). The effectiveness and features of formative assessment in US K–12 education: A systematic review. *Applied Measurement in Education, 33*(2), 124–140. https://doi.org/10.1080/08957347.2020.1732383

Lehman, E., De Jong, D., & Baron, M. (2018). Investigating the relationship of standards-based grades vs. traditional-based grades to results of the Scholastic Math Inventory at the middle school level. *Education Leadership Review of Doctoral Research, 6*, 1–16.

Lemann, N. (2000). *The big test: The secret history of the American meritocracy.* Farrar, Straus & Giroux.

Lindquist, E. F. (Ed.). (1951). *Educational measurement.* American Council on Education.

Linn, R. L. (Ed.). (1989). *Educational measurement* (3rd ed.). American Council on Education.

Lord, F. M. (1959). Problems in mental test theory arising from errors of measurement. *Journal of the American Statistical Association, 54*(286), 472–479.

Lord, F. M., & Novick, M. R. (1968). *Statistical theories of mental test scores.* Addison-Wesley.

Magnusson, D. (1967). *Test theory* (H. Mabon, Trans.). Addison-Wesley.

Marzano, R. J. (2000). *Transforming classroom grading.* ASCD.

Marzano, R. J. (2006). *Classroom assessment and grading that work.* ASCD.

Marzano, R. J. (2010). *Formative assessment and standards-based grading.* Marzano Resources.

Marzano, R. J. (2018). *Making classroom assessments reliable and valid.* Solution Tree Press.

Marzano, R. J., & Abbott, S. D. (2022). *Teaching in a competency-based elementary school: The Marzano Academies model.* Marzano Resources.

Marzano, R. J., Brandt, R. S., Hughes, C. S., Jones, B. F., Presseisen, B. Z., Rankin, S. C., et al. (1988). *Dimensions of thinking: A framework for curriculum and instruction.* ASCD.

Marzano, R. J., Cahill, B., Gotto, J., Kosena, B. J., Lynch, M. J., & Pearson, L. (2025). *Test-specific thinking: Teaching students to think the way tests make them.* Marzano Resources.

Marzano, R. J., & Hardy, P. B. (2023). *Leading a competency-based secondary school: The Marzano Academies model.* Marzano Resources.

Marzano, R. J., & Haystead, M. W. (2008). *Making standards useful in the classroom.* ASCD.

Marzano, R. J., & Haystead, M. W. (2023). *A validity study of GLEs as predictors of student performance on external assessments: Secondary analysis.* Marzano Academies.

Marzano, R. J., Heflebower, T., Hoegh, J. K., Warrick, P., & Grift, G. (2016). *Collaborative teams that transform schools: The next step in PLCs.* Marzano Resources.

Marzano, R. J., & Kendall, J. S. (1996). *A comprehensive guide to designing standards-based districts, schools, and classrooms.* ASCD.

Marzano, R. J., & Kendall, J. S. (2007). *The new taxonomy of educational objectives* (2nd ed.). Corwin Press.

Marzano, R. J., & Kendall, J. S. (2008). *Designing and assessing educational objectives: Applying the new taxonomy.* Corwin Press.

Marzano, R. J., & Kosena, B. J. (2022). *Leading a competency-based elementary school: The Marzano Academies model.* Marzano Resources.

Marzano, R. J., Norford, J. S., Finn, M., & Finn, D., III. (2017). *A handbook for personalized competency-based education.* Marzano Resources.

Marzano, R. J., Norford, J. S., & Ruyle, M. (2019). *The new art and science of classroom assessment.* Solution Tree Press.

Marzano, R. J., Zima, B., & Simms, J. A. (2025). *Marzano mastery approaches: A decision-making process for competency-based schools.* Marzano Resources.

McEntarffer, R. (2021). Replacing the term *formative assessment*: A modest proposal. In S. A. Nolan, C. M. Hakala, & R. E. Landrum (Eds.), *Assessing undergraduate learning in psychology: Strategies for measuring and improving student performance* (pp. 57–65). American Psychological Association.

McMillan, J. H. (2013). Why we need research on classroom assessment. In J. H. McMillan (Ed.), *SAGE handbook of research on classroom assessment* (pp. 3–16). SAGE.

Mehrens, W. A., & Lehmann, I. J. (1991). *Measurement and evaluation in education and psychology* (4th ed.). Holt, Rinehart and Winston.

Messick, S. (1975). The standard problem: Meaning and values in measurement and evaluation. *American Psychologist, 30*(10), 955–966.

Messick, S. (1989). Validity. In R. L. Linn (Ed.), *Educational measurement* (3rd ed., pp. 13–103). American Council on Education.

Mid-continent Research for Education and Learning. (2014). *McREL compendium of standards: List of benchmarks for geography standard 3.* Author.

Mid-continent Research for Education and Learning. (2024). *McREL compendium of standards.* Author. Accessed at www.mcrel.org/wp-content/uploads/2024/05/McREL-Compendium-of-Standards_PurposeHistoryProcess.pdf on April 4, 2025.

Mitzel, H. C., Lewis, D. M., Patz, R. J., & Green, D. R. (2001). The bookmark procedure: Psychological perspectives. In G. J. Cizek (Ed.), *Setting performance standards: Concepts, methods, and perspectives* (pp. 249–281). Erlbaum.

Myers, D. G. (2009). *Psychology: Ninth edition in modules* (9th ed.). Worth.

National Governors Association Center for Best Practices & Council of Chief State School Officers. (2010a). *Common Core State Standards for English language arts and literacy in history/social studies, science, and technical subjects.* Authors. Accessed at https://corestandards.org/wp-content/uploads/2023/09/ELA_Standards1.pdf on November 25, 2024.

National Governors Association Center for Best Practices & Council of Chief State School Officers. (2010b). *Common Core State Standards for mathematics.* Authors. Accessed at https://corestandards.org/wp-content/uploads/2023/09/Math_Standards1.pdf on November 25, 2024.

National Research Council. (2001). *Knowing what students know: The science and design of educational assessment.* The National Academies Press. https://doi.org/10.17226/10019

National Task Force on Assessment Education for Teachers. (2016). *Assessment literacy defined.* Author. Accessed at https://ies.ed.gov/ncee/edlabs/regions/northeast/onlinetraining/ResourcesTools/Assessment%20Literacy%20Definition.pdf on April 4, 2025.

NGSS Lead States. (2013). *Next Generation Science Standards: For states, by states.* The National Academies Press.

Nitko, A. J., & Brookhart, S. M. (2011). *Educational assessment of students* (6th ed.). Pearson.

No Child Left Behind (NCLB) Act of 2001, Pub. L. No. 107-110, § 115, Stat. 1425 (2002). Accessed at www.congress.gov/bill/107th-congress/house-bill/1/text on April 4, 2025.

Parkes, J. (2013). Reliability in classroom assessment. In J. H. McMillan (Ed.), *SAGE handbook of research on classroom assessment* (pp. 107–123). SAGE.

Pearson, K. (1896). Mathematical contributions to the theory of evolution. III. Regression, heredity, and panmixia. *Philosophical Transactions of the Royal Society of London. Series A, Containing Papers of a Mathematical or Physical Character, 187,* 253–318.

Pellegrino, J. W., & Chudowsky, N. (2003). The foundations of assessment. *Measurement: Interdisciplinary Research and Perspectives, 1*(2), 103–148.

Perie, M., Marion, S., & Gong, B. (2009). Moving toward a comprehensive assessment system: A framework for considering interim assessments. *Educational Measurement: Issues and Practice, 28*(3), 5–13. https://doi.org/10.1111/j.1745-3992.2009.00149.x

Perie, M., Marion, S., Gong, B., & Wurtzel, J. (2007, November). *The role of interim assessments in a comprehensive assessment system: A policy brief.* Center for Assessment, Achieve, Inc., & The Aspen Institute. Accessed at www.nciea.org/wp-content/uploads/2021/11/PolicyBriefFINAL.pdf on October 28, 2025.

Plake, B. S., Hambleton, R. K., & Jaeger, R. M. (1997). A new standard-setting method for performance assessments: The dominant profile judgment method and some field-test results. *Educational and Psychological Measurement, 57*(3), 400–411. https://doi.org/10.1177/0013164497057003002

Polikoff, M. S. (2020). The present and future of alignment. *Educational Measurement: Issues and Practice, 39*(2), 18–20.

Popham, W. J. (2006, November). Phony formative assessments: Buyer beware! *Educational Leadership, 64*(3), 86–87.

Popham, W. J. (2017). *Classroom assessment: What teachers need to know* (8th ed.). Pearson Education.

Porter, A. C. (2002). Measuring the content of instruction: Uses in research and practice. *Educational Researcher, 31*(7), 3–14.

Rains, C. L. (2020). Leadership in High Reliability School districts. In R. Eaker & R. J. Marzano (Eds.), *Professional Learning Communities at Work and High Reliability Schools: Cultures of continuous learning* (pp. 351–383). Solution Tree Press.

Rasch, G. (1960). *Studies in mathematical psychology: I. Probabilistic models for some intelligence and attainment tests.* Nielsen & Lydiche.

Rice, J. M. (1893). *The public-school system of the United States.* Century.

Rice, J. M. (1897). The futility of the spelling grind—II. *The Forum*, 409–419.

Rios, J. A., & Miranda, A. A. (2021). What are the conditions associated with subscore added value noninvariance? Implications for improving subscore interpretation fairness. *Educational Measurement: Issues and Practice, 40*(1), 69–78.

Sacks, P. (1999). *Standardized minds: The high price of America's testing culture and what we can do to change it.* Perseus Books.

Sato, M., Wei, R. C., & Darling-Hammond, L. (2008). Improving teachers' assessment practices through professional development: The case of National Board Certification. *American Educational Research Journal, 45*(3), 669–700.

Shapovalov, Y. A., & Evans, C. M. (2022, August). *Research synthesis: Developing the educator assessment literacy professional learning screener.* The National Center for the Improvement of Educational Assessment. Accessed at www.nciea.org/wp-content/uploads/2023/04/Research-Synthesis-and-Tool-Final.pdf on April 4, 2025.

Shepard, L. A. (2006). Classroom assessment. In R. L. Brennan (Ed.), *Educational measurement* (4th ed., pp. 623–646). Rowman & Littlefield.

Shepard, L. A. (2009). Commentary: Evaluating the validity of formative and interim assessment. *Educational Measurement: Issues and Practice, 28*(3), 32–37. https://doi.org/10.1111/j.1745-3992.2009.00152.x

Simms, J. A. (2016, August). *The Critical Concepts: English language arts, mathematics, and science*. Marzano Resources. Accessed at www.marzanoresources.com/the-critical-concepts.html on April 4, 2025.

Sireci, S., & O'Riordan, M. (2020). Comparability when assessing individuals with disabilities. In A. I. Berman, E. H. Haertel, & J. W. Pellegrino (Eds.), *Comparability of large-scale educational assessments: Issues and recommendations* (pp. 177–204). National Academy of Education.

Skaggs, G., Hein, S. F., & Wilkins, J. L. M. (2020). Using diagnostic profiles to describe borderline performance in standard setting. *Educational Measurement: Issues and Practice*, *39*(1), 45–51.

Spearman, C. (1904). "General intelligence," objectively determined and measured. *The American Journal of Psychology*, *15*(2), 201–292. https://doi.org/10.2307/1412107

Sridhar, S., Khamaj, A., & Asthana, M. K. (2023). Cognitive neuroscience perspective on memory: Overview and summary. *Frontiers in Human Neuroscience*, *17*, Article 1217093. https://doi.org/10.3389/fnhum.2023.1217093

Stanford, L. (2024, September 17). All states allow competency-based learning. Will it become a reality in schools? *Education Week*. Accessed at www.edweek.org/technology/all-states-allow-competency-based-learning-will-it-become-a-reality-in-schools/2024/09 on November 25, 2024.

Stevens, S. S. (1946). On the theory of scales of measurement. *Science*, *103*(2684), 677–680.

Stiggins, R. J. (1991). Assessment literacy. *Phi Delta Kappan*, *72*(7), 534–539.

Surianarayanan, C., Lawrence, J. J., Chelliah, P. R., Prakash, E., & Hewage, C. (2023). Convergence of artificial intelligence and neuroscience towards the diagnosis of neurological disorders—A scoping review. *Sensors*, *23*(6), Article 3062. https://doi.org/10.3390/s23063062

Suzuki, H., Hong, M., Ober, T., & Cheng, Y. (2022). Prediction of differential performance between advanced placement exam scores and class grades using machine learning. *Frontiers in Education*, *7*, Article 1007779. https://doi.org/10.3389/feduc.2022.1007779

Tavakol, M., & Dennick, R. (2011). Making sense of Cronbach's alpha. *International Journal of Medical Education*, *2*, 53–55.

Terman, L. M. (1916). *The measurement of intelligence*. Houghton, Mifflin and Company. https://doi.org/10.1037/10014-000

Tetzlaff, L., Schmiedek, F., & Brod, G. (2021). Developing personalized education: A dynamic framework. *Educational Psychology Review*, *33*(3), 863–882.

Thissen, D., & Wainer, H. (Eds.). (2001). *Test scoring*. Erlbaum.

Thompson, S., Blount, A., & Thurlow, M. (2002, December). *A summary of research on the effects of test accommodations: 1999 through 2001* (NCEO Technical Report No. 34). University of Minnesota, National Center on Educational Outcomes. Accessed at https://nceo.info/Resources/publications/OnlinePubs/Technical34.htm on April 4, 2025.

Thorndike, E. L. (1904). *Theory of mental and social measurements*. The Science Press. https://doi.org/10.1037/13283-000

Thorndike, R. L. (Ed.). (1971). *Educational measurement* (2nd ed.). American Council on Education.

Thurlow, M. L., Lazarus, S. S., Christensen, L. L., & Shyyan, V. (2016, January). *Principles and characteristics of inclusive assessment systems in a changing assessment landscape* (NCEO Report No. 400). University of Minnesota, National Center on Educational Outcomes. Accessed at https://nceo.umn.edu/docs/OnlinePubs/Report400/NCEOReport400.pdf on October 30, 2025.

Thurstone, L. L. (1928). Attitudes can be measured. *American Journal of Sociology, 33*(4), 529–554. https://doi.org/10.1086/214483

Thurstone, L. L. (1931). Multiple factor analysis. *Psychological Review, 38*(5), 406–427. https://doi.org/10.1037/h0069792

Thurstone, L. L. (1934). The vectors of mind. *Psychological Review, 41*(1), 1–32. https://doi.org/10.1037/h0075959

U.S. Congress, Office of Technology Assessment. (1992). *Testing in American schools: Asking the right questions* (Publication No. OTA-SET-519). U.S. Government Printing Office. Accessed at https://files.eric.ed.gov/fulltext/ED340770.pdf on April 4, 2025.

Valencia, R. R. (2010). *Dismantling contemporary deficit thinking: Educational thought and practice*. Routledge.

Valencia, R. R. (2019). *International deficit thinking: Educational thought and practice*. Routledge. https://doi.org/10.4324/9780367855581

Valencia, S. W., Stallman, A. C., Commeyras, M., Pearson, P. D., & Hartman, D. K. (1991). Four measures of topical knowledge: A study of construct validity. *Reading Research Quarterly, 26*(3), 204–233. https://doi.org/10.2307/747761

Vanlommel, K., & Schildkamp, K. (2019). How do teachers make sense of data in the context of high-stakes decision making? *American Educational Research Journal, 56*(3), 792–821.

Volante, L., DeLuca, C., Adie, L., Baker, E., Harju-Luukkainen, H., Heritage, M., et al. (2020). Synergy and tension between large-scale and classroom assessment: International trends. *Educational Measurement: Issues and Practice, 39*(4), 21–29.

Way, W. D., & Croft, M. (2020). Alignment issues facing testing organizations. *Educational Measurement: Issues and Practice, 39*(2), 28–30.

Webb, N. L. (1997, April). *Criteria for alignment of expectations and assessments in mathematics and science education* (Research Monograph No. 6). National Institute for Science Education. Accessed at https://files.eric.ed.gov/fulltext/ED414305.pdf on October 30, 2025.

Webb, N. L. (1999, August). *Alignment of science and mathematics standards and assessments in four states* (Research Monograph No. 18). National Institute for Science Education. Accessed at https://files.eric.ed.gov/fulltext/ED440852.pdf on October 30, 2025.

Webb, N. L. (2007). Issues related to judging the alignment of curriculum standards and assessments. *Applied Measurement in Education, 20*(1), 7–25.

Welch, C. J., & Dunbar, S. B. (2020). Alignment and implications for test takers. *Educational Measurement: Issues and Practice, 39*(2), 8–17.

Wilson, M., & Wolfe, R. (2020). Comparability within a single assessment system. In A. I. Berman, E. H. Haertel, & J. W. Pellegrino (Eds.), *Comparability of large-scale educational assessments: Issues and recommendations* (pp. 75–121). National Academy of Education.

Wise, S. L., & Kingsbury, G. G. (2022). Performance decline as an indicator of generalized test-taking disengagement. *Applied Measurement in Education, 35*(4), 272–286. https://doi.org/10.1080/08957347.2022.2155651

Wylie, E. C. (2020). Observing formative assessment practice: Learning lessons through validation. *Educational Assessment, 25*(4), 251–258.

Wylie, E. C., & Lyon, C. J. (2020). Developing a formative assessment protocol to support professional growth. *Educational Assessment, 25*(4), 314–330.

Xuan, Q., Cheung, A., & Sun, D. (2022). The effectiveness of formative assessment for enhancing reading achievement in K–12 classrooms: A meta-analysis. *Frontiers in Psychology, 13*, Article 990196. https://doi.org/10.3389/fpsyg.2022.990196

Yao, Y., Amos, M., Snider, K., & Brown, T. (2024). The impact of formative assessment on K–12 learning: A meta-analysis. *Educational Research and Evaluation, 29*(7–8), 452–475. https://doi.org/10.1080/13803611.2024.2363831

Yerkes, R. M. (Ed.). (1921). *Memoirs of the National Academy of Sciences, Vol. XV: Psychological examining in the United States Army.* U.S. Government Printing Office.

Index

A

B

C

D

E

F

G

H

I

J

K

L

M

N

O

P

R

S

T

U

V

W

Y

Making Classroom Assessments Reliable and Valid
Robert J. Marzano
Classroom assessments (CAs) have key advantages over large-scale interim, end-of-course, and state assessments. This resource details why CAs should become the primary method for formally measuring student learning and outlines how to revamp your CAs to ensure validity and reliability.
BKF789

Where Learning Happens
Julia A. Simms
Explore the types of attention—sustained, selective, divided, and effective—in depth and gain research-suggested strategies to maximize student attention and engagement. By understanding cognitive load theory, information-processing principles, and other key concepts, teachers can leverage attention-related strategies to help students achieve their academic goals.
BKL078

The New Art and Science of Classroom Assessment
Robert J. Marzano, Jennifer S. Norford, and Mike Ruyle
Shift to a new paradigm of classroom assessment that is more meaningful and accurate. Step by step, the authors outline a clear path for transitioning to a holistic mode of assessment that truly reflects course curriculum and student progress.
BKF788

Test-Specific Thinking
Robert J. Marzano, Bridget Cahill, Jeni Gotto, Brian J. Kosena, Michael J. Lynch, and Lucy Pearson
The authors provide recommended practices, methods, and means for educators to help students better prepare for tests and formulate stronger responses to common question structures. Using this book, teachers will have greater confidence in preparing students for taking standardized exams.
BKL080

Visit MarzanoResources.com or call 888.849.0851 to order.

Professional Development Designed for Success

Empower your staff to tap into their full potential as educators. As an all-inclusive research-into-practice resource center, we are committed to helping your school or district become highly effective at preparing every student for his or her future.

Choose from our wide range of customized professional development opportunities for teachers, administrators, and district leaders. Each session offers hands-on support, personalized answers, and accessible strategies that can be put into practice immediately.

Bring Marzano Resources experts to your school for results-oriented training on:

- Assessment & Grading
- Curriculum
- Instruction
- School Leadership
- Teacher Effectiveness
- Student Engagement
- Vocabulary
- Competency-Based Education